PENGUIN BOOKS

# PLAYING THE PRIVAT
# ADMISSIONS GAME

Richard Moll is Executive Director of Legal Personnel at the Manhattan-based law firm of Lord, Day and Lord. He spent twenty-seven years in college admissions. Moll was Dean of Admissions at the University of California, Santa Cruz, has been director of admissions at Vassar and Bowdoin colleges, and has worked in the admissions offices of Harvard and Yale. He is the author of *The Public Ivys* (Penguin) and has written for many publications, including *Harper's, The New York Times, The Washington Post,* and *The College Board Review.*

# Playing
## the _Private_ College
## Admissions
## Game

### Richard Moll

PENGUIN BOOKS

PENGUIN BOOKS
Viking Penguin Inc., 40 West 23rd Street,
New York, New York 10010, U.S.A.
Penguin Books Ltd, Harmondsworth,
Middlesex, England
Penguin Books Australia Ltd, Ringwood,
Victoria, Australia
Penguin Books Canada Limited, 2801 John Street,
Markham, Ontario, Canada L3R 1B4
Penguin Books (N.Z.) Ltd, 182–190 Wairau Road,
Auckland 10, New Zealand

First published in the United States of America
    by Times Books, a division of Random House, Inc., 1979
Published in Penguin Books 1980
Reprinted 1980, 1981, 1983, 1984
This revised edition first published in the
    United States of America in Penguin Books 1986
Published simultaneously in Canada

ISBN 0 14 00.9385 0

CIP data available

Printed in the United States of America by
R. R. Donnelley & Sons Company, Harrisonburg, Virginia
Set in Times Roman

TO

the family—especially Mom and Dad, whose
encouragement to the young I have attempted to
emulate in these pages—

and to Susan,

and to all those teenagers who have more to
offer than they know or perhaps are willing to
admit.

# Acknowledgments

When the final version of "the first book" has been submitted to the publisher, one sits back to count the blessings and the friends that made it all possible.

Four patient and forgiving bosses top my list: Arthur Howe, Jr., of Yale; David D. Henry of Harvard; LeRoy A. Greason of Bowdoin; and Natalie Marshall of Vassar. I have learned so much from them, and am grateful for the support and the space each offered. Thanks also to John Oliver Nelson and Donald K. Walker for illuminating that first path to the college admissions field.

Some recent and current Directors of Admission have had more influence as colleagues than they perhaps know: Bill Wilson and Ed Wall of Amherst, Helen McCann of Barnard, John Maguire of Boston College, Betty Vermey of Bryn Mawr, Bill Elliott of Carnegie-Mellon, Emery Walker of Claremont/Harvey Mudd, Jan Hersey of Connecticut College, Ron Potier of Franklin and Marshall, Fred Glimp and Fred Jewett of Harvard, Dick Haines of Lafayette, Bill Ihlanfeldt of Northwestern, Jack Osander and Tim Callard of Princeton, Rix Snyder and Fred Hargadon of Stanford, and Jack Hoy of Wesleyan.

Where does one begin in acknowledging the scores of dedicated secondary school counselors? They are overworked, underpaid, and so often more effective than their audiences know or acknowledge. Thanks, and Godspeed to them all.

And finally, for providing incentive and/or counsel for this book, my thanks to Gerry Friedman, Lewis Lapham of *Harper's,* Bobbi Marks, Molly Friedrich, and Professor William Gifford.

I should like to gratefully acknowledge the following college candidates for their exemplary application essays used in Chapter 3: Wade Komisar, Bethlehem Central School, New York; Jessica Miller, United Nations International School, New York; and Carlos Griffith, Stuyvesant High School, New York.

My thanks to Leslie Gell for permission to include her essay entitled "Reflections on North High."

# Contents

ix

# Playing
## the *Private* College
# Admissions
# Game

# Introduction

The envelope in my mailbox on April 17 was a thin one. Without opening it, I knew: I was a Princeton reject.

Correction: I am a Princeton reject. Somehow we never quite forget that introductory hour of judgment when a selective college announces (quite tersely in 1952, as I recall) that our first major Here-Am-I Statement has "passed" or "failed." The College Admissions Office plays a heavy and quick hand in adolescent flirtation with self-worth.

Around the family dinner table that evening there were tears, then anger . . . then a quiet, slightly resentful withdrawal to take stock.

Maybe Princeton just couldn't bear to include my Hoosier trappings on their freshman roster? I was graduating from Broad Ripple High School ("The Ripple Rockets") and had prepped for Broad Ripple at John Strange Elementary School. To top all, the Strange School had a principal named Mr. Quear (I swear to God: Check Ripley's roster of wonders, late '40s). And it didn't seem to matter to Princeton that Ripple's colors were orange and black.

It *did* matter to Princeton that my academic involvements had been rather thoroughly displaced in favor of running every schoolboy organization in sight—that is, when incessant schoolboy song-and-dance performances provided intermission for more serious activity. But tough courses and disciplined study?—No.

In short, Princeton was right.

Looking back, how was it that my family and I avoided arranging a session—just one—with the guidance counselor? How did she avoid getting to me for a little tough talk regarding objectivity in college planning? And what right did the Princeton alumni rep (everyone's favorite local clergyman/sportsman) have to assure my family that I was a "clear admit"? (The Reverend's nod of approval caused us to hop to New Jersey during high school spring vacation to see which dorm might be nicest for fall. As I recall, we even made a deposit on a black-with-a-touch-of-orange tweed couch at the local Tigertown mart.)

This book is being written with the knowledge that there are too many Broad Ripples (some called St. So-and-So), too many how-did-she-avoid-me counselors, too many families who mistake local-turf fame for Ivy suitability, and, alas, too few Princetons who (most abruptly at times) issue forth a judgment that is, more often than not, sound.

We in Admissions are inherently garrulous. We talk a lot not only to candidates, parents, and counselors, but also to each other. In fact, we talk candidly *mostly* to each other, and say far too little beyond Why-My-College? to all you others.

This book is an attempt to share insider talk on private college admissions with outsiders.

And this is, essentially, a how-to book. But before the tips can be implied or spelled out, several basic concepts must be understood:

1. Most private colleges in America today, including some with rather prestigious names, are *not* highly selective; if they feel you can survive their program, you'll be admitted. High price, a declining number of college-age Americans, apprehension regarding the worth of a bachelor's degree in the job marketplace, and the growth and strength of the state university system nationwide have created this phenomenon.

2. Unfortunately, many colleges pose as being more selective than they really are. They feel good students will not be attracted to them if there is not an aura of selectivity at the front gate. But as a result of the hidden anxiety that the upcoming class may not

be filled with the quantity and quality of students hoped for, the Admissions Office tends to *over*state the qualities of the institution. So students and families must analyze a private college as carefully as they would analyze an automobile before buying it. Probing questions must be asked to confirm what is advertised and to check tone, performance and justification of price. "Test rides" must be made by visiting classes, libraries, Union buildings, campus art galleries, athletic facilities, laboratories, and dorms. Hunches must be confirmed by talking with those who earlier decided in favor of the product.

3. A few private undergraduate institutions in America today are as highly selective as they ever have been, and a handful are even more selective. But not more than forty private colleges enjoy the luxury of admitting one out of two of their candidates, and not more than a half-dozen private colleges admit one out of five applicants. Aspiring kids and parents flock in droves to the latter little inner circle, hoping to get a bit of the juicy and seemingly irresistible prestige. Even though fame-of-a-name is not always consistent with an Ivy college's quality, the hordes keep applying, not realizing (or caring?) that the academic program may be as good or better at a place considerably more accessible.

4. Nothing speaks louder than a strong high school record in the college admissions game. "Other considerations" are almost always secondary in importance to the degree of difficulty of a candidate's courseload, grades, class rank, recommendations from teachers and school officials, standardized test scores, and the depth of extracurricular involvement.

5. Given the (rare) highly selective college situation, and given an average candidate in that college's admissions competition, "other considerations" can indeed enter the picture, some of which the candidate can capitalize on. Who is admitted from the muddy-middle of a selective college's applicant pool is partly a matter of chance, and the applicant has some control over "positioning" himself.

It might be most helpful to concentrate on the end of the admissions process first, and to reserve our discussion of the beginning of the process for later. Thus, the first section of this book speaks to where the average reader probably aspires to be: on the borderline of being admitted—and consequently the subject of debate by the Admissions Committee—to a college we'll call "quite selective" (for the sake of realism, not one of the tiny few "highly selective"). One might substitute a Trinity (Connecticut) or a Carleton (Minnesota) or a Vassar (New York) or an Oberlin (Ohio) or a Lehigh (Pennsylvania) or a Columbia/ Barnard (New York) for what I'm calling "Oldebrick College." Such a college is Ivyish, private, undergraduate, and admits approximately half of its applicants; the applicants are, overall, of quite sound quality because Oldebrick has always been known as one of "the fine old demanding schools" and has traditionally been able to attract bright, interesting (and mostly affluent) young people.

My hope is that when the reader sees what happens at the end of the line in the college admissions game, he or she will know how to make wiser starting moves: how to search for the right college(s) amidst a barrage of rumors from friends and family and a barrage of professional marketing techniques by colleges; how to recognize which elements of the secondary school record are most important and which elements of *self* should be dramatized; and how to understand how colleges ultimately structure a "classful of differences."

First, a simulated Admissions Committee meeting which draws heavily on actual cases, Committee personalities, moods, and processes of the meetings I've attended or commandeered during the last two decades. . . .

# 1.

# Playing the Game for Practice

Benson was late again.

The Mathematics, Political Science, Art History, and Classics faculty reps to the Admissions Committee had shown up on time as expected, and were now on their second round of coffee in the sparse and functional President's Conference Room, Main Building. But the Dean of Admissions knew he'd have to wait for Professor Truman Benson of the English Department.

The appearance of the conference room was less than grand. Amidst the clutter of cardboard file boxes holding 3,700 tired manila folders was a huge coffee pot surrounded by colorful hot-and-cold dixie cups, two stacks of ashtrays, rubber-banded cylinders of yellow pencils, and computerized printouts of the entire applicant pool. The paraphernalia so necessary to this Committee's mission did nothing to enhance the appearance of an already sterile setting.

In two's and three's, faculty members were simulating serious conversation with members of the admissions staff, so often perceived as "extras" to the faculty, and slightly distrusted. ("After all, you've moved into marketing now," a faculty member said to the Dean of Admissions at the Student Union recently.)

5

It was spring break at Oldebrick College, and "representative" faculty consultants to the Admissions Committee had been called upon to give precious vacation time to augment the admissions staff's votes in deciding which candidates would be admitted from the final muddy-middle group of the applicant pool. The assignment: Vote in half of the 125 applicants whose folders would be reviewed in an intense five-day period. The rules: 1. No vote and no discussion until *all* members were present (six admissions staff, five faculty) so that every vote would be uniform; 2. Committee members were urged to vote in favor of only those candidates who seemed truly desirable— those with the most votes would win in the end, and all others would fall to the waiting list (or be rejected, if something unusual were afloat).

Professor Benson finally blustered forth, in uniform: horn-rims, yellow striped shirt, rumpled grey suit, pink polka dot hanky flopping from the pocket. He thought he could warm up the cool reception by springing his oft-published flip: "I know we're here to sweat over College Board scores, absurd hairline differences between A − and B + averages, and Miss Tillihofer's credibility when she says, 'This is the best student I've taught in twenty years at Central High.' But I say to hell with it. This year I'm going to sit impassionately outside your rantings over seventeen-year-old accomplishment, and vote with one consideration in mind: *Whom* do I want in the bow of my canoe?"

Drawing a guffaw from Butch Lassiter of Classics (also volunteer assistant line coach of football), no response from Harry Chin of Mathematics, only the hint of a forced smile from Norton Taylor of Political Science, and an outright hostile stare from Rita Dorsett of Art History, he retreated to a serious posture.

"Whom do I want in the bow of my canoe? I mean it! That's the hurdle each kid must jump. And which of you will prove to me before we begin that my number one criterion is less reliable than yours?" Benson skipped the coffee, grabbed a Danish, and slumped in the one remaining black-with-Oldebrick-seal chair at the large oval table.

While Ms. Dorsett fidgeted with her handkerchief, mustering courage to snap back at Benson, the Dean started the meeting, twenty minutes late. This was an 8:00 P.M. orientation session on the eve of the five-day voting marathon.

"A few of you have been through this exercise before, but most of you are new. Thanks to you all for giving up five days of vacation time. As you know, I've consulted with the Dean of the Faculty to structure a balanced group of representatives to this Committee, hoping the entire faculty will feel indirectly involved in selecting the new class. We in the Admissions Office too often feel like an island at the College, and I struggle to find lines of communication to the faculty. This is one.

"You're here to help us decide whether Jane Jones should be admitted before John James, and why. Frankly, I'm a bit weary of those friendly locker-room-after-squash conversations when you earnestly query why our College Board averages aren't as high as Yale's, how so-and-so got into the class when he can't quite seem to put a sentence together, and why we can't attract more who want to major in Physics or Classics."

"Jesus, that's all we need to lure some of our disenchanted alums to cough up extra endowment capital: more drones for Physics and wimps for Classics," sputtered Benson.

Scowling at the representative from English, the Dean began again hurriedly:

"This will be a tight five days, reviewing twenty-five candidates per day. We won't begin until everyone is in his or her seat—hopefully, at nine each morning. I'll read the comments of teachers and guidance counselors from applicants' folders aloud while you check out the students' statistics in the computerized docket in front of you. We'll break one hour for lunch (I'll jog, and would enjoy your company), and we'll disband promptly at five. If we can hold down editorial and emotional chatter and limit discussion to clarification of the kids' credentials or honest talk about what a specific candidate symbolizes in terms of overall admissions policy, we can finish the job on time. Actually, we *must* finish on time: Our secretaries need over two weeks to prepare the decision letters, all of which will be mailed to applicants on April 10. As always, we and twenty or so of our colleague colleges will mail on the same day."

Norton Taylor of Political Science shook his head. "This already sounds tedious to me. Can I smoke in here?"

"Sitting next to a smoker for *five days?*" gasped Rita Dorsett of Art. "Oh please, Norton. Why don't we take a five-minute break every hour on the hour for the smokers to leave the room?" The Dean nodded quick approval, and continued.

"Before we get into the line-up of candidates, let me tell you where the admissions staff has brought us to date. You might want to jot these numbers down for reference during the next few days. We have 3,707 completed applications this year, up 3 percent over last year—a comforting sign in this era of fewer 17-year-olds and declining interest in private colleges (the latter probably related more to cost than to any other factor). The target number for next fall's class is 600, down a little from last year as we seem to have fewer students transferring out, so less room for entering freshmen. To get a class of 600 we must admit approximately 1,275 kids, anticipating a yield of 47 percent. In other words, slightly fewer than half of those we admit will choose us on May 1, the National Candidate's Reply Date.

Mr. Chin adjusted his glasses. "Excuse me. Less than half of those we admit actually choose us?"

"I know it's disappointing," replied the Dean, settling somewhat more comfortably into his chair now. "But don't be discouraged by our 47 percent yield: Columbia's yield last year was 43 percent; Trinity's 34 percent; Colgate's 34 percent; Carleton's 42 percent and Swarthmore's 41 percent. Most secondary school seniors apply to five or six places now, and can obviously attend only one. Harvard/Radcliffe is the only college in America with a consistently high yield, around 75 percent year after year. Even Yale normally lands only about 60 percent of those they admit, losing over 300 admittees to Harvard alone each year.

"But back to us. Each folder has been read by three different admissions officers. And each reader has rated the candidate on a one-to-five scale in three categories: academic, personal, and overall evaluation. Prior to this evening we on the staff admitted 1,212 applicants, rejected approximately 2,130, proposed 240 for the waiting list, and sent 125 to this Committee for final deliberation."

Adam McDermott of the admissions staff started circling the table with coffee refills. The faculty delegation looked as though they were taking an examination, busily scribbling notes and numbers on paper provided.

The Dean moved on. "You will note in your computerized docket of candidates, arranged by state and then alphabetically by secondary school, that there are some inconsistencies in our decisions, at least in terms of straight statistics such as GPAs (Grade Point Average) or class rank. If you spot any proposed decision that seems out of line, question me after one of these meetings and I'll pull the folder from the file for you to see—all folders are here in these boxes. If you feel the entire Committee should review the case, we'll add it on at the end."

"Oh, my," said Mr. Chin softly. "I'm leaving for a mathematics conference two hours after our sessions are over on Sunday, so I certainly hope we do not add many cases to our deliberations."

The Dean stood to stretch. "We can finish up on time, but I don't want to close off discussion on any candidate you spot on the docket—particularly a reject—whose proposed action you cannot understand. Remember, though, that stats alone do not tell the whole story. We're interested in an appraisal of motivation. We must analyze whether one school's grading system is as tough as the next. And we also have to pay attention to the forest as well as to the trees: will the class have adequate minority representation? decent football and hockey squads? enough students who can pay their own way so our scholarship resources are not overdrawn? an adequate showing of alumni children? a spread of proposed academic majors so the entire class won't end up in the pre-med or pre-law hoppers?"

Norton Taylor of Political Science interrupted. "Well, I'm not going to overlook the cold statistics with ease. I'm really concerned about the gradual decline in SATs over the last several years at Oldebrick and I'm here, quite frankly, with the intent of being score-conscious. Those who were on this Committee last year have led me to believe that we're going to second-guess socioeconomic advantage or disadvantage, the influence of an alcoholic mother on a teenager's in-school performance, how important it is to throw a ball well, and how much better a student's record might have been if only she had been able to attend a more demanding high school.

"Law schools look at test scores! One of my responsibilities here is to slip kids into law school as a reward for their $60,000 investment in Oldebrick. Law schools seem to use standardized test scores as an initial screening, and do not even move to appraise a student's four-year undergraduate record if the Law Boards aren't above a certain fairly high cut-off level. Certainly, à la Bakke's case, special students will be spliced into the class on the basis of somewhat different and imaginative standards. But for non-minorities, the standardized tests seem to stand supreme in importance. In other words, there is no substitute for brains!

"My informal studies at Oldebrick show that, on the whole, a high performer on the SATs will be a high performer on the Law Boards four years later, regardless of what happens in the four intervening years of undergraduate study.

"Now, if this theory is correct—and I'm rather certain it is, probably as much for the medical school as for the law school aspirants—I'm voting for the highest College Board scores I can find in the pack. I can only enjoy my summer canoe, Truman, if my graduate school placements have gone well in the spring."

The Dean sat patiently and watched Taylor as he made this statement. It seemed the Dean welcomed basic questions at this stage in the proceedings. There was a short silence.

"Perhaps you'll all be surprised that I'm the one most eager to disagree with what Taylor said," Mr. Chin of Mathematics said suddenly. "When I look around the table, I think that my department must seem the most cut-and-dried, perhaps the most confining in terms of a student's ultimate vocational choice. I'll save the speech refuting that for later. But right now I would like to say just one thing. This is a liberal arts college. We are here to teach students to broaden their horizons. Much as I, too, would like to improve our graduate school placement record, *for* the record, I would like to remind you that it is not the business of this institution to be career-oriented. The pressure will increase to become so, but I want no part of it. A man spends only one-fifth of his life on the job, if my calculations are correct, and I'm more interested in educating toward the *other* four-fifths, when one is confronted with priorities and the values of decision-making. We in Mathematics have stumbled upon such wonderful human surprises at this college that to chart success by means of our own statistics would be subterfuge."

Truman Benson stirred. "I'm moved, but I'm staying with my canoe." He prepared to take the floor once again, but Rita Dorsett of Art, a fiftyish, prime fixture at Oldebrick, broke in.

"I'm moved too; in fact, I've just been quietly jolted to become a fan of the Math Department. To think I have been fooled all along about what was going on over there!" Ms. Dorsett and Mr. Chin exchanged formal, nodding smiles, looking somewhat like peace ambassadors at a conference table.

"Of course this is a liberal arts college, and the strength of my department is a symbol of its remaining so. Students often don't find something like Art History until the sophomore or junior year of college. Worrying about students' job preference would inhibit the intellectual expansion our less visible departments can provide. Give the students time to stumble upon us, off the track of job myopia."

Ms. Dorsett stiffened in her chair and reached to adjust the bun she wore as a crown. "I am prompted to say something else before our candidate review begins. I'm just wondering how on earth we are supposed to spot 'motivation and thirst'? The attitude in my classroom is beginning to remind me of the fifties, and I don't particularly like it. As our tuition soars, I fear we're attracting more of the very rich who are not at all nervous about the important step of college, do not even give much thought to it, and who seem considerably more intrigued by the next party than by the next reference book or social issue.

"I serve on the Records Committee where we are noting a pattern among those who fail which is strangely reminiscent of a bygone era. Yes, there were a few students in difficulty whose advisors had not cautioned them that they were over their heads in a heavy pre-med curriculum, or who just had not had satisfactory preparation in secondary school to cope—and we were sympathetic in their cases. But there were too many bright students whose SATs were above the class average and who just plain disappointed us—they didn't work hard because they didn't care. Most of them, judging from their schools, were affluent. Cyclical patterns scare me a little."

"You mean, is it a matter of money?" the Dean asked, obviously interested in Rita's statement. "Do we *have* to take the rich? Well, nothing contributes more to class diversity than scholarship resources. We're in a reasonably good position here but not as good as some of the competition. Yale, Rice, Wellesley, Williams, Amherst, and Duke are examples of institutions which can fund all admitted students who have proved financial need. We can't. We're more in a league with Amherst, Bowdoin, and Princeton in having the money to give scholarship assistance to approximately 40% of the entering class: We'd be strained to move beyond that proportion. (All of our scholarships, remember, are on the basis of financial need. A good many private colleges have moved to awarding scholarships on the basis of merit rather than need—they call them 'no-need awards,' but I would call them bribes.)

"The fact remains that my admissions staff must find at least two-thirds of a freshman class (or 400 bodies) who can pay their own way. What this does to the general motivation level of the class, I don't know."

The financial aid topic was obviously falling on a few deaf ears around the table, but the Dean was earnest in pursuing it, with Mr. Chin, Rita Dorsett, and the younger members of the admissions staff listening intently.

"Now, let me anticipate one of your questions: Does the need of financial aid handicap a student in the admissions process? Somewhat, it seems to me, although you will be in a position to decide that as we vote on a few of these cases. I had a rather embarrassing public spat with a Director of Admissions from one of the Seven Sister colleges not long ago on this very topic. She was pontificating that she would leave the admissions field if ever 'ability to pay' were to become an admissions criterion at her college. So be it. But if an institution does not have the financial aid endowment of a Wellesley, and cannot possibly fund all candidates who are 'muddy-middle' in the applicant pool, I'm not convinced it is so evil to tip the scales toward a candidate who can pay his or her own way. After all, even Wellesley probably tips the scales now and then in favor of Utah over Massachusetts, or a candidate with a

Wellesley mother rather than a Bryn Mawr mother. The admissions process is, and perhaps has to be, sprinkled with inequities.''

Rita dDorsett straightened in her chair again. "Wellesley does so many things so well. Let's not be critical of them, Dean.''

"I'm less critical than envious of institutions like Wellesley, which have more extensive financial resources than Oldebrick. Most selective private colleges do have the resources to fund all outstanding candidates, however, as do we. But well down the scale, when we have a broad choice of above-average but not thoroughly outstanding candidates to complete the class, we may favor the student, all else being rather equal, who can pay. Now, whether the consequence of accepting one more who can pay means less motivation in the classroom or not—who knows? Maybe we can talk about this again as individual candidates' cases beg the issue.''

Butch Lassiter of Classics, who did not appear to have quite tuned into the discussion yet, rose to open a window. Looking out on the freshman yard, he executed three quick knee-bends and four touch-your-toes.

"I think it is time to get to the first case," said the Dean, noting Lassiter's impatience. "Policy talk is easier when we're not discussing specific candidates. Let's let the applicants suggest policy decisions as we go.''

"Hold it," said Butch Lassiter, jumping back to his seat with a broad grin. "I won't make a speech, but I just wanted to say one thing.''

Lassiter was a thirtyish alumnus of Oldebrick with a boyish face and the ability to skirt offensive topics. "I just want to say that I'm in favor of school spirit, and in my experience, that means good athletics. There is a growing apathy and me-centeredness here at Oldebrick that may also mean a declining loyalty to the college. Careerist eighties have simply exhausted us and we're in a period of catching our breath, but I see no need to retrench altogether. I hear this mood is everywhere— at other colleges and in secondary schools, too. But one special ingredient at Oldebrick has been its spirit and sense of community, and I am beginning to miss it.''

Now Norton Taylor rose to view the freshman yard as Lassiter continued.

"Oldebrick *needs* a rallying point or two right now, and I think that a winning athletic team or two can do the trick. We don't have to compromise academic stature for athletic strength—Harvard, Stanford, and Amherst are pretty good at winning games while pumping out more than their share of Rhodes Scholars. A good team or two in highly visible sports like football and basketball wouldn't hurt us one bit and might help us muster a little more enthusiasm throughout all levels of the college family."

Rita Dorsett smiled politely. "Now Butch, that *is* a flashback. I don't mind the presence of a few superb ballplayers here, providing we see some of them on the *female* team rosters also. What I do hate is spotting the goof-offs on campus who probably were admitted to help a team win, but who end up playing cards for four years at the Sig House. And if their ability on the field doesn't pan out, they're lost and rather pathetic souls, and we are the losers, too."

The Dean, missing an attempt to hit the wastebasket halfway across the room with his empty Dixie cup, responded. "Well, you're certainly going to find others besides ballplayers failing to fulfill the potential you thought you had spotted at this table. You'll be charmed during the coming days by math potential, leadership potential, journalistic potential, et cetera. But who can predict which students, experiencing at age seventeen and a half a total change of environment and perhaps their first real freedom ever, will work and produce? So we're back to motivation and how to spot it."

"Let's go!" blurted Truman Benson, sharing his prolific doodlings with admissions staff members on either side of him (whose expressions seemed to suggest "How did *this* guy get appointed to the Committee?").

"Yes, Truman, let's go," nodded the Dean with a somewhat apologetic smile. "The seven candidates picked for discussion at this evening's orientation session seem to me almost to represent a microcosm of the entire applicant pool. At least they suggest why some of the central policy guidelines have no clear applicability once we come down to the choice of one candidate over another.

"The first candidate on your docket is MIMI BECHOLDT."

Suddenly everyone at the table straightened up, as though a starting gun had been fired.

"Mimi attends a superb country day school, one we'd like to do more business with. Note also that Mimi is from the Midwest, the area of the nation most underrepresented on many eastern campuses, partly because of the superb state university system out there, and partly because the area is just plain provincial. Anyway, Mimi is a midwesterner, and we need more of them *if* you feel geographical diversity is important at the College. Your predecessors on this Committee felt that we will only be as lively as we are different, and splicing a little Orange County together with the Bronx can assure it.

"Let's look first at Mimi's transcript." *(See pages 16–17.)*

"What do we look at first?" Taylor asked, puzzled. This was his first year on the Committee.

"Well, look at the actual course listings to appraise the degree of difficulty of the courseload. Then you'll probably want to look at grades to see level of performance and whether she has performed consistently. Then, notice her class rank based on six semesters to the right of the transcript.

"Frankly, I find it difficult in Mimi's case to appraise the quality of the courseload although I know this is a no-nonsense school. Mimi appears to have bailed out of Math, Science, and Foreign Language after the junior year. Her lowest grades throughout, note, were in Math, so I can understand why she wanted to evacuate that area. But why this good school also let her leave Science and Foreign Language is unclear. Her senior courseload appears on the surface to be adequate although it is obviously centered in areas of key interest to her."

Around the table there was subdued chatter as faculty members checked transcript impressions with the admissions staff. And the Dean continued:

"As the colleges offered more electives to students, allowing students to chart their own courses, the secondary schools followed suit. The "core curriculum" is returning now, but we can not presuppose that the best high schools and prep schools give kids sound training in 'basic disciplines.' On the one hand, she is probably happy that she was able to develop specific interests in the Humanities and the Arts, and thereby improve her overall

| Date of Birth | Sex | | | Month | Ye |
|---|---|---|---|---|---|
| 3-18-68 | F | ☐ Withdrew<br>☒ Was or Will Be Graduated | | June | 198 |

| YEAR | SUBJECTS | IDENTIFY LAB TV SEMINAR SUMMER | IDENTIFY HONORS ACCEL AD. PL. ETC. | 1ST. SEM. | FINAL OR 2ND. SEM. | CRED OR UNIT | STA EXA SCC |
|---|---|---|---|---|---|---|---|
| | English I - Genre | | | C+ | C+ | 1 | |
| | Math I - UICSM | | | D | C | 1 | |
| 9 | Earth Science | | | C- | B- | 1 | |
| | Latin II | | | C+ | C | 1 | |
| | French II | | | B- | B+ | 1 | |
| 19 82 | Studio Art | | | A | A | n/c | |
| 19 83 | | | | | | | |
| | | | | | | | |
| | Hum 45-Creative Writing | | | A | A | 1 | |
| | Review Alg. & Pl. Geom. | | | C+ | B- | 1 | |
| 10 | Modern World History | | | B- | B- | 1 | |
| | Biology I | | | B- | B | 1 | |
| | French 31 | | | B | B | 1 | |
| 19 83 | Studio Art | | | A- | A- | n/c | |
| 19 84 | | | | | | | |
| | | | | | | | |
| | | | | | | | |
| | Studio Art | | | B+ | B+ | n/c | |
| | French 41 | | | P | - | ½ | |
| 11 | Hum 42 - Am. Heritage | | | B+ | - | ½ | |
| | Hum 45 - Shakespeare | | | - | B+ | ½ | |
| | Math 31 - Adv. Algebra | | | B- | C+ | 1 | |
| 19 84 | Scie 25 - Electricity | | | B | B | ½ | |
| 19 85 | S.S.30 - U.S. History | | | B- | B- | 1 | |
| | S.S.42 - African Studies | | | A | - | ½ | |
| | Ind. Study - Theater | | | - | P | n/c | |
| | | | | | | | |
| | (mid-year;7th Semester) | | | | | | |
| 12 | Art History | | | B+ | | | |
| | Alienation & Affirmation | | | B+ | | | |
| | Photography I | | | B | | | |
| 19 86 | Journalism | | | A- | | | |
| 19 86 | Senior Seminar SS | | | B+ | | | |
| | Creative Reading (Ind. Study) | | | B | | | |
| | Phy. Ed. | | | P | | | |

| Passing Mark | Honors Mark (if any) | LOWEST NUMERICAL EQUIVALENT | | | |
|---|---|---|---|---|---|
| | | A | B | C | D |
| D- | B | | | | |

## EXPLANATION OF HONORS COURSES

---

## RANK IN CLASS     BASED ON    6    SEMESTERS

☑ EXACTLY   20   ☐ APPROX. _____ IN CLASS OF _67_

FINAL RANK _____

*Check Appropriate Rank Information*

☑ ALL SUBJECTS GIVEN CREDIT     ☑ ALL STUDENTS

☐ MAJOR SUBJECTS ONLY     ☑ COLL. PREP. STUDENTS ONLY

*Explain Weighting of Marks in Determining Rank*

record. But was she shortchanged in not being forced into a more balanced secondary education?—I think so. The current back-to-basics discussion throughout the nation may change the pattern we note on this transcript.

"Mimi's record improved with time, and she now ranks twentieth in their class of sixty-seven. By the way, a profile from the school in Mimi's folder indicates they had eighteen National Merit Semifinalists or Commended students last year in a class of sixty-five. Their own SAT medians for last year's seniors were 530 Verbal, 580 Math. Mimi's best SAT Verbal is a 580; her best Math score is 510; her College Board Achievements were 490 in English Composition; 560 in Math I; and 530 in American History. To put all this in context, remember that Oldebrick's median Verbal for last fall's entering freshman class was 580; our median SAT Math was 600."

"Oh God, let's work on that," said Norton Taylor with his eyes still glued to the docket in front of him.

"I'll read bits and pieces from Mimi's folder now," said the Dean. "She had two sisters who graduated from here three and four years ago, so this is a family who knows Oldebrick well. Mimi's father is a bank executive with an M.B.A., and her mother is a housewife with a B.A. She does not need financial aid."

Mr. Chin squirmed. "Is it really necessary for you to tell us whether her mother and father went to college, and what they do for a living? Why is that important?" Mr. Chin was an understated and highly regarded professor who, as the son of a waiter and waitress, had gone to a public high school for the 'gifted' in New York City prior to winning a full scholarship to NYU.

"Well I think it is important," said Al Hodges, the precise and bow-tied Director of Financial Aid, who was annually invited to attend these meetings so his office, too, would feel more in communication with Admissions. "Has this candidate benefited from informed discussion night after night at the dinner table? Whether Mom and Dad and brothers and sisters went to college can give us a feel for the type of household the applicant has been exposed to. If we're talking about a non-college taxi driver's or construction laborer's kid, there is a

strong likelihood that we may be talking about an applicant who
did not have certain advantages and encouragements that most
other Oldebrick candidates did have."

As Mr. Chin nodded courteously, the Dean said, "Unless
anyone strongly objects, I'll continue to comment on the education and employments of parents and siblings, where listed.
But back to Mimi. When asked about her main academic interests, she says:

> My main interest at Oldebrick will be in the Fine Arts. I feel that
> communications is a very new and developing field, and that one of
> the best ways to communicate is through fine arts such as theater,
> dance, and film. I am interested in performing, directing, writing,
> designing, business, or any other of the many facets these fields offer.

"Mimi has obviously had advantages, and she seems to have
used them well. In the application slot designated for out-of-
classroom activities, she says:

> During the last four years I have acted in 14 plays, and have also
> taken part in other aspects of the theater such as costuming, props,
> set construction, and student directing. My participation has been
> at school, community theater, and with the American Repertory
> Theater in Europe. Other activities at school have been in chorus,
> and student government. I am the Editor of the school's literary
> magazine, and Advertising Editor of the school's news magazine.
> Outside of school I have tutored for OEO, and studied piano. This
> past summer I performed with The American Repertory Theater
> Company in Europe. There were four classes every morning in voice,
> acting Mime, and movement. There were six hours of rehearsal in
> the afternoon and evening. We rehearsed for five weeks on two
> plays, Medea and The Birds.
>
> When rehearsals ended, we left Lugano, Switzerland for Taori-
> mina, Sicily. After Sicily we performed in Pompeii and Fiesole, Italy.
> All the places in which we performed were old Greek and Roman
> outdoor theatres.

"The essay our candidates were assigned this year is inten-
tionally wide open. We're one of about 110 private colleges
using what is called the Common Application. A candidate fills
out the original, and mails photocopies to several colleges, and
the schools do likewise with their forms. To get so many colleges
to agree on a common form was obviously a minor miracle. Our

greatest argument came over the choice of a common essay topic, and the result is a rather sweeping assignment:

> This personal statement helps us become acquainted with you in ways different from courses, grades, test scores, and other objective data. *It enables you to demonstrate your ability to organize thoughts and express yourself. Please write an essay about one of the topics listed below.*
> 1. Evaluate a significant experience or achievement that has special meaning to you.
> 2. Discuss some issue of personal, local, or national concern and its importance to you.
> 3. If you could interview a prominent person (past or present) in the arts, politics, religion, or science, for example, whom would you choose and why?

"I'll read you snatches of Mimi's essay:

> I am I!/ And I may not know why/ But I know that I like it./ Three cheers! I am I.

> The above quotation from Dr. Seuss is what I think is important about me, "I am I." Being yourself and recognizing what is your "self" is necessary for all people, so that they can live their lives fully. For if you do not understand yourself, how can you begin to understand others?

"Spare us the pain," groaned Truman Benson. "My *God,* how do you Admissions people read 2,800 of these dreadful things? Please, good Dean, telescope the essay reading the next few days."

"Well, Mimi goes on to say, down the page here:

> If I sound like Herman Hesse there is a reason, for he has played a part, as many authors have, and will, with how I see myself . . . Through literature I have found a piece of myself which will help me endure life with others. But reading is a mental activity, and many physical ones contribute to form one's "self". I tend to think of art, the fine arts, and how they have expanded me personally. Each theater production was an awakening to new characters, new behaviors, etc., etc.

"Mimi ends by saying:

> I have begun to understand myself, and by taking that step I have also begun to understand others. As for the future, not just mine,

but anyone's, I have to agree with the Moody Blues: "Just what you want to be, you'll be in the end."

"At least she can put a sentence together most of the time," Ms. Dorsett injected. "But I'm very tired of drama aspirants, not to mention the let-me-be-me syndrome, at least when presented in such shallow terms. I keep forgetting, however, that she's only seventeen, and from the sounds of it, one who has viewed the world from a very limited, carefully screened, perspective."

"Now we come to the School Report," continued the Dean. "You'll find as we move along that prep schools on the whole report more thoroughly, and perhaps even more sensitively, than the large public schools. Public school counselors just have too huge a student load to know kids well, and they also seem somewhat intimidated by the Buckley Amendment, or Family Educational Rights and Privacy Act. But there are only 67 seniors in Mimi's class, so this school knows its kids well. I'll read from the Headmaster's report:

Mimi is a truly unique person who lives life to the full and enjoys it. Her philosophy is that one gets out of life exactly what one puts into it. Her standardized testing is not impressive, but she has a working ability as a student and as a person that far exceeds her numerical scores. In spite of the fact that she has always carried a remarkable schedule of activities, she has usually earned honor grades and certainly observes well-ordered priorities. She thrives on over-involvement. From a purely traditional academic viewpoint she is not deeply intellectual, and her reading and writing skills are adequate for serious college study but not outstanding. But in self-confidence, self-discipline, willingness to work, and interest, she is outstanding. Her driving interests are in the creative communication arts as well as the humanities.

She is truly one of the most vivacious, lively, and interesting members of her class, if not the entire student body. She is most respected for her honesty, self-confidence, and energy. Always easy to communicate with, she is a delightful friend and companion with her peers, and she also has highly successful, informal relations with the adults she knows. One teacher said recently, "All the world is a stage for Mimi and she turns in an excellent performance in all of life's roles." Yet, there is nothing "stagey" or insincere in her approach to people or responsibilities.

"The Headmaster continues his raves about Mimi's energies, the fact that she wishes there were 25 hours in every day, and concludes by saying:

> I believe that the college in which Mimi enrolls will be fortunate to have her and I think she is ideal for Oldebrick in spite of test scores obviously below your average (and ours). She is thoroughly familiar with Oldebrick, which was attended by two older sisters. In short, we enthusiastically recommend her for admission.

"Was all that verbiage necessary?" queried Political Science's matter-of-fact Norton Taylor, already impatient with 124 candidates yet to be read. "All that the Headmaster said can be narrowed down to: 'Here is an energetic, involved, artistically inclined, affluent girl with middling abilities whom we'd like to slip into Oldebrick. You took her sisters, so why not Mimi?' "

As Butch Lassiter resumed his position at the window, the Dean continued after a cool glance at Taylor. "The verbiage does get a bit long-winded, Norton. But so often counselors and teachers truly capture a candidate in these characterizations. Let's hear what Mimi's Senior Seminar teacher has to say. By the way, we ask each candidate to submit at least one teacher's recommendation. We find that teachers are often less cautious than guidance counselors or principals, not to mention the fact that they know the kids better, having seen their ups and downs in the classroom. Some day we should consider eliminating everything in the candidate's folder except the kid's own application, a transcript, and comments from the English teacher. We might learn just as much as we do with today's fat folders which include comments from everyone around the schoolyard. Anyway, Mimi's African History teacher says:

> During the last several years, Mimi has taken every opportunity to diversify and take control of her own learning. She has studied education, politics and mountain climbing in East Africa. She has traveled in Europe with a repertory company. She took practical electricity as a junior and thoroughly enjoyed it. She has also designed independent study projects in costume design, contemporary literature, and grassroots politics. She is independent, sophisticated, well-traveled, strong-willed, sometimes intolerant, always proud, and an extremely confident girl. She has grace under pressure, at 15,000 feet

on Mt. Kilimanjaro, or in a difficult dance sequence in a school play.

As a reader, she is quick and critical. As a writer, she is straight-forward and to the point. She can use dramatic analogies very effectively in both writing and speech. Her sense of balance and proportion is always true, both at the seminar table and in the art studio.

"Note that everyone thus far seems in unison regarding Mimi. Finally, here is a summary paragraph from the interview report in our office. Kelly Darby saw Mimi back in November:

A very good prospect: strong-willed, very involved, innovative in approach to a sedate school setting, and obviously intelligent. She seems to have the combination of discipline and imagination needed.

Benson reached for his third Danish. "Now how can anyone be *that* profoundly convinced of another's qualities in a twenty minute interview?"

Kelly Darby, a bubbly 26-year-old Assistant Director of Admissions, spoke up, breaking the silence of the admissions staff who always found it a bit difficult to speak with confidence in the presence of faculty.

"I remember this girl well. Her energy, her composure, her willingness to try different things, her articulation: all were obvious. Granted, the interview—which is, by the way, usually considerably longer than twenty minutes, Professor Benson—often allows us to notice just the very obvious. If an applicant is particularly high-strung, particularly jolly, particularly shy, particularly intense about his or her studies, it sticks out. Regrettably, some of the subtle characteristics of the candidate don't show in this staged situation. But we *can* sight the obvious, often factors not indicated (for good or for bad) by teachers or by the candidates themselves in the folders. In Mimi's case, the interview confirmed all of the qualities mentioned by her school." Kelly bowed her head slightly, and smiled broadly.

"That, Ms. Darby, was a fine response to a sharp query. I'm going to believe everything you say about a candidate from now on," quipped Benson with an inviting glance.

"Well, that's all we know about Mimi Becholdt," said the Dean. "Let me add that there are four candidates from her school this year. There is a brilliant all-everything boy who is second in the class and who probably applied here because his mother went here—perhaps in deference to her, perhaps because he thinks he's a sure bet to get in because he's a legacy. Anyway, we're admitting him but I'll wager he'll end up at one of the Ivies. We're also admitting a girl who is fourteenth in the class, high Board scores, and a bit of an underachiever, but she has spent all her time playing tennis and is currently ranked third in her age group in the state. She, according to a phone call from the guidance counselor last week, is torn between Carleton and Oldebrick: We may get her. Mimi is next in line in class rank. And we're rejecting another Oldebrick legacy who is in the bottom fifth of the class and dull, dull, dull."

Mr. Chin adjusted his glasses once again. "What does it mean today in admissions to be the son or daughter of one of our alumni?"

"This is a favorite question of the alums who return to campus," Butch Lassiter said in turning from the window. "What can we tell them?"

"Last year we admitted 68 percent of our legacies," the Dean said. "We define legacies as sons or daughters of alumni, *not* sisters or brothers or grandsons or nieces. We seem to end up admitting roughly the same percentage each year, somewhat coincidentally. Our legacies are often above-average candidates. But also, we're kind to them in the admissions process. I'm not saying we'll sell out to take a legacy, but all things being rather similar between two applicants, we'll tip toward the legacy. After all, our own alumni must support this place, and admitting their kids seems to *them* the most visible symbol of Alma Mater's caring in return."

"What do the Ivies and Sisters do—and the rest of our competition?" asked Butch Lassiter, his interest obviously piqued.

The Dean lifted his hands to his head and started a slow twisting exercise. "Oh, most of our colleagues respond similarly. Some are extraordinarily generous with offspring of alumns: For example, Amherst admitted only 22 percent of all its applicants last year, but 54 percent of its legacies. That is a little extreme, granted, but most of the selective private colleges admit a considerably higher percentage of legacies than nonrelated applicants: 40 percent v. 58 percent at Colgate last year, 20 percent v. 40 percent at Dartmouth last year. Some colleges check with the Development Office before rejecting legacies."

Adam McDermott, a handsome, well-spoken 22-year-old and the latest in a string of Admissions Fellows hired at graduation from Oldebrick for a two-year term ("to get out and hustle where Oldebrick doesn't seem to be getting to first base in recruitment—Michigan and Indiana, for example"), nervously entered the conversation.

"Granted, I'm a newcomer and don't know all the ropes—and don't think I'm ungrateful, as I was on scholarship and know it was alumni who made it possible for me to graduate from this place. But after seeing dozens of deserving, well-qualified, and naive kids throughout the nation this year who would benefit so much from attending Oldebrick if just given the chance, it irks me to see us giving *any* favoritism to the 'old families' of the College, with the cash register ringing in our ears. If we're concerned about loyalty and dollars and future, what's wrong with attracting *new* families?"

Adam paused for a moment to catch his breath, and then said in an apologetic tone: "Sorry to interrupt, but having met some of our stuffy alums on the road, and having had my fill of their expectations of favoritism in the admissions process as some sort of pay-off, I just had to say something."

For several moments no one spoke. Then the Dean said, "Thanks for your thoughts, Adam. Continue to speak up. That's the sort of thing we need to hear. In defense of the legacies, however, I should add that their record of performance at the College, once admitted, is strong. But it is also relevant to add, I think, that the admission or rejection of a legacy—after all the shouting is over—seems to make little difference in the giving pattern of the parents to Alma Mater. Studies here and elsewhere confirm that."

"Look, let's vote on Miss Becholdt," said Benson. "Aside from her tweedy enthusiasm, I think she's dull as beans."

"Give her greater exposure, and she may develop nicely," responded Mr. Chin. "It seems to me that her basic instincts are quite good, and she has made the most of her aptitude and her manifold opportunities. What, exactly, is her flaw, except the absence of 750 Verbal and Math scores? I think she suffers here from being the first in line."

"She *does* suffer because she's first," Rita Dorsett agreed.

"Since we know this is a 'control group' tonight, and since we're just getting our feet wet, why don't we hear and discuss each candidate, then vote on all seven at the end of the evening? That way we'll be able to put them all in context, at least with each other. Tomorrow morning we can go to the regular procedure, voting after each applicant is read. We'll have an educated base of reference then. I can see this is going to be draining." She frowned and glanced about, but there were no receivers.

"Unless there is strenuous objection, I find that a good suggestion to follow," said the Dean. With even Benson quiet at this point, the group proceeded to the next case.

"Our next candidate also attends a private day school, or rather did attend one. (I've put our private school candidates together tonight just for the ease of comparison.) DIANE PERKINS graduated a semester early and is now working in New York City for several months before entering college in the fall. Her school would be considered fairly decent, but not nearly as strong at Mimi Becholdt's. You have Diane's transcript in front of you." *(See page 27.)*

Butch Lassiter interrupted: "I notice you always seem to start with a comment about the candidate's school. What benefit does a kid actually have coming from a private school?" Butch had taught and coached at a boarding school prior to being hired by Oldebrick.

"The benefit of being a prime candidate for our Records Committee," Ms. Dorsett snapped back tartly and uncharacteristically. "Some of the prep school products are spoiled children, regardless of what advantage they might have had in academics. So what if they read *Catcher in the Rye* one or two years early? At most of the boarding schools they learn social values by cold rules and regulations. Is that right for a fifteen-year-old? Once they get to college, they flounder in pretentious emancipation, while their public school colleagues earnestly, apprehensively, intelligently, and quietly dig right in because the comfort level isn't quite as high."

Rita Dorsett often twisted her handkerchief or poked her bun. At this point, she twisted, then poked.

Others around the table appeared unmoved.

## 3. STUDENT'S ACADEMIC HISTORY

| ADE & YRS. | COURSES TAKEN (AND SPECIAL LEVEL WHERE APPROPRIATE) | MARKS | CREDITS |
|---|---|---|---|
| 9th | English 1 | B | |
| | French 1 | A | |
| | Geometry | A | |
| | Biology | B | |
| | Civics | A | |
| 10th | English 2 | A | |
| | French 2 | B | |
| | Algebra 2 | A | |
| | Physics 1 | A | |
| | European History | A | |
| 11th | English 3 | A | |
| | French 3 | A | |
| | Analytic Geometry | A | |
| | Physics 2 | A | |
| | Art Major | A | |
| | U.S. History | A+ | |
| 12th one em.) | Humanities (Eng. 12) | A | |
| | Literature Tutorial | A | |
| | Philosophy | A | |
| | French 4 | A | |
| | Greek 1 | A | |
| | SAT:  V = 730; M = 700 | | |
| | ACH:  En = 640; M1 = 560; Fr = 580 | | |

"Rita, that indictment strikes me as a little heavy," replied the Dean. "It is true that some of the prep school products, particularly the boarding school kids, may fly a little high on their new-found freedom—and with a coterie of last summer's friends transplanted here from Cape Cod or The Hamptons. But maybe part of the problem is that we offer too much choice and freedom to our freshmen, particularly those who were part of a rather tight situation such a short time before, be it a school or a family. True, the home may provide a more flexible hit-or-miss social laboratory than the boarding school, but let's look at how the prep school product ultimately fares here rather than just judge the entering student with his cool, sophisticated facade."

Butch persisted. "I just want to know if prep school kids are somewhat advantaged in our admissions situation."

"Well, Butch, I like to think we're looking at kids more than at schools," said the Dean. "Not long ago, some prep schools served essentially as farm clubs for Ivyish colleges. No longer. College admissions has democratized on one side, and the schools have broadened their college counseling on the other. Also, remember that a good many prep schools were more selective in their admissions some years ago than they are now. St. Grottlesex today may not be helping us with the one-out-of-four screening in *their* admissions process that used to be rather automatic. The high price of education has hurt them too. Their popularity will increase considerably, however, if the quality of the public schools continues to be perceived as on the decline.

"But we get some fine kids from the prep schools. Some of our private school products, often with a lackadaisical start here, flourish to become our most accomplished. Actually, we're like a good many colleges in our league today, enrolling approximately 40 percent from private schools, and 60 percent from public high schools.

"Back to Diane, whose private school, I repeat, strikes us as middling in quality. Interestingly, her home area has some outstanding public high schools, so I don't know why her family decided she should go to private school. But she obviously has done well—only three B's flaw her otherwise perfect record. Note also that she has taken a fairly 'straight' courseload, though she bailed out of science and math in the senior year. Her SAT scores are superb—far above our averages here. Interestingly, her Achievements are good but not consistent with her SATs: one wonders, as a result, how tough it is to get an A at this school, or whether she just had a 'bad afternoon' with the tests, which could well be.

"Let's see what else is here." He shuffled the folder.

"Diane was born in Seattle and moved to North Carolina before secondary school. Her father is a college-educated senior engineer, her mother a part-time secretary. She is one of seven children and all the older ones have gone to or are going to college. She will need scholarship aid of approximately $2,500. Diane obviously charts her own course, and is allowed to by the family. Her application reads:

> I just moved to NYC three months ago, found myself an apartment and a job, and commenced to live on my own. In my most recent memory, these 3 months have been the biggest event ever; I have never had to support myself completely before, and I have never lived in New York. In between work and sleeping, there is not much time for real consideration of what I am doing, but when there is a little quiet time to think, I can see how much more aware of myself, my strengths and my weaknesses, I have become. In short, I'm enjoying my freedom.

"Forgive me if I stumble over some of this," the Dean said. "She's written her application in longhand. It's hard to read." He twisted and held the paper toward the light:

> Right now I want to become a doctor, which means a required set of courses probably, but I also want to learn something about Philosophy and Art. The medical interest has come as a result of my youngest brother's learning disability, which may be either organic or emotional, if not both . . .

"Regarding her extracurricular involvements, Diane says:

> Right now there is not much time for anything beyond work. Almost every free second is spent at a potter's, 2 blocks from my teeny apartment. However, when I was in school, I played lots of volleyball, began my interest in pottery, tutored and did bits and pieces of substitute teaching, belonged to a woman's group, had major and minor parts in many plays, as well as doing lots of makeup and

costume work, did a short stint with the Young Democrats, etc. For the largest part of my senior year I tutored for an hour every morning in the second grade of my school. It was the first thing I did every morning and I greatly relished it. My kids were all very loud and precocious, but also often lonely and in need of a lap. . . .

For two winters, I worked weekends in a bakery. And for more years than I care to remember, I have done baby-sitting.

"I won't read all of Diane's essay. She did a clever thing, though. To document her interest in art, she sent what might be called a maze-essay. She drew and painted high points of her life on a huge, unfolding piece of paper. Here it is. But what it says doesn't really add much to what I've already read from other parts of her application. Although this was a clever idea and she executed it well, it strikes me as a bit gimmicky.

"The headmaster from Diane's school sends us raves on the School Report:

It isn't just that Diane is in the top of her class, because we do not stress such things very much. It isn't that she has come so far and yet is still so young. We think she is really a strong person who is able and sensitive in a number of very important ways. Whether this comes of her being raised in a large family or whether it is inborn, we have found Diane to be a most remarkable person who is peculiarly fitted to do the more than usual in college.

As a student Diane is gifted both in class under guidance and also on her own with the loosest of reins. I do not think that I have ever seen quite such a balance of receptive skill and forward self-start in one person.

Even though Diane is not clear on her specialty as yet, I see her as the kind of person who will need the opportunity to specialize early. In the second place, she has the natural talent for concentration when she needs it. I do not need to say more to indicate that we think she is a very unusual student. Her independent work this year has been marked by a very fine approach.

In addition, Diane has a good many artistic sensitivities. Last year she did very well in her art work and this year she is going on with ceramics in such a way that I am quite surprised to see. Only a beginner, she seems to show a natural feel for what she does. She has the grace to pick up the job by the right handle.

I can think of no one in the past ten years that I would recommend more highly. She is an excellent student but she is outstanding in any number of other ways.

Mr. Chin was pressing his hands together as though in prayer. "I hate to be critical and cut you short, but it strikes me that the candidate is probably more precise in telling us about herself than this headmaster. Do you have any teachers' comments?"

"Yes," the Dean continued, smiling.

I have taught Diane English for three years. She is one of the best writers I have met in my teaching career. Her capacity for clear, precise, and subtle expression is great. In her present development, she writes more subtly than clearly, more clearly than precisely. She first exercised her writing powers in flowery expressions, puns, exotic and delicious words. Control came late, and is still coming. Last year her sentences grew more lucid—one could find the thought more easily and the thought had greater force as a result. She does not always manage to express the right thought, the very thought she had in mind. Few writers do. Precision is the hardest of the accomplishments on the list you have provided me for comment.

As to her speech—well, I can only say she always improved any class she entered. And she is not merely a good student, but her citizenship in my classes has benefited others. She has to a noticeable degree the public virtues helpful in a community of learning.

"Oh my God," exclaimed Norton Taylor. "Are *all* these kids going to be paragons of virtue? That's what I mean about tests: We ought to stick with test scores rather than this glib mush. I must say, however, that after hearing all this, I'd like to meet Diane." His comment, intended to entertain, drew only one or two weak smiles.

"Let me add our campus interviewer's comments. Adam McDermott interviewed Diane in January," said the Dean.

A free and gentle spirit with an inquiring mind, a stripe of daring, but above all, enormous personal charm. She's looking at Radcliffe and Yale, so we may have to kiss her goodbye, but *I quit* if she's not admitted! Her family was somewhat dismayed that she chose to spend a year in the Big Apple, but she pinned down the job and the apartment and then they fell in line. Still wallowing in self-discovery, perhaps, but with a sense of joy and awareness. Probably pre-med, though this is somewhat a romantic notion grounded in her kid brother's medical problems. Also vitally interested in ceramics and philosophy—has read quite a bit in the latter field in her spare time. Trying out Kierkegaard, and admits to being lost but intrigued. In short, this one has all the ingredients. Of course we want her—but will she want us?

"Well, sounds as though someone is making our decisions for us," Ms. Dorsett said, a bit haughtily. "Nonetheless, this young woman does have spunk and grace and intelligence and all other goods things going for her. She is even more intriguing because of the semester off, and the way she has handled it. Friends of mine have a son who wants to take the year off before college and work on a *kibbutz* in Israel. The parents are leary. . . ."

Sid Goldstein of the admissions staff suddenly sat up. "Right! I headed off to Israel to work on a *kibbutz* after high school nine years ago, before entering Oberlin. I know that was a trendy thing to do. It still is. At first, the trip and the orientation week on the *kibbutz* gave me a new sense of my Jewish heritage, and I was elated. But then my assignment! They stuck me out in the hills picking olives. I was almost alone out there. After several weeks, I was so damned tired of picking olives that I didn't know what to do! I wrote Oberlin and asked if I could enroll at midyear, and happily they said 'come on.' I haven't eaten an olive since."

There were a few chuckles, and then a silence while the group returned to Diane Perkins. But the Dean added: "We've seen some disastrous years off. I guess it all comes down to good planning—and Diane's venture in New York strikes me as a worthwhile example of that. But for an affluent kid just to go travel in Europe for a year—I have questions about that sort of thing. I remember one boy recently, however, who went to Montreal to work as an apprentice for a violinmaker. He was himself an aspiring concert violinist, so this was a great experience for him. But most kids who are seventeen or eighteen can't get a decent job, and the year is of little value as a true learning experience. I wish some of them would wait and take off the year between the sophomore and junior years of college—go work in a hospital, for example, if they're on the threshold of serious pre-medical training."

The Dean snapped back to the matter at hand, glancing at his watch. "Any other questions about Diane? She is a strong candidate, and I'm almost spoiling you by introducing a student of her credentials at this orientation session. Remember, most of our time will be spent with truly borderline candidates. Diane has been thrown in to demonstrate balance within the applicant pool. Let's move on. . . ."

Butch Lassiter circulated with coffee refills as the Dean changed folders.

"We're about to look at SOPHIE ROOSEVELT, a black applicant. Before we go into Sophie's record, let me pause and discuss Oldebrick's minority situation with you *briefly*. I realize you have heard a great deal on this topic already at faculty meetings but I'd like to attempt to summarize.

"You know that Oldebrick announced in a very fuzzy statement some years ago that, in an attempt to help blacks catch up in education nationally, and in an attempt to make due reparations for Oldebrick's less than noteworthy record in accommodating minorities through the years, we would now strive to get a 'representative number' of minorities—which seemed actually to mean blacks—into each incoming freshman class. Frankly, I'm irked that our mandate was not made more clear at that time, or since. Our Trustees did say, several years later, that because Oldebrick could not 'be all things to all people,' preference would be given to black students over other minorities, since we are better prepared to accommodate them with the Black Studies Program, the Crispus Attucks Cultural House, et cetera.

"Although we've put aside considerable monies each year in our Admissions budget for black-oriented recruitment activities, we've never succeeded in drawing a freshman class with a 'representative number' of blacks. I'm inferring the Trustees meant 11 percent by that phrase 'representative number,' or the approximate percentage of blacks in the national population. We have been enrolling 5 to 7 percent which is, frankly, somewhat better than most of our colleague colleges. Wellesley, Harvard, and Stanford, however, are examples of colleges which have been more consistently successful in this area—not just in attracting a larger number of blacks than the rest of us, but in attracting particularly well-qualified black students.

"In all honesty, we have had to 'stretch' some to reach our 5 to 7 percent at Oldebrick. By 'stretch' I mean we have had to dip somewhat lower on the scale of traditional indices, particularly College Board scores. I would quickly add, however, that we have always 'stretched' around here—as you might also vote to do during the next few days—for a few exceptional athletes (even for a few extraordinary violinists!), for a few who live far away, for a few wealthy alumni children, and for some candidates who, although not promising scholars, have extraordinary promise as leaders and seem absolutely irresistible as human beings."

"I resist that term 'stretch,' Dean," said Lois Ruffin, the attractive, young, and outspoken black admissions counselor who had been with Oldebrick two years now after graduating from Swarthmore. "Yes, we may indeed 'stretch' to take some dumb jock from one of the nation's best prep schools (which itself probably took him as a one-year postgraduate student in order to win more games), but don't use that word regarding the majority of our black applicants who are stuck in the pits of the nation's secondary schools and who have no idea in hell how to get themselves out. *They've* 'stretched' to get an education in those sewers, amidst teachers who, by default, spend most of their time keeping order, amidst facilities that are shamefully underbudgeted by racist school boards, and among kids who would rather smoke than write."

Ms. Ruffin's voice grew intense and loud as she reached into her purse for notes.

"Let me remind you of what's happening in the big world out there: 58 percent of the black folks are stuck, just plain stuck, in central cities; 47 percent of 17-year-old blacks are functionally illiterate; there are *more* blacks below the poverty level than there were 5 years ago; and only 6 percent of the kids who score over 500 on the SATs are black kids. Now don't tell me you have to 'stretch' to accommodate a group that this nation and this college have abused for so long. It is not the *privilege* of black kids to work into Oldebrick's freshman class next fall— it is their *right.*"

Silence. Everyone seemed to have his eyes on the docket in front of him until Truman Benson said calmly, "I and all my colleagues read *The New York Times,* Miss Ruffin. We may be more aware of the plight of your people than you give us credit for. We may also be more aware of the manifold missions of Oldebrick College than you, who are new. We can learn from each other at these meetings, Miss Ruffin. I will listen to you if you will listen to me. We are intelligent people, open to issues of the day, but I for one am not willing to be consumed by any single issue. And to my knowledge, none of us is hard of hearing."

With Lois Ruffin's eyes ablaze, the Dean suggested abruptly that Sophie Roosevelt's credentials be reviewed.

As the Dean read on, the tension in the room subsided.

"Sophie, who was born in Illinois but now lives in California, attends one of the nation's most prestigious boarding schools. Sophie's school, although famous, leaves some questions now and then in our minds regarding academic demands. It went through a rather flaky period of curricular change in the early seventies, but seems to be swinging back to a fairly straight and basic program now.

"Sophie's family is complicated, and we don't know all the dimensions. On the surface, she seems a rather advantaged young lady; her mother and father attended (black) colleges, and both are employed in white collar jobs. Her father is an industrial psychologist, her mother a part-time teacher. However, something is awry, because there appears to be little or no money in the family. Sophie was given a fee waiver (we and many other colleges will waive the application fee if the candidate's school confirms that he or she needs nearly a full scholarship to attend college), and she is sponsored at her prep school by ABC, 'A Better Chance' program, which places disadvantaged kids, particularly blacks, at good secondary schools in order to give them added educational and vocational incentive. ABC strikes us as a worthy and responsible program, and we trust they rather thoroughly analyzed Sophie's economic background before picking her.

"By the way, Sophie has filled out her application in pencil, so it is a little difficult to decipher. But here goes:

> I have found my involvement in student government here to be the most important of my extra-curricular activities. As president of the student body, I find my attendance at all meetings of student concern to be quite important. During these meetings I introduce new reforms in school policies to benefit my peers, and I attempt to appeal unfair decisions made about a student's conduct, if I believe she is innocent.
>
> This position is important to me because the best of my abilities is demanded, which I feel is a service to others. As a leader I have

learned one important lesson in how to remain objective, yet sensitive in my evaluation of the needs of my constituency—my peers.

"Sophie goes on to tell us that she has worked as a salaried library aide for two hours per day at the school. During summers she says she reads a lot—last summer, books on political philosophy by Fanon, Malcolm X, and Hitler. Also, she sews many of her own clothes, and informally enjoys modern dance. Perhaps the biggest event in her life was being chosen as a summer exchange student to Japan. She writes her application essay on that experience:

As an observer of the Japanese culture, I gained insight into another society and I acquired a better understanding of myself. During my exchange summer to Japan, I became a member of an upper-echelon Japanese family.

My first lesson in Japan was to have respect for my fellow man. I was expected to bow to all my elders and to refrain from familial discord. At first, I was reluctant to comply with the bowing ritual, but I learned to adjust to it. Familial discord was frowned upon, so before I became angry with someone, I learned to find the source of my anger, and many times discovered it to be quite shallow. I thus learned to control my emotions and to carry myself as a more civil, in turn, noble person.

The next tradition from which I extracted a valuable lesson was male supremacy. Male supremacy was exemplified for me in two ways. I was told to serve my Japanese father at any time, and to allow him or any other male to dominate any conversation that dealt with controversial, political, social, or economic issues. I was not accustomed to total intellectual subserviency to a member of the opposite sex. As a member of the female sex, I was considered a second-class citizen in Japan. I felt that the Japanese society suffered as a whole because women were not permitted to acquire key positions in the intellectual world.

I learned from this experience that women must play an equal role in a society, in order that society may benefit from women's contributions.

My blackness was difficult for many Japanese to accept. At one time during my stay, I was called a "nigger" by a young Japanese man. It was not a new experience for me, but I found a new meaning in the experience. I learned to find peace and worth in myself as a young, black American, barring the opinions and beliefs of others about my kind.

In this transition to another mode of living and thinking, I strengthened my weaknesses as a young adult. I learned lessons of life in Japan that will help me make positive contributions to humanity and the world.

"You have Sophie's transcript in front of you. *(See page 38)*. A phone call yesterday resulted in our getting the following first semester, senior year grades: C− in Poetry, C+ in French, C+ in Biology, and D in History. Note that she is taking Advanced Placement French and doing reasonably well; it is fair to say, however, that Sophie's overall record has not been consistent. Naturally we would like to have seen a swing up this last year. In her favor, however, it seems to me that she has taken a decent courseload with the exception of avoiding science until now. And C's from this school should not put her out of the running."

"This is a school which knows its kids well, knows Oldebrick well, and has fed us honest and comprehensive reports in the past. So let's hear what the Headmaster has to say about Sophie:

Sophie is a very complex young woman who has been a boarding student here throughout all four years of her secondary school career. She has been the chief hope of her father, who expects great things of her and is a stern task-master. The expectations of her father have created a perpetual tension for Sophie as she tries to reconcile his plans for her with her own abilities and inclinations.

Sophie is a student who, because of continual strain, has had more than her share of academic ups and downs. She has tended to work in spurts corresponding to moods of self-confident "new starts," then receive a series of disappointing setbacks and go into a depression, producing little until her sense of shame drives her to a new effort to succeed. Family problems and personal insecurities have prevented Sophie from remaining on an even keel for long. When she attains a balance, she will be on her way.

Sophie's chief academic difficulty is her tendency to generalize without mastering all the details of a complex situation. Thus she is often unable to sustain an argument or have a meaningful discussion. She is stronger when dealing with factual material to be applied within a given context. She is currently drawn to the field of politics and international relations, perhaps because she admires certain legislators and identifies her student marshalship with their mandate, but she will need to realize that success in this field will not come as easily to her as she thinks. Sophie has yet to make a realistic evaluation of her academic potential. She can be a good average

| | CLASS RECORD<br>*Include Subjects Failed or Repeated* | IDENTIFY LAB TV SEMINAR SUMMER | IDENTIFY HONORS ACCEL AD. PL. ETC. | MARKS | | CRED CR UNIT |
|---|---|---|---|---|---|---|
| YEAR | SUBJECTS | | | 1ST. SEM | FINAL OR 2ND. SEM | |
| **9**<br>19 82<br>19 83 | English 100 | | | | B− | 1 |
| | French 200 | | | | C+ | 1 |
| | German 100 | | | | B+ | 1 |
| | Math 100: Algebra I | | | | B− | 1 |
| | Hist 100: Anc-Med. | | | | B+ | 1 |
| | Music 100: Intro. | | | | B | 1/2 |
| | | | | | | |
| | French I (8th Grade) | | | | 93 | 1 |
| **10**<br>19 83<br>19 84 | English 200 | | H | | C+ | 1 |
| | French 300 | | | | B− | 1 |
| | German 200 | | | | B− | 1 |
| | Math 200: Geometry | | | | C+ | 1 |
| | Hist 200: U.S. | | | | C+ | 1 |
| | Mus 160: Afro-Amer. | | | | B− | 1/2 |
| | | | | | | |
| | | | | | | |
| | | | | | | |
| **11**<br>19 84<br>19 85 | English 300 | | H | | B− | 1 |
| | French 400 | | | | C+ | 1 |
| | German 300 | | | | C+ | 1 |
| | Math 300: Alg. II & Trig. | | | | D+ | 1 |
| | Journalism | | | | C | 1/2 |
| | | | | | | |
| | | | | | | |
| | | | | | | |
| **12**<br>19 85<br>19 86 | English 402: Poetry* | | | | | 1 |
| | French 450* | | AP | | | 1 |
| | Sci 300: Biology* | | | | | 1 |
| | History 410: Am.Pol.Inst.* | | | | | 1/3 |
| | | | | | | |
| | *Courses in progress | | | | | |
| | | | | | | |
| | | | | | | |
| | | | | | | |

| | DATE | NAME OF TEST | RAW OR STD. SCORE | PERCENTILE SCORE | NORM GROUP | |
|---|---|---|---|---|---|---|
| **TEST RECORD** | | CEEB PSAT V 47; M 47 | | | | |
| | | SAT V 460; M 440 | | | | |
| | | ACH EN 460; FR 560 | | | | |
| | | | | | | |
| | | | | | | |
| | | | | | | |

student with consistent effort; she will never set the academic world on fire, no matter how hard she tries. She must come to terms with that reality before she can attain the equilibrium she requires for her best work.

The heart of her pride and self-esteem is her election as president of the student body. She had long been popular as an advocate for various student causes and she felt she could exercise a meaningful leadership if given the chance. She is now discovering the disappointing depths of student apathy, the need for tact, patience, and compromise in attempting to cut through procedural red tape, the burdensome obligations of her office, and the difficult expectations of a marshal and moral exemplar. Once again she had not grasped all the ramifications of a complex situation, and coming to terms with the difficulties of this position has again put Sophie under a strain this fall.

To her credit, Sophie has never given up her struggle to become the best possible student and person she could be. A lesser individual would have taken the line of least resistance. Sophie deserves the opportunity to develop her mind and her personality in an atmosphere of challenge and vitality. She has much to give and will make a fine contribution to the academic community she joins. I recommend her for college admission.

Sophie's folder obviously intrigued the full Committee. Everyone listened earnestly as the Dean continued.

"The profile of last year's senior class, sent along with Sophie's transcript, indicates that the mean grade there was a B. Although the school does not provide us with a class rank—which we regret—it is obvious that Sophie's record would place her well into the bottom half of the class. Actually, her CEEB scores seem to me rather consistent with her in-school performance, emotional ups and downs notwithstanding. As a postscript on the school, their profile indicates that of last year's class of 275, 12 went to Harvard/Radcliffe, 16 to Tufts, 7 to Yale, 10 to Duke. In other words, we're talking about a high-powered group of kids that Sophie had to compete with academically, and remember, they chose her as student body president. Finally, let's hear what her Advanced Placement French teacher says:

Being Sophie's Fourth Year Honors French teacher, I feel well-qualified to evaluate her academic potential. She may not have extraordinary natural ability—it is nevertheless above average—but she really does have <u>extraordinary</u> drive and determination, some of it coming from her family, but most of it from herself. She is one of the most determined students I have taught. Although her teahers and peers have great confidence in her, she often lacks confidence in herself. She enjoys and indeed does her best in independent work, particularly when she feels it relates to her own situation, but curiously enough she prefaces even excellent work with profuse apologies. Her desire to learn pushes her to participate in class (where her contributions are valuable), but at the same time her lack of confidence makes her somewhat tense when she does. What I have particularly enjoyed about teaching Sophie is that she has been developing more and more confidence in herself so that learning has become enjoyable for her. Now let me speak to your question about her "clear, precise, subtle expression . . ." Sophie does not make many mistakes when she writes in French; her writing shows a sensitivity to nuances of style. What she lacks often when she writes is an ability to organize her ideas, particularly when she is forced by an examination to write quickly. In her most recent papers, she shows that she is developing the ability to synthesize and distinguish between the essential and the nonessential.

The Dean stopped reading. There was a silence. Finally, everyone heard Harry Chin take a deep breath. (Was it because he was a member of a minority group himself that he had covered his eyes with his hands during the reading?)

"I'm enormously impressed," he said, "with the successful effort of this school to help us know Sophie. Those reports are superb. Perhaps, however, they have grown to know Sophie *too* well because she is there around the clock, because she is so visible as a student officer, and probably because she is a minority student. But all to Sophie's benefit! My, how that girl must have grown. Here is a prime example of why boarding schools exist. Now I know what school to promote for my bright niece who is stuck in the New York City public system."

"Yes, those are impressive reports," said Norton Taylor, "partly for what they tell us about Sophie, and partly because they are so well written. If only the candidates knew they are at the mercy of a counselor's or teacher's ability to *write* in this admissions process!

"But what impresses us—what Sophie represents, or how

they present her? That's what puzzles me. If one searches carefully in those guarded and well-turned phrases, I think we hear
that we are looking at a growing but nonetheless very insecure
young lady, who hasn't yet seen her way clearly to a consistent
performance in the classroom or in student office. Wasn't the
guidance counselor trying to tell us something we should know
before we introduce Sophie to this sophisticated, rather cold,
highly competitive environment? Much as I like Sophie, I can't
help wondering if she wouldn't fare better at a college with
more advanced support services and a slightly warmer atmosphere—and one perhaps even smaller in size than Oldebrick.
Dean, could you read the counselor's remarks on Sophie's academic potential and her performance in the student government again? Those warnings need to be spotlighted, I think."
  The Dean complied:

. . . Sophie has yet to make a realistic evaluation of her academic
potential. She can be a good average student with consistent effort;
she will never set the academic world on fire, no matter how hard
she tries. She must come to terms with that reality before she can
attain the equilibrium she requires for her best work. . . .
  . . . She is now discovering the disappointing depths of student
apathy, the need for tact, patience, and compromise in attempting
to cut through procedural red tape, the burdensome obligations of
her office, and the difficult expectations of a marshal as a moral
exemplar. Once again, she has not grasped all the ramifications of
a complex situation, and reestablishing her vision of the position has
again put Sophie under a strain this fall. . . .

"I'm really confused by all this," young Adam McDermott
hesitantly remarked. "On the one hand, Mr. Chin commends
the school for all they've done for Sophie, and he is undoubtedly
right—not to mention what Sophie surely did for this Waspy
place in return. But here she is now, presenting her credentials
for college admission, and we know her flaws so well that she
is about to be crucified. What if she had stayed in her local high
school back in California—even though it might be a zoo—had
struggled to take the honors curriculum, had come up with the
same SATs, had gotten A's and B's, and more importantly,
raves from the school because they didn't know her subtle shortcomings and problems? I have the uncomfortable feeling that

Sophie is about to pay a price for her 'advantaged' schooling, even though it undoubtedly benefited her in many ways."

"Well, I think I agree with Adam," said Butch Lassiter warmly. "But 'pay the price' or not, I'm won by Norton's honest question of how well we can accommodate this girl with our less-than-adequate advisory system and support services. She'll pay an even greater price if she enrolls at a college where she'll suffer. If we don't take Sophie, however, let's remember that she'll pay the price for *our* inadequacies rather than her own."

The comments on Sophie came in rapid fire.

"I'm suspicious of the label, or implied label, of 'disadvantaged' in this case," said Benson. "Yes, she is black, but if I heard the report correctly, both parents went to college and hold responsible jobs, the father is very involved in guiding the daughter—probably *too* involved—she has gone to a superb school, and has tooted off to Japan. On the surface of things, she has had a hell of a lot more advantages than my daughter (whom I consider 'advantaged'). I find Sophie interesting, and a little sad. I'm glad we're reviewing her case. But my vote will not be bought just because she is black and we need more of them. It seems to me that our black program is trying to reach out not to the Sophies of the world, but to those in far less grand circumstances. As a regular candidate for Oldebrick, I find Sophie beneath our standards. Color, in this case, strikes me as irrelevant."

"Being black, Mr. Benson, is *never* irrelevant," Lois Ruffin retorted firmly.

"I somehow would have felt shortchanged if you had not made that comment, Ms. Ruffin," responded Truman Benson, attempting a smile which came as a smirk. "On the other hand, I'm looking forward to your guidance in this case. Your experience and commitment will help us here. What are your thoughts about Sophie?"

"Well, I'm of a mixed mind," Lois Ruffin responded with a softened tone. "On one hand, I agree there is little evidence that Sophie is truly disadvantaged and should be given special consideration just because of her color. In fact, I question her fee waiver and wonder why the school approved it—there is nothing in the folder documenting her severe financial shortcomings. On the other hand, she is black and 1. that has meant certain strains for her in an elitist school, and she has survived that trial with distinction, and 2. for some reason or reasons, we and a good many of our colleague colleges are down in black applications this year, so we need her. Black for black's sake?— a little of that. But more important, it seems to me, is the fact that she has fought a battle in a tough, stuck-up school; consequently, I find her emotional flip-flops no surprise at all. Also, it is going to take the needs of a few Sophies at this college to finally force us to get the supportive services that will help the black kids survive here once recruited and enrolled. Sophie is an unusual minority case, because of her background, but we need her."

"Since we decided to hold voting until we've heard all seven folders, I'd suggest we move along," said the Dean. "Any more questions or comments regarding Sophie?"

"Not really regarding Sophie," said Mr. Chin, in the prayerful position again, "but would you comment on why a good secondary school as large as Sophie's does not rank its students? I find class rank a helpful barometer in this process, particularly when we don't know the degree of difficulty of attaining an A grade in one school compared to another school five miles down the road."

The Dean complied, glancing again at his watch. There was a general shuffling around the room. Adam McDermott and Kelly Darby started playing catch with a Danish over by the coffee urn until the Dean scowled. They quickly stopped and returned to their seats.

"Well, I think that is an important question, Mr. Chin. And I wish you all would listen, although I realize time is moving on. A good many schools, particularly the private ones, are reluctant to rank their kids since grade point averages can differ by only a hundredth of a point or so. Many schools feel—and I can see their point—that it is simply unjust to call one candidate "top fifth" and the next kid "second fifth" when only a B in ninth grade American History separates them. On the other hand, a good many validity studies at individual private colleges, many of them overseen by the College Entrance Examination Board, indicates that class rank is a very high predictor of in-college success, particularly in the freshman year.

"As you have suggested, we aren't certain of the quality of

an A – GPA at Iowa City Central High unless we see where that average puts a kid in context with others. The top fifth at Iowa City Central High may *all* have A records!—we don't know unless rank is recorded. The National Association of Secondary School Principals recommends a ranking system which many schools use. It gives added weight to Advanced Placement courses, Honors level courses, et cetera. The NASSP formula strikes many of us at the college level as being fair and well formulated. I wish everyone would use it. I do understand, though, why tiny schools—those with 30 in the class, say—find it unfair to rank.

"Let's look at JOHN WESTERHALL now." Everyone stirred to attention in his seat.

"A boy! I wondered if the class wasn't beginning to take on flagrant tones of feminism. Does this kid paddle?" queried Benson.

Benson's presence was no longer felt, it seemed, particularly by the other faculty members. Whenever he spoke, Dorsett, Lassiter, Chin, and Taylor did not stir or look up.

"Probably," said the Dean. "Westerhall is perhaps the classic case of a middling student who seems to have a lot going on the personal side. We can't fill the class with this type, but now and then we run across an applicant who is so compelling personally that we're willing to forgive a few academic holes.

"John attends a large public high school in a rather wealthy suburban area of New York. His school is regarded as superb: 70 percent head on to four-year colleges, so the curriculum is quite college-oriented. We've had a good draw from this school recently. Often, if a college attracts a few good kids one year and they talk positively when they return home for that first Christmas vacation, good kids the next year will follow.

"There are sixteen applicants from the school this year. Regrettably, John's class rank is toward the lower end of the group. But he draws such personal raves from all parties that we doubt if the school would question our inconsistency here. We're admitting a handful at the top of the class who are bright and a trifle drab; maybe John would help us strike a balance.

"On his application, John says he wants to major in Political Science, English, or Psychology. He says his most important extracurricular activity is being president of the Senior Class. He also is on the Varsity tennis team, varsity fencing team, and reports for the school newspaper. He is the chairman of the School Student Committee for a Safer Community—we'll hear a lot more about this later. His father is a lawyer; his mother does some freelance publicity work; he has one young brother. John urges us to read a few comments about his academic record before we dig into it. Here is his essay:

I feel I have qualities which make me the "right" person to attend Oldebrick. One quality is that of progressive academic improvement. My transcript shows that I received an 83% in the ninth grade, 86% in tenth grade, and 89% in eleventh grade. My present average is in the nineties. This shows a pattern of growth and I feel that such a trend will continue during my college years. This quality of improvement will help me fit into college life and enable me to get the most out of my college education.

Another of my qualities is that of social maturity. I started in high school as an unknown freshman and became one of the best known students in the school. I achieved this because of both school and community activities. I have worked in my school's General Association since I was a freshman. Last year I was given the opportunity of giving a speech to the entire student body of 2400. As Junior Class Social Affairs Committee Chairman, and as Senior Class President I have addressed the 618 members of the Class on numerous occasions.

I am able to get along with people and have come to know many of my teachers on a personal basis.

Another quality essential to success is that of determination. I do not like to "give up." When I start something I finish with the best effort I can give. If I am involved in a report, essay or activity, I try to attain the best result possible out of the task. For example, I was able to obtain a traffic light to be placed in front of my school by overcoming the initial disapproval of village officials and trustees. I spearheaded the drive that resulted in the final approval of the light.

Another quality I possess is sensitivity to other people. I enjoy people and try to do what I can to help others. I like to do volunteer work. I have taught tennis to underprivileged children of my town and have tutored students in history. This is part of the give-and-take philosophy in my life as a member of the community. I like to get involved, and have either worked on or chaired a number of committees or organizations aiding my high school. These include committees dedicated to making the school a better place in which to study, committees planning activities for the student body, committees to provide better career education for those not planning to go on to college, and the student publications.

Finally, I believe I am an all-round person. In addition to my activities which I have described, I have been active in school athletics as a member of the Varsity tennis and fencing teams. I was part of the team that captured the tennis sectionals and swept the State tournament.

I am sure that I will be able to contribute to, and benefit from, the Oldebrick College community. I believe that my transcript, extra-curricular activities, the personal interview, and the qualities described in this essay, indicate that I am the "right" person for Oldebrick College.

Benson blew his nose. "Would that I had a beer tonight for every time that young man used the pronoun 'I.' He might be tough and aggressive when the rocks and the rapids threaten, but in calm waters he sounds like he'd be a pain in the tail."

"John's transcript brings few surprises, considering his warning to us. Look it over," the Dean said.

The group seemed more self-confident now in reading transcripts. Everyone quietly studied his copy of Westerhall's record, as the Dean talked on. *(See pages 48–49.)*

"Note that there has been steady growth from an early smattering of grades in the 70's to straight 90's now. John has taken a balanced courseload; notice, however, that, with the exception of senior European History, no courses are designated as Advanced Placement or Honors. His New York State Regents Exam scores are moderate indeed, and his SATs are paltry. His class rank is clearly affected by his slow start in high school—all those lowish grades in the freshman and sophomore years hurt his standing now. (This school, to my surprise, indicates they do not give added weight in rank to their more demanding courses.) Finally, notice that John had enough spunk and interest to attend the Phillips Exeter summer school, where all grades are listed as 'Satisfactory.' He drew no Honor grades there, but it does say something that he chose to go to enhance his own high school program."

For the second time, Harry Chin passed Rita Dorsett a note. This time she returned a faint smile, then adjusted her bun. One could sense pairings by point of view developing around the table, unstated but there.

John's counselor writes:

John is an alert, articulate young man, consistently conscientious, anxious to do well, goal-oriented, and motivated to achieve. His personal warmth and sincerity, combined with an unusually mature outlook, have helped make him well respected by students and faculty alike. . . . John has been praised by his teachers for his genuine interest, his excellent attitude, his depth of understanding, his full acceptance of responsibility and his self-initiated participation in class discussions.

His American History teacher commented: "John is an excellent student who contributes a lot to the class. He possesses real compassion for his fellow man and is willing to work for his ideals. He deserves the best education he can obtain."

His Math II teacher describes him as "highly motivated." His Biology teacher wrote: "John has shown a steady improvement from a B student to doing A work. Has excellent ability and is capable of working on his own with little guidance. He is a real pusher— works quite beyond his level, and thus, through sheer diligence, does very well."

John is well known at the school. He is President of the Senior Class, and has distinguished himself in athletics, particularly tennis. . . . During the past year he was the leader in the campaign to get a much needed traffic light in front of our school. For his leadership and dedication to this cause, he earned the praise and admiration of many community leaders.

John spent last summer at Exeter taking American Foreign Policy, among other courses. An already strong interest in history received further impetus at Exeter, with the subsequent result that he is currently enrolled in Advanced Placement European History.

Also, John has taught underprivileged children locally, has helped the tennis pro at a local club, and at present is employed weekends and after school working at a local pharmacy to make money for college.

John is a doer without ostentation. He is involved, industrious, and trustworthy. He seeks counsel when necessary, yet preserves his own integrity and independence. He is intellectually capable and emotionally ready to accept a challenging undergraduate program.

| YEAR | SUBJECTS | IDENTIFY LAB TV SEMINAR SUMMER | IDENTIFY HONORS ACCEL AD. PL. ETC | 1ST. SEM | FINAL OR 2ND SEM | CRED OR UNIT | STATE EXAM. SCORES |
|---|---|---|---|---|---|---|---|
| | **CLASS RECORD** *Include Subjects Failed or Repeated* | | | | | | |
| | English 1 | | | | 89 | 1 | |
| | Afro Asian History | | | | 90 | 1 | |
| **9** | French 1 | | | | 74 | 1 | |
| | Math 9 | | | | 73 | 1 | 82 |
| | Earth Science | Lab | | | 80 | 1 | 74 |
| 19 82 | Phys. Education | | | | PA | 1/4 | |
| 19 83 | | | | | | | |
| | | | | | | | |
| | English 2 | | | | 93 | 1 | |
| | Biology | Lab | | | 84 | 1 | 93 |
| **10** | Math 10 | | | | 75 | 1 | 80 |
| | European Studies | | | | 92 | 1 | |
| | French 2 | | | | 85 | 1 | |
| 19 83 | Phys. Education | | | | PA | 1/4 | |
| 19 84 | | | | | | | |
| | | | | | | | |
| | English 3LL | | | | 90 | 1/2 | |
| | Language & Literature | | | | 88 | 1/2 | |
| | Environmental Study | | | | 92 | 1/2 | |
| **11** | French 3 | | | | 81 | 1 | 71 |
| | American Studies | | | | 92 | 1 | |
| 19 84 | Speech/Drama | | | | 91 | 1/2 | |
| 19 85 | Anthropology | | | | 92 | 1/2 | |
| | Math 11 | | | | 83 | 1 | |
| | Phys. Education | | | | PA | 1/4 | |
| | English Sen. Cr. Wr. | | | 91 | | | |
| | American Life & Prob. | | | 91 | | | |
| **12** | Russian Studies | | | 96 | | | |
| | European Studies | | AP | 90 | | | |
| | Drivers Education | | | 95 | | | |
| 19 85 | Phys. Education | | | | | 1/4 | |
| 19 86 | (Courses in progress) | | | | | | |
| | | | | | | | |

| | DATE | NAME OF TEST | RAW OR STD. SCORE | PERCENTILE SCORE | NORM GROUP | DATE |
|---|---|---|---|---|---|---|
| **TEST RECORD** | | | | | | |
| | | | | | | |
| | | | | | | |
| | | | | | | |
| | | | | | | |
| | | | | | | |

| PUBLIC | NON-PUBLIC | Enrollment in Grades | Percent Graduates Entering College | | |
|---|---|---|---|---|---|
| X | ☐ | 9 –12 | 70 4 Yr. Col. | 10 | 2 Yr. Col. and Other |

| Passing Mark | Honors Mark | LOWEST NUMERICAL EQUIVALENT | | | |
|---|---|---|---|---|---|
| 65 | (if any) 90 | 90 A | 80 B | 70 C | 65 D |

## EXPLANATION OF HONORS COURSES

AP–Advanced Placement curriculum of CEEB
H–Honors group
("Regular" class groups do not carry any
  suffix designation)

(See Summer School record below)

## RANK IN CLASS    BASED ON __6__ SEMESTERS

☒ EXACTLY 168 ☐ APPROX. _____ IN CLASS OF __529__

FINAL RANK _____

*Check Appropriate Rank Information*

☒ ALL SUBJECTS GIVEN CREDIT    ☒ ALL STUDENTS

☐ MAJOR SUBJECTS ONLY    ☐ COLL. PREP. STUDENTS ONLY

*Explain Weighting of Marks in Determining Rank*

*Rank determined on basis of all subjects
 given credit <u>except</u> Physical Education,
 Glee Club, Choir, Band, Orchestra.

X̶X̶X̶P̶S̶T̶A̶N̶D̶X̶N̶G̶X̶X̶X̶C̶T̶X̶H̶X̶X̶E̶S̶X̶X̶H̶X̶N̶X̶R̶S̶X̶X̶A̶W̶A̶R̶D̶S̶

PHILLIPS EXETER ACADEMY SUMMER SCHOOL

| | GR | CR |
|---|---|---|
| Amer. For. Pol.-Age of Rev. | S | 1/2 |
| Psychology-Concepts & Methods | S | 1/2 |
| English 12-Literary Int. | S | 1/2 |

| NAME OF TEST | RAW OR STD. SCORE | PERCENTILE SCORE | NORM GROUP |
|---|---|---|---|
| Otis Lennon | | 105 | |
| DAT VR&NA75ile | | | |
| CEEB SAT V460 M400 | | | |
| CEEB SAT V590 M410 | | | |
| | | | |
| | | | |
| | | | |

"You know," Norton Taylor said, "after hearing the candidate's essay first and then this recommendation, I get the uncomfortable feeling that John handed a list of his involvements to his counselor and the counselor just dutifully wrote them up. Frankly, I learned nothing new from that report except that he works in a pharmacy after school and on weekends. If a report that long ends up being so shallow regarding a kid who is seemingly quite visible, think what happens when the counselor writes about kids who are understated!"

Growing repetitious, as was Taylor's custom, he said: "As the evening progresses, grades and SATs are beginning to speak louder to me. A lot of these time-consuming reports from schools hide candidates more than they reveal them. I agree, however, that the school reports on Sophie were exceptional."

"Remember," said the Dean, "that John is in Advanced Placement History. I think it's interesting that he has given his instructor's form to that teacher for a recommendation, because AP History is probably his most demanding course Here are the teacher's comments:

> John is a good student who works to the level of his ability, and then some. He is conscientious, well organized, and mature. When assigned research papers, he begins work at once and tries to obtain every source available.
>
> John expresses himself clearly and precisely both in writing and in speech. Considering the fact that students today are rarely taught to write correctly, John's work is far above the average. Had he been taught traditional English by our school, he might produce even better papers!

"Bravo!" exclaimed Truman Benson. "Who *is* this man? We should send him a medal."

"This man is a woman, Truman, by the name of Bernadette Jacobs. Write her! Surely some of these teachers wonder if we ever read their recommendations. Ms. Jacobs would be really glad to know we care. I'll give you her address at the school so you can write.

"But let me finish this folder. It's a fat one," the Dean said. "Which reminds me—there is a little quip that circulates among admissions people: 'The thicker the folder, the thicker the kid,' meaning we're suspicious, if the folder is chuck full of outside recommendations, that the applicant has not felt secure in letting his record stand alone—that strings must be pulled to get in. We're coming to a pile of those recommendations now, but in John's case there is a difference: these letters seem to have been spontaneously sent. I don't have the feeling that John or his father went out hustling support. So often it is the father who feels such letters are necessary, and the result is embarrassing indeed: the solicited reference talking more about the civic spirit of the father and mother than about the quality of the candidate, who is sometimes not known at all by the senator, or the chairman of the board or even by the business partner who happens to be an alumnus of Oldebrick. We in Admissions are human and reasonably intelligent: some of these letters create a bias against the candidate rather than for him. One no longer gets into college via 'the Old Boy system,' but somehow that word hasn't gotten out.

"Anyway, in John's case, we have a stack of letters singing his praise, often related to his great campaign of talking the town fathers into the traffic light in front of the high school. John must have spent months on that traffic light. Obviously he charmed the authorities. We have several letters from our own alumni regarding the campaign and ohn's effectiveness, as well as letters from the Principal (that is unusual, I must say), from several members of the Town Council, from the area's state senator, and from the town's Director of Parks. Also, we have from John himself a sampling of newspaper clippings. And finally, let me read you a few comments from his interview here at Oldebrick:

John is hardly an outstanding scholar, but he could probably handle our work if he lands courses of interest to him. He might bomb in science or math, but he seems vitally interested in politics and history, and perhaps will discover sociology and philosophy. He wants Law School, but unlike so many others we meet, he's leaving the options open. . . . Despite his disappointing record and test scores, I have the feeling this fellow has genuine intellectual curiosity. . . . In sum, John is probably a candidate we should seriously consider. He has certainly accomplished in the extracurricular zone at his school. Reading his folder prior to the interview, I expected more of a dynamo: not so. He is outgoing, but in a rather quiet way, solid, inquisitive, firm, and clearly one whom others would follow.

Ms. Darby of the admissions staff suddenly spoke again. "You know, I wrote that, and I'm disappointed now that I hear it. It's been four months since I interviewed John, but he is one of those candidates who lingers in your mind. I feel I really understated his personal strengths. And I think Oldebrick needs this fellow for diversity. True, he's not a super-jock or a legacy or a minority student and his father is not worth a million dollars. And he is not brilliant. But he *is* one super guy, and I hope we have room for him. I feel I've done him a bit of an injustice by not using more superlatives in the interview report. He must have been my sixth or seventh interview on a full day."

"I'm perplexed," said Taylor, who'd been examining the docket carefully. "His SATs are absolutely pathetic and his Law Boards will probably be similar. Four years from now the law schools will throw him out of the running before they even give his college grades and recommendations a fair reading. On the other hand, although I wouldn't want him as a college roommate, I'm becoming rather taken by his energy, his discipline, and his sense of purpose. In short, I guess he'd make a dandy lawyer. Curses on you, Dean, for introducing a good pre-law candidate with lousy scores. It upsets the vow I took upon entering here."

The Committee members looked at each other. They seemed satisfied. One could sense a camaraderie developing. But then Benson. . . .

"Somehow he isn't quite right for my canoe, and I really wonder if he's quite right for Oldebrick. Haven't we enough suburban, alligator-shirted, reasonably-bright-but-not-really, help-the-underprivileged-play-tennis types already lurking around the punch bowls here? This may be just the type Ms. Dorsett was rightly scorning before."

Rita Dorsett looked stricken. "Oh, oh. My speech served to hurt the wrong applicant. Truman, I really like this boy, alligator shirt and suburbs or not. He sounds genuine." She smiled, then lifted her handkerchief to her cheek. "Somehow I have the feeling I'm not going to like this job."

Butch Lassiter was slowly circling the table now, pausing at his favorite window each round. Chin and Taylor seemed frozen to their seats, unlike the admissions staff, who were twisting and turning, already having read these cases and discussed them at length at staff meetings.

"Let's move on," urged the Dean. "It's late. Our fifth candidate of the evening is KEN JACOBSON. Like Diane Perkins, he is introduced tonight to give you a sense of balance. Our admissions staff would also like to hear your reaction as faculty members to a conflict that pops up late in his folder. As you see from Ken's transcript, we're looking at an exceptional student. His urban high school in Cleveland is probably not quite as strong as John Westerhall's school, but it is above average nonetheless. This school sends approximately 45 percent of its students on to four-year colleges, another 25 percent to two-year colleges. Ken obviously has sought out every tough course he could find. Rarely do we see a more high-powered senior course-load. Note that he has gained extra weighting in his class rank for the Advanced Placement courses, which puts him in the top 3 percent. Also, note his College Board scores, which are sky-high. Ken is a Commended student in the National Merit Program, the most prestigious honor program in the nation (which disppoints many of us, I might add, because National Merit gives much more weight to standardized test scores than to any other credential).

"Let's review Ken's transcript. *(See pages 54–55.)*

There was obvious elation around the table as faculty members muttered about the high College Board scores under their breath. Norton Taylor, with a wry smile, held up two fingers to form a "V."

"Ken's parents are both college educated. They are now divorced. His mother is a school librarian. His father is a hospital administrator. The father will be paying college bills, and although he applied for financial aid, our analysis of the Financial Aid Form indicates this is a 'no-need' case. There are two younger children. Ken wants to major in Biology or Chemistry and wants to become a doctor. Last summer he worked as an hospital orderly, so he has done a lot more than most of our candidates to find out what the medical profession is all about.

Regarding his extracurricular involvements, he says:

| CLASS RECORD<br>*Include Subjects Failed or Repeated* | | IDENTIFY LAB TV SEMINAR SUMMER | IDENTIFY HONORS ACCEL AD PL. ETC | MARKS | | CRED OR UNIT | STATE EXAM. SCORES |
|---|---|---|---|---|---|---|---|
| YEAR | SUBJECTS | | | 1ST. SEM | FINAL OR 2ND. SEM | | |
| **9**<br>19 82<br>19 83 | English I | | | | B | 5 | |
| | Algebra I | | | | A | 5 | |
| | World History | | | | A | 5 | |
| | French 9 | | | | B | 5 | |
| | Physical Science | | | | B | 5 | |
| | Electricity | | | | A | 2½ | |
| | Phys. Ed./Health | | | | B | 1 | |
| **10**<br>19 83<br>19 84 | English II | | | | B | 5 | |
| | Plane & Solid Geom. | | | | A | 5 | |
| | U.S. History I | | | | A | 5 | |
| | French 10 | | | | B | 5 | |
| | Algebra II & Trig. | | | | A | 5 | |
| | A.P. Biology | Lab | | | A | 5 | |
| | Phys. Ed. II | | | | A | 1 | |
| **11**<br>19 84-<br>19 85 | English III | | | | A | 5 | |
| | AP Calculus | | | | B | 5 | |
| | U.S. History AP | | | | A | 5 | |
| | Chemistry | Lab | | | A | 5 | |
| | French IV | | | | B | 5 | |
| | Phys. Ed./Dr. Ed | | | | O | 1 | |
| | Dr. Ed. II (BTW) | | | | S | | |
| **12**<br>19 85<br>19 86 | AP English | | | B | | | |
| | AP Calculus | | | A | | | |
| | AP Biology | Lab | | A | | | |
| | PSSC Physics | Lab | | A | | | |
| | Personal Typing (Sem) | | | | | | |
| | Phys. Ed. | | | O | | | |

| | DATE | NAME OF TEST | | RAW OR STD. SCORE | PERCENTILE SCORE | NORM GROUP | | DATE |
|---|---|---|---|---|---|---|---|---|
| **TEST RECORD** | 1984 | PSAT/NMSQT | V | 62 | | | | |
| | | | M | 72 | | | | |
| | 2/86 | SAT | V | 630 | | | | |
| | | | M | 730 | | | | |
| | 4/85 | SAT | V | 620 | | | | |
| | | | M | 750 | | | | |

| Passing Mark | Honors Mark (if any) | LOWEST NUMERICAL EQUIVALENT | | | |
|---|---|---|---|---|---|
| 70 | | A 93 | B 85 | C 74 | D 70 |

## EXPLANATION OF HONORS COURSES

---

RANK IN CLASS    BASED ON ___6___ SEMESTERS

[X] EXACTLY    [ ] APPROX. ___15___ IN CLASS OF ___550___

FINAL RANK _____

*Check Appropriate Rank Information*

[X] ALL SUBJECTS GIVEN CREDIT    [XX] ALL STUDENTS

[ ] MAJOR SUBJECTS ONLY    [ ] COLL. PREP. STUDENTS ONLY

*Explain Weighting of Marks in Determining Rank*

Only Advanced Placement courses
are weighted.


S - Satisfactory
O - Outstanding

---

## OUTSTANDING ACTIVITIES. HONORS. AWARDS

COMMENDED STUDENT 1986 MERIT PROG.
Soccer Team 9, 10, 11, 12
Winter Track 11, 12
Spring Track 10, 11, 12
Academy of Science 11, 12
Debate Team 10, 11, 12
Newspaper Photographer 11, 12

| NAME OF TEST | | RAW OR STD. SCORE | PERCENTILE SCORE | NORM GROUP |
|---|---|---|---|---|
| SAT | V | 710 | | |
| | M | 750 | | |
| | | | | |
| Eng. Achievement | | 620 | | |
| Math II | | 750 | | |
| Physics | | 650 | | |
| | | | | |

I find my athletic involvement on the soccer and track squads to be the most meaningful of the previously mentioned activities I pursue. By their inherent nature as extra-curricular activities, they have broadened me as a person and allowed me to meet many new people. As sports they have developed me physically, but there is a further development involved. That development involves me as a person and my values. Perhaps the most important thing to be learned from athletics is that success is the result of hard work. Something athletics has instilled in me is the pursuit of excellence in whatever I do, whether it be on the track, the field, or my future profession. Lastly, my experience with athletics reflects what is hidden in each of us in some form. When I first went out for track last year, it was merely to stay in shape for the tennis team so that I could learn how to play tennis. Within a few months of hard work, I advanced from a novice to a member of a mile relay which won the state sectional championship.

"Sterile prose," Benson pointed out.

"Maybe his application essay will give him a little life," responded the Dean. "Here it is:

I'm weird.

That's a rather funny thing to say on an application to one of the finest institutions of learning in this country. Let me explain.

The dictionary defines "weird" as odd or unusual. Yet when I indicated my career ambition, medicine, there did not seem to be anything unusual about that. After all, "premeds" compose one of the largest categories of students in colleges today. Nearly all of these "premeds" choose to major in either Chemistry or Biology. This is my first weirdness since I intend to major in Astronomy. Another weirdness is that along with being a good student, I am also an athlete who can make a substantial contribution to the Oldebrick track team.

On a more personal level, I don't smoke or drink and am not afraid to assert my individual weirdness. I believe this is especially important in a college atmosphere where even on the smallest level, a person can be easily swallowed up and be vulnerable to many pressures.

Undoubtedly the most important factor in the selection of candidates for Oldebrick is that of scholarship. I believe that in this respect I qualify, as evidenced by my SAT scores and by my high grade average in high school, even with a schedule so rigorous that I was able to go through my entire high school program in three years.

"Yes, that's a lot better," Benson said. "The wooden statue is still there, but at least we know now it doesn't smoke or drink. Frankly, I think it took some gumption to say that."

The Dean continued. "Ken sent us what appears to be a professionally prepared resume (you can get this sort of thing for a price at counseling bureaus today) with headings of 'College Goals,' 'Career Goals,' 'Academic Awards,' et cetera. We don't learn anything new through this formal presentation except that he really seems to have distinguished himself in track: gold medals, silver medals, bronze medals at state and county meets. He was the anchor of a mile relay team that broke the school and county records. Despite these accolades, however, our track coach feels that Ken would not be outstanding at Oldebrick in track—he might be a contributor, but the times he has achieved so far would probably not put him in the forefront here."

"What?" Mr. Chin was astonished. "You actually check with our coaches on a candidate's athletic suitability for Oldebrick?"

The Dean stood and stretched. "Yes, we sometimes check with them—but the initiative often comes from them rather than from us. Actually, I wish other departments were as interested in our candidates! We rarely have Math or Physics or History or French calling over here to inquire about the quality or status of an applicant (unless the applicant is a relative). You know, when we really want to pursue a kid, faculty interest would be most helpful.

"With the coaches, we now have a fairly well-organized system. I meet with each coach individually in January and March, honing down each of their lists according to which students seem genuinely interested in Oldebrick, and which seem realistic admits academically. At times, the 'bargaining' gets a bit sticky and there are always some strained feelings. A few not so coincidental phone calls will come in from alumni pushing candidates I've told the coaches are 'maybe's' for admission. But let me repeat: If every department at this college took the interest in recruiting talent that the Athletic Department takes, we'd blow the doors off most of our competition, academically as well as athletically.

"I should add, by the way, that the coaches know that not all of their sports have equal clout in the Admissions Office.

We'll push to structure winning teams in the most visible sports at Oldebrick—football, hockey, and basketball for men, and tennis and volleyball for women. As you might guess, we never give enough 'special priority' to please all the coaching staff. But we are generous enough with some of these top athletes to twist my own conscience now and then. Sometimes it upsets me to see us taking mediocre students who can win games when we might be taking candidates who could win some graduate fellowships. Remember, though, that a good many of the highly rated athletes are not dummies. Some who are disciplined on the field are equally disciplined in the classroom, with outstanding and often surprising results. Ken Jacobson, the fellow whose credentials are in front of you, is a fairly decent athlete who is second to very few in academics.

So let's continue with Ken's folder. Here is his guidance counselor's report:

> Ken is great college material. He is extremely bright and an excellent athlete. He has a fine attitude toward learning and he has learned that much effort is necessary to achieve one's goals. He is more than willing to put forth this effort. In fact, he enjoys academic challenges. To illustrate, Ken is the only person to carry two enriched mathematics courses as a junior, and this year he is again taking Advanced Placement calculus in order to do independent work—a rarity in our system. He is quite science/math oriented, but he is also very verbal and he reads voraciously.
>
> Ken's teachers find him conscientious and one who has learned to use his time well. He has worked hard to develop a good background.

I'll skip around in this report. . . .

> Ken is quite good in photography—has collected some excellent cameras and uses them for very good purposes . . .

Jesus! . . .

> Ken has spent much time as a volunteer at our local hospital. He has worked in most of the departments and has had many opportunities to see the intricate and sophisticated happenings in a modern hospital.
>
> Another aspect of Ken that is noteworthy is his keen interest in athletics. He has been on our soccer team for three years and worked hard to become our "most improved player." He played goalie for

our varsity team and has done much to promote our good record. Track is his major sport. He puts forth much effort in training and won the trophy as "The Most Improved Runner" last year. He is a member of our mile relay team and also of our distance team. As a quarter-miler his best time was 50.9 seconds. His coaches feel he has great potential as an athlete, and with his excellent attitudes he should be an asset to your teams too.

Ken deserves an enthusiastic recommendation. He is the kind of student and person who does not come along very often and it is a great pleasure to recommend him to your college!

"That report is embarrassing," said Mr. Taylor a bit pompously. "Thank God for the Buckley Amendment, so families can now demand to see these reports. I'm marching with my senior daughter into the guidance office next week to see what kind of pap they threw at colleges about her."

"Maybe Ken was smarter than we think in having a professional resume composed," Ms. Dorsett said, capping off the remark with her pressed smile.

"Well, remember that these counselors often have 300–400 seniors to report on. What can we reasonably expect of them? Here is what Ken's Biology teacher has to say," said the Dean.

Ken is a highly motivated student. He is absolutely stimulated by a demanding academic environment. He never needs prodding. He made very good use of his time, particularly since there were interferences caused by his track and soccer involvements. He has a critical, analytical mind. He was able to convey his ideas verbly and defend his position with skill and clarity.

"That seems like scant praise for a student who appears on paper to be so exceptional," commented Mr. Chin.

"I'm not certain the Biology teacher is verbose. By the way, he did a dreadful job of trying to spell 'verbally.' Anyway, the Assistant Principal of Ken's school also writes a letter which says, once again, what we've already heard.

"But now the curve ball. Ken came here for an interview last month. Sid Goldstein of our staff wrote the following:

One of the myopic candidates: there is nothing in the world to him but becoming a doctor. Ken's father is a hospital administrator, so perhaps this is part of the limited perspective. Doesn't have much to say for his high school, but did seek out the most demanding courses. Clearly has his sights set on the Ivies: wanted comparisons of our Biology Department to Yale's, Princeton's. Guess he has done a good job in soccer and track—perhaps more effort than actual accomplishment. Somehow this fellow seems to go through all the motions—but is any excitement generated?

Ken was quite ill at ease. In fact, he had very little to say. He was stiff. Was he just nervous, or did I do a bad job of getting him to open up, or is he just a set of impressive statistics? He seems egocentric and naive. What little he did say was in praise of his own accomplishments. I nearly upchucked when he went through the bit about being disappointed with his Math SAT of 750 . . . Baloney.

Yes, he's smart. But socially immature—perhaps that is an understatement. Frankly, I'm just not convinced that he would contribute anything to Oldebrick except one more admission ticket to medical school. Are we this hungry to improve our med school entry stats? Let Yale have him. But if he's as smart as he thinks he is, he won't go to New Haven for an interview.

"Sid, that's a strong statement," said the Dean. "Is there anything you want to add or subtract, one month later?"

"Not a thing," Sid Goldstein answered. "I think my report says it all."

"Well, I'd like to add a little," piped up Adam McDermott, the Admissions Fellow, growing at ease now with the group. "It seems to many of us in the student body—and I was just there—that Oldebrick spends too much time comparing itself to Amherst and Williams and Brown, and nurturing its own inferiority complex because we're not quite in line with them, at least as popularly perceived. And usually the comparisons are made via statistics—our Board averages aren't quite as high, et cetera. So here comes a candidate who will help us *get* in line: He has all the right numbers. But dammit, we sacrifice a great deal that is important to Oldebrick if we go for this guy. He has no soul whatsoever. I don't want to stand up and sing the Alma Mater now, but I do want to say that Oldebrick has something going for it that we shouldn't lose sight of. We're casual but serious, bright but not insufferably brainy, into our studies but not morosely academic, and we care about each other and have a pretty good time. Do we crave med school entries *so* much that we will risk sacrificing a few of our subtle attributes—attributes, by the way, that may make us an even better place than Amherst or Williams or Brown?"

Adam's face reddened as he tried to settle back in his chair. Kelly Darby and Sid Goldstein applauded to support their friend, but the faculty delegation ignored them.

"Adam, we know what you're saying and you said it very well," responded Rita Dorsett. "But you're using this young man as too heavy a symbol. In voting one Ken Jacobson in or out, we're not charting the future of the college. Yes, he is something of a machine, but we have so few here with so much intellectual capability and accomplishment!"

"I wish the pre-med advisor were here," said Mr. Chin, "because I'm about to try to talk us out of this one, and the pre-med faculty should be given equal time.

"Frankly, I'm a bit tired of the get-the-good-grades-for-med-school syndrome. Those kids strike me as unoriginal, they try to elbow each other out of the way, they're strangely insensitive, and, well, I guess I end up agreeing with Adam McDermott and Sid Goldstein. Maybe Ken Jacobsen is a good match for Columbia or NYU, but for our residential college, where we all try to live together in the woods somewhat peacefully, I'm not certain. His numbers *are* impressive—and I'm surprising myself by speaking against him."

The Dean looked upset. After a pause he began. "I guess it is fair to say that I'm disappointed by the tone of this conversation, or at least the direction it seems to be taking. The consensus appears to be that 'you have to be nice to be necessary' at Oldebrick. Just because this kid isn't going to be everyone's choice for Social Chairman, you dump him and send him packing to the Ivies. Well, *why?* We spend so much time complaining that we don't draw a large number of students who profile out as impressively as those the Ivies get. And here is one. Not only is he distinguished academically, but he has also diligently worked at his athletics until he has become something of a champion in his own league. So what if he's stiff and naive and caught up with himself? It irks me to think that personality is more important to our Committee than powerhouse academic potential and accomplishment."

The Dean began gently pounding his fist on the table, and continued. "And who is to say that the personality Jacobson conveys now won't be considerably improved four years from now? What kind of faith do we have in Oldebrick? I think this kid will meet some other highpowered types around here, will tone down a little, will turn to others more, and will, in time, mature. If we have a community here, Adam, then let it contribute to this kid's growth. He has a hell of a lot to give in brainpower. And that's what we're supposed to be all about."

It was the first time the Dean had let loose. No one seemed to feel comfortable in speaking next. And no one did.

"Let's look at our final two applicants of the evening, and then vote on all seven," the Dean said with a noticeable tremor in his voice.

"ANN BAKER is another candidate from the suburbs of a big city. She applied for Early Decision here and didn't make it, so we're looking at her once again. Ann attends a huge and well-known high school outside Dallas, and 'The Big D' should be underlined here, because our alumni in Dallas are very interested in her. Why have they singled out Ann Baker? Frankly, I can't quite figure it out, but several recent calls and letters have convinced us of the seriousness of their interest. And I might add that the Dallas Alumni Club, as you may have heard, is one of our most influential and supportive alumni groups. Remember, it was they who gave the new arts building four or five years ago.

"Ann's father is a lawyer, her mother a housewife, and she has older brothers who are now out of college. Ann wants to major in Psychology (she spells the word p-s-y-c-o-l-o-g-y throughout her application) to prepare for guidance counseling at the high school level. She is very involved in equestrian activities—shows her horse throughout the country at A-rated AHSA shows. She works at a jewelry store to help defray expenses on the horse. Also, Ann is a cheerleader. Her application essay is, to a large degree, an attempt to justify her mediocre high school record. As a rhetorical strategy, she pretends that she has already been rejected by Oldebrick and is responding to our Committee's decision:

Dear Admissions Committee:

Although my transcript did not please you and your staff, I feel as though you are overlooking the most important factor in evaluating these grades, this factor being improvement! Although the grades on the transcript were not as outstanding as a competitive college (like Oldebrick) might expect, the improvement from two slumping (4th and 5th) semesters to the past two semesters (6th and 7th) has been quite steady and shall continue into my final semester. However, grades alone are not the most important criteria in judging an applicant, contrary to many college's beliefs! The growing maturity that one shows through his grades is a much more important criteria to be judged. I believe that through outside experiences I have gained the maturity to sort out my emotional life from my school work and bear down to improve my grades. A person must be a more mature person to go to college in a changing atmosphere. Considering the change that Oldebrick must be undergoing due to the upheavals of the late sixties and early seventies, I feel that perhaps I will be better able to handle the situation than a "straight A" student. Many of these students may not have ever had to learn to sort out the priorities of school work vs. outside influences and therefore would be unable to handle a changing situation. Hence, I feel that I am the right person to attend Oldebrick and reap the most profit from my education at Oldebrick in the period of change.

"Oh Pain!" blurted Benson. "Her letter to the Committee has just confirmed that we all made the right decision in the first place. Why on God's green earth must we spend time on this one? She has Pi Beta Phi at U. Texas written all over her."

The Dean shook his head, conveying his own mixed thoughts. "Well, I really felt I had to give her a hearing in front of the full Committee, considering the interest in her among alumni. And she undoubtedly could succeed here, if she put her mind to it. It *is* easier to survive here than to get in, is it not? This candidate is probably one who could graduate if admitted. Her transcript comes as no surprise after her warning. She did not tell us, however, that her improvement in grades came via a fluffy course-load." *(See pages 64–65.)*

Taylor and Benson had abandoned the transcript after one quick glance, but the rest of the Committee members were still poring over it.

"Note that she dropped Math and Science and History after

| SUBJECTS NOW IN PROGRESS | | | | | | | | UNITS |
|---|---|---|---|---|---|---|---|---|
| SUBJECTS | | Level | 9 | 10 | 11 | 12 | Extra | Earned |
| English | I, II, III | 4 | BB | BC | D | | | 2½ |
| | III, IV | 3 | | | B | C* | | ½ |
| | | | | | | | | |
| | | | | | | | | |
| Lang. | French I | | CrCr | | | | | 1 |
| | French II, III | 3 | CB | PC | | | | 2 |
| | Spanish I | 3 | | | | A* | | |
| | | | | | | | | |
| | | | | | | | | |
| Math | Algebra I, II | 3 | BB | | | CC | | 2 |
| | Plane Geometry | 3 | | BC | | | | 1 |
| | | | | | | | | |
| | | | | | | | | |
| | Lab. Periods | Yes | | | | | | |
| Science | Biology | X | 4 | BB | | | | 1 |
| | Chemistry | X | 4 | | D | | | ½ |
| | Chemistry | X | 3 | B | | | | ½ |
| | | | | | | | | |
| | | | | | | | | |
| Soc. Studies | Modern History | 3 | | C | | | | ½ |
| | US History | 3 | | | BB | | | 1 |
| | Sociology | 3 | | | B | | | ½ |
| | | | | | | | | |
| | | | | | | | | |
| | | | | | | | | |
| Other Subjects | Consumer Econ | 3 | | | | B* | | |
| | Painting (10xwk) | 3 | | | | B* | | |
| | Drawing (10xwk) | 3 | | | A | | | ½ |
| | | | | | | | | |
| | Drawing | | PP | | | | | ½ |
| | Phys Ed | | xx | xx | | xx | | ½ |
| | | | | | | | | |
| | | | | | | | | |
| | | | | | | | | |

# DETERMINATION OF WEIGHTED AVERAGE

A weighted average is computed according to the ability level at which each major course is taken. Courses not designated by level are minor credit courses which are not used in computing rank.

The 2 level is regarded as the average high school level of competition. At this level A = 4, B = 3, C = 2, D = 1.

Grades in other levels are weighted by the following multipliers.

| | |
|---|---|
| 5 level (Advanced Placement) | 1.8 |
| 4 level (Superior or Honors) | 1.5 |
| 3 level (Above Average) | 1.2 |
| 1 level (Below Average) | .8 |

her junior year. Note also that this school rather carefully 'levels' courses. She has been mostly in '3' level courses, defined as 'above average.' The class rank is weighted according to level of courses. Ann is 296th in a class of 847, but remember that 85 percent go on to college from here. That means that her second-fifth ranking is no disgrace. But her College Board scores are all just above 500. The college counselor, who is an old friend of ours, says:

> Ann works very diligently and has managed to maintain a good average and rank in class over the past three years. She has been in our "above average" academic classification in all subjects. The candidate has many cultural interests, with music and art being the most important to her. She has a talent in art, painting, and drawing.
>
> Ann spends a great deal of time improving her riding skills. She owns her own horse and has won many prizes competing in contests around the country. However, she does not make an occupation in this interest area and uses wise judgment in budgeting her time between this activity and others.
>
> We are of the opinion that Ann has more ability than her SATs indicate. She has a strong 27 composite on the ACT, which places her in the 92nd percentile for college-bound students. I suggested she repeat the SATs, and her second test scores may be reported to you by now. This young woman has much to offer any college or community.

"We did receive a new set of SATs on this candidate: 530 Verbal, 510 Math. Not much improvement."

"Well, your 'old friend' did the best he could, considering there is so little to work with," said Norton Taylor.

"Ann's senior English teacher reports as follows," continued the Dean:

> Ann is a perceptive and sensitive student of literature. Insightful understanding rather than precise intellectual analysis is her forte. Certain intellectual tasks that require precision make her shrink; she seems to have some diffidence about her ability to tackle such tasks. This makes her academic performance somewhat uneven.
>
> Ann's writing competence is well above average for a twelfth-grade student. She does not, however, participate regularly in classroom discussion. When she does, her contributions are valuable, but she seems reluctant to participate at times.

"Oh, how welcome honesty is in this exercise," said Ms. Dorsett. "That was a graceful but candid and fair report. I feel that I'm getting to know this girl. And I know plenty of Dallas alumnae." This time Rita Dorsett's smile and quick glance around the table found a nodding reception. The Dean was relaxed and smiling now.

"Let's hear what our alumna has to say. Ann was not interviewed on campus, so one of our former graduates interviewed Ann in Texas. Here is her report:

> This is a lovely girl. Also, I think she will attend Oldebrick if admitted. Seems to know what she's talking about in psychology, her intended major. I would guess that she is a responsible student. It is her outside activities, however, that seem rather outstanding. Being a cheerleader at her huge high school is a very big deal—several have gone on to cheer for the Cowboys. And Ann just loves horses; she's so enthusiastic about her horse that she works in a jewelry store to help her parents pay the transportation and entry fee costs for shows around the country. Ann speaks well; she seems socially mature; she was most attractively dressed. In short, I think she's a perfect match for Oldebrick.

Harry Chin raised his hand. "Dean, could you comment on these alumni interviews? I realize that a good many colleges have a force of representatives around the country. But frankly, I find this lady's interview report a disappointment. I mean, it's so 'horsey.' Does she know what to look for in a candidate?"

Mr. Chin was earnest, as always, but pleased with his own little stab at humor. So were the others.

"Our alumni interviewers are hard-working people," the Dean said thoughtfully, "and they do seem more an asset than a liability. Candidates want the opinion of someone from their hometown before choosing a national college, so our alumni are obviously valuable to us. Their personal touch can persuade a candidate to choose Oldebrick over another college. So we try our best to keep them informed of what's going on here— fly them back to campus for conferences, have training sesssions when we're in their home towns recruiting, et cetera. Too often, however, they have a tendency to represent the college as it *was* rather than as it *is*—I guess that's only natural. And they really are not as exposed to the academic credentials of a candidate as we are, so their comments dwell mostly on the personal."

The Dean paused, drumming his fingers on the table. It was obvious this topic perplexed him somewhat. "We do, of course, sometimes draw the wrong alumni volunteers to interview for us: the always-wanted-to-be-a-jock-but-never-quite-made-the-team types, who are embarrassing in their fervor to chase quarterbacks and goalies, and a few too many nonworking women who volunteer just to have something to do. On the whole, however, the alumni take their work seriously and are important to us. But as you will see, their reports tend to be quite uneven in quality.

"There is more in Ann's folder from alums. Excerpts from a couple of letters that arrived quite recently:

> I am writing regarding Ann Baker, whose family I have known for many years.
>
> Ann realizes her SAT scores and her grades/class rank are not the highest, but she feels capable of tackling the demanding education at Oldebrick. On the plus side for Ann is her diligence and perseverance in other areas. She has been working after school and on Saturdays at a jewelry store to help support her horse. She is a cheerleader, plays piano and organ and guitar. She has been an adequate student and now really wants to concentrate on her studies and self-development. She is interested in Psychology, especially relating to teenage problems and also how this relates to animals.
>
> I feel Ann has a lot of spunk and is capable of accomplishing whatever she really wants to do. To demonstrate: Ann says that if she doesn't make Oldebrick on this round, she'll apply later as a transfer. Take her now!—she is a personable young lady of good character and discipline.

"Another alumna throws us a bit more grit:

> I understand Ann Baker is applying to Oldebrick and will attend if admitted. Thank God! We Alumnae/i in Dallas have been befuddled by some of your recent choices in our area—clearly, grades and long hair seem to mean more to you than character and personal promise. We're a bit fed up. Now we throw you a challenge: Ann Baker. She is bright, purposeful, an accomplished equestrian, and she is *clean*. We trust she will hear positively from you. If not, the College will not hear positively from some of the alumnae/i here.

"That self-serving biddy probably hasn't given us a penny," quipped Benson.

"*Wrong,* Truman," replied the Dean. "During the recent capital campaign she gave an endowed scholarship for the disadvantaged, with priority to blacks and Chicanos from the Southwest. She is also a Trustee for the Dallas Art Museum, has donated heavily to our gallery, and has been most helpful in advising our curator. You certainly missed the target on this one."

Everyone glanced at Benson, hoping to catch him wincing in humility. They were not rewarded.

"And finally, we have just received a letter from Ann Baker herself:

> While I fully appreciate and realize the tremendous burdens placed upon you in selecting from the great number of applicants those fortunate enough to be admitted, I hope you can take time to ponder my earnest desire to attend Oldebrick. If I understand college admissions correctly, you will undoubtedly admit some with records better than mine, and they may end up on your campus only because they're not admitted at, say, Harvard. Why not generously stretch a bit and admit one who so desperately wants Oldebrick as a first-choice college? Well, I just thought I'd like to make a final plea. . . . Thanks.

Rita Dorsett leaned forward. "Oh, poor dear. . . . And doesn't she have a point regarding those who *want* to be here and tried for Early Decision versus those who come reluctantly, and would rather be in Hanover or New Haven or Palo Alto?"

"That's a tough question," the Dean responded. "We obviously favor Early Decision candidates because they are declaring Oldebrick first choice and we'll get 100 percent of those we admit. Last year, remember, we admitted about half of all our candidates, but we admitted nearly 70 percent of our E.D. candidates: 'One in hand is worth two in the bush' in this business. Williams and Bowdoin and Amherst and a few others normally take a surprisingly high percentage of the class Early Decision because they know their losses will be heavy to the Ivies come April.

"Once here, however, our Early Decision admittees can become some of our most disappointed freshmen. They found what they thought was the perfect college early in their senior year of high school, and they continued to fantasize it into Utopia during the succeeding months. Once they are here, any flaw they find disappoints them greatly. On the other hand, some kids here who were dying to go to Harvard or Yale come to Oldebrick with a bit of a chip on their shoulder. But then, almost inevitably, they love the place by the end of the first year and become some of our strongest supporters."

"Let's move on," urged Benson. "Desire or not, wealthy alumni support or not, I can only hope we'll uncover better candidates than Ms. Baker. I'm all for prompting smiles from the rich, but not at the expense of selling my soul."

Ms. Darby of the admissions staff spoke up. "Someone else can recruit in Dallas next year if we don't take this one. At a tea in my honor several of those ladies gave me a piece of their mind about how Oldebrick was going down the drain with the 'hippie types' we have been admitting. Turn down Miss Clean here, and I think we should just skip Dallas for a while until the ladies simmer down."

Adam McDermott winked at Kelly Darby and whispered audibly that he'd travel to Dallas on the next round.

"The *final* candidate of the evening is a total contrast to any other candidate we've considered thus far," said the Dean, a touch of excitement in his voice. "This is a kid from Alabama who discovered us late and applied late (we excuse a few who seem to have legitimate reasons for not getting their materials in on time). Just how THADDEUS RODGERS stumbled upon Oldebrick from down in the boonies of Alabama, I'n not certain, but we're glad he did. He lives on a farm, has several younger brothers and sisters, and attends what appears to be slow-w-w high school. No one in Thad's family has attended college. A nearly full scholarship, by the way, will be needed. His application is sketchy and the reports from his school are even sketchier.

"I must admit I'd like to take a chance on this fellow because he's so different for us. But in actuality, we know little about him, so I want you to hear his story before I get carried away.

"Thad says he wants to major in Math or Astronomy. His Math SAT of 620 and his Math II Achievement of 700 indicate he might know what he's talking about. His other scores, by the way, are SAT Verbal 580, English Achievement 470, and Physics Achievment 650. You have his transcript in front of you. *(See page 72.)*

"Frankly, we know little about the quality of Thad's school. They sent no profile, but they did indicate on the school report that 28 percent go on to college—that's well below the national average. Note that Thad took the basic courses. He ranks 24th in a class of 138; they weigh all grades evenly, so his two C's in Typing didn't help the rank. Considering the fact that this fellow is so bright, one does wonder why he didn't get straight A's, particularly if the school is below average. We'll never know, but I'm guessing there are two reasons: 1. on school days he works from 5:00 to 7:30 A.M., and again from 3:00 to 6:00 P.M., on the family farm, and that is bound to make a dent in his school performance; and 2. the great majority of his school-mates are not going to college, nor did anyone in his family—in other words, there is not much company for discussing educational goals.

"Thad is a National Merit Semi-Finalist, and he has been named to "Who's Who Among High School Students," a national honor society in which we put little stock due to its questionable means of selection and recruitment of secondary school students. Beyond that, there is little to report from Thad's application except the fact that he spends three to four hours per week as a newspaper reporter and always participates in the county science fairs with great success."

The Dean's enthusiasm had perked up the Committee. Butch Lassiter returned to his chair once again. "Here is Thad's essay, written in longhand, and a bit of a mess.

An area of moderate interest to me is whether or not genetic engineering is safe. I see the question as two-fold: will we use it for good or will we use it to destroy each other. It can do good by possibly providing a means to increase food crop yieldage. It can be used to evil by giving the military leaders a means of kill off the enemy with terrible diseases or destroy the local ecology.

The solution that will be accepted won't be acceptable to everyone because some people are naturally cautious and others are trail-blazers who won't or can't see the evil potential of something of this

## 3. STUDENT'S ACADEMIC HISTORY

| MINIMUM PASSING MARK | OTHER PASSING MARKS USED (AND NUMERICAL EQUIVALENT) | | |
|---|---|---|---|
| GRADE & YRS. | COURSES TAKEN (AND SPECIAL LEVEL WHERE APPROPRIATE) | MARKS | CRED |
| 1982-83 | English I | C    B | 1 |
| | Algebra I | B –    B | 1 |
| | Science | A    A | 1 |
| | Civics | A –    A | 1 |
| | Typing I | C    C | 1 |
| | P.E. | S    S | 1/2 |
| 1983-84 | English II | B    B | 1 |
| | Biology | B    A | 1 |
| | Geometry | B    B | 1 |
| | Spanish I | A    B | 1 |
| | P.E. | A    S | 1/2 |
| 1984-85 | English III | B    B | 1 |
| | U.S. History | A    A | 1 |
| | Chemistry | B    A | 1 |
| | Algebra II | B    A | 1 |
| | Spanish II | A    A | 1 |
| 1985-86 | English IV | B | |
| | Spanish II | B | |
| | Trig. | A | |
| | Physics | B | |
| | Calculus | A | |
| | Athletics | | |

nature. The solution that I feel will be accepted is "proceed with caution."

Genetic engineering can be a panacea for society's ills or a weapon more terrible than anything physics can produce. The choice is in the hands of the layman, of the politicians, but most of all, in the hands of the scientists.

"What an obscure topic for John-Boy Walton to try to write about," said Benson. "I'd enjoy a hayseed at Oldebrick as much as the next don, but I can only hope someone else will get him for the opening course in English. Actually, I really do think we need this type of variety here. How many deep southern accents have you heard in your classrooms lately?"

"Well, Truman, Thad's writing is the only area adequately discussed in his folder by school authorities, and you're not alone in your reaction. His History teacher writes:

> Thad is "outstanding" in intellectual ability and academic achieve-ment, "excellent" in disciplined work habits and potential for growth, "good" in original thought and taking initiative, but "below average" in written expression of ideas. Thad always makes it his business to know the subject matter, but is inconsistent and disorganized in his presentation and evaluation. He has a real thirst for learning (and is the *only* student in our school who spends spare time quietly reading in the library, alone) but has a way to go in written expres-sion. His deportment in class, by the way, is (most of the time) alright.

"Thad's counselor really doesn't help the boy at all. It appears he just didn't take the time:

> Thad is a fine boy, who will go far if given the opportunity. He is well liked by student and faculty. He has a 3.3 average out of a possible 4.0. I am certain you will enjoy him.

"And that's all we know about Thaddeus Rodgers. Intriguing in the context of our usual suburban applicant. What do you think?"

"I'm with you, Dean," said Harry Chin promptly and delib-erately. "He will probably end up in our department. Not only does he have ability, but he has the potential for growth that we so enjoy working with. I think we should admit him, high cost and rough diamond or not."

"I'm *certain* we should admit him," Lois Ruffin said quietly. "This white kid is just like most of the blacks we'd like to attract. He is from a different, somewhat disadvantaged situation, and Oldebrick could open nice new doors for him. And he'd teach us all a whole lot."

"Whom would you room him with?" queried Norton Taylor. "Yes, I find him interesting, and a change of pace for us, and I think he'd achieve. But how comfortable will he feel here? Whom will he share campus life with? Frankly, I think he'll be miserable at Oldebrick, at least for a while. We should take him *only* if we put a flag on his folder indicating that the Dean of Freshmen should follow him carefully and take special care in asssigning a roommate."

"Mr. Taylor, he only looks different," Mr. Chin said, leaning forward. "So many of our freshmen, including those who arrive with the 'right' demeanor, are scared and uncertain and lacking confidence. This boy, it seems to me, already has developed a sense of independence that will be obvious very, very soon. Also, our department is small and we'll watch him."

"This thoughtful conversation pleases me," said Rita Dorsett a bit ponderously. "But it raises questions: For example, what is this young man like as a person? We really don't know. He didn't let us know much, and his school didn't help except to say he might need assistance in English. Here is a case where I wish we had an interview report. We need to know more about Thaddeus. Would he be able to adjust to Oldebrick? We should be searching for an answer to that question, for his sake as well as for our own. We're investing, if I heard the report accurately, a full scholarship in this young man. Is this money properly spent? I personally feel it may be, but I'm not convinced we've done our homework quite thoroughly enough yet."

"Well, you're probably right," said the Dean. "We have very few, if any, alumni in Thaddeus' area of Alabama, I'm afraid. But let me call the Alumni Office in the morning and see if we can get Thaddeus interviewed down there, pronto. If we can, I'll ask the alum to phone in the report quickly and we'll talk about Thad again before the week is out. I must admit, my own enthusiasm for 'differences' became a bit unbridled. Yes, Rita, you're right. Let's have this kid interviewed. It's better than a quick vote, impetuously giving away a place in the class and a bundle of financial aid for four years here, plus running the danger of making the boy miserable. I'll report back to you in a few days."

With positive nods all around, the meeting moved on.

"Okay, it is past 10:00 P.M. and we must vote. But is there any relevant general topic we have not stumbled upon yet and ought to discuss to make tonight's (and tomorrow's) decisions more informed?"

"Yes, the SATs," said Taylor. "My own daughter was sick to her stomach the night before the test, just worrying about getting into college. Probably my own dinner-table talk over the years hasn't helped her any; I'm obviously high on tests. But what really are the facts? Do those with the highest scores tend to do the best work here? Are we right to turn down kids who score under 500 on either Verbal or Math? You know how I've always been talking up tests. But frankly, I'm running a little scared now, with so many human dimensions sticking out of these damned folders."

"The topic is huge, Norton, and I know you don't expect to cover all the bases at this late hour. But let me try to respond briefly," said the Dean, a little impatiently.

"Here at Oldebrick we've found that almost all the students who do exceptionally well by traditional standards—Phi Beta Kappa, graduate Magna Cum Laude, et cetera—entered Oldebrick with high Board scores. Among that group there are few surprises when one checks back to both SATs and the secondary school grades. However, there are plenty of surprises when one checks the SATs of those who get into academic trouble here. Too often, that group *also* entered Oldebrick with well above average Board scores. Obviously, something didn't click in terms of attitude and discipline: the kid's fault? Oldebrick's fault? Who knows? But plenty of youngsters who enter with very strong SATs bomb out. In short, we've had enough experience to know that numbers alone do not tell all. And that is why I believe in rather thoroughly scanning the 'characterizations' submitted by teachers and counselors. Their adjectives can give us important clues regarding the applicant's determination, genuine academic interest, and self-discipline.

In 1970, Bowdoin College shocked Admissions circles by announcing that it would no longer require candidates to submit College Board results. The move was noteworthy because Bowdoin has long been considered very selective. Although some of Bowdoin's competitors felt this was a 'grandstand play,' the Bowdoin statement was rather convincing. Essentially, it said that the SATs had become overemphasized and that a highly selective college could go about its business of choosing a new class without standardized test scores. Bowdoin also questioned whether minority kids and those who 'freeze' were not significantly disadvantaged by required SATs. The announcement also cited what the college considered an 'evidence gap' regarding the SATs.

"As a postscript, let me read you this little poem a student sent to Bowdoin in support of its announcement:

Do the numbers of the SAT reveal what one is like:
Can one who times a sprinter know how far the man can hike?
Can one who weighs a person know how much that man can eat?
Can one who counts the seeds predict the total crop of wheat?

"I love it!" exclaimed Ms. Dorsett. "That poem says it all for me, Norton, I'll be disappointed if you categorically vote 'yes' for high scores, 'no' for low scores. Let's use the Board scores as just a piece of the pie. To do otherwise would be simply unfair, law school admissions frenzy or not."

"Let's vote, for Chrissake!" yelled Benson. The others jumped, but everyone agreed the time had come.

The Dean began. "Remember that you should be voting for approximately half the candidates who are presented, so try to pace yourself accordingly. Raise your hand if you are in favor of a candidate, and I will record that individual's total number of votes. At the end of the week I'll admit those with the highest vote totals, approximately 125.

"As I explained to you at the beginning of the evening the seven candidates we read tonight are fairly representative of our applicant pool. In his or her own way, each suggests different problems of admission policy. But remember, I included a couple of outstanding candidates in this group tonight just to add balance and give you some perspective. Those you see the

rest of the week will be more marginal and truly 'muddy-middle.'
Obviously, there are no clear answers."

The Dean had a full audience. There was not a sound in the
room but his voice.

"Because these seven candidates constitute a microcosm of
our applicants, let's do more than just see which three or four
you feel should be admitted. After we determine the three with
the most votes, let's further eliminate two of the candidates
(just for fun, not for good) to simulate the kind of class Oldebrick *might* have if our applicant pool grew larger and we were
able to move closer to the Ivies in selectivity."

---

### READER:

### STOP!

It is decision-making time, so to play your own hand in the college
admissions game, vote now on the candidates.

Oldebrick is in a position to admit three of the six candidates
just presented. (The seventh and last candidate's folder was
considered incomplete, you will remember, and discussion of
his application was postponed pending further investigation. It
is only fair to tell you right now, however, that the alumnus
interviewer who drove miles to see Thaddeus was extremely
impressed by him. Not only did he seem an extraordinarily eager
student, but also a hard-working fellow who was able to put in
five hours per day on the family farm. After the interview report
had been called in, the Committee unanimously voted to admit
the Alabamian. Thaddeus will come to Oldebrick on full scholarship.)

VOTE! And have your arguments ready so that you can participate in the Committee discussions that follow.

---

"I'll try to do a very brief recap of each candidate before I
ask you to raise your hands," said the Dean. "While I recap,
you can review the transcript in your folder.

"First was Mimi Becholdt, from the good day school in the
Midwest. Mimi has two sisters who went here. Her Boards are
a little lower than our medians; she ranked twentieth in a class

of sixty-seven, with a moderately difficult courseload. This year she is taking things she obviously enjoys. You will remember that Mimi has traveled a great deal, is strong in the theater, and wrote the 'I am I' essay. She seems to have a lot of bounce and self-confidence, and she had a positive interview here. There is no indication of how seriously interested in Oldebrick she is— but she obviously was interested enough to come out and see us, all the way from Wisconsin. Besides being a decent student who wears a big smile, Mimi raises two important questions: how loyal should we be to a family that has already sent two students to us, and how far are we willing to go to increase enrollment from an underrepresented area like the Midwest? Well, enough. How many favor Mimi?"

"I don't like this!" exclaimed Rita Dorsett. "Five whole days of playing God. Really, each young person tonight, with the possible exception of one, seems to me to be a positive addition to Oldebrick. And I'm to raise my hand for *three?*"

Mr. Chin clapped his hands softly, delighted. "No, no! This is interesting. Each one of us has complained at one time or another that Oldebrick is not quite as selective as Swarthmore or Princeton. And now we balk at rejecting even some who appear truly mediocre by all traditional yardsticks. Come on Rita, get tough," he urged with his first broad smile of the evening.

"Up with the hands," said the Dean. A few hands went up halfway, then came down. Everyone seemed to be waiting for others to vote. After a few false starts, most hands remained raised. Seven of the eleven favored Mimi.

"Seven. Next is Diane Perkins, who is working in New York for a semester, attended a decent but not terribly demanding day school, had a near-perfect record, a straight courseload, powerhouse SATs wth Achievements not quite as strong, a real interest in art, and is somewhat bent toward medicine, largely because of her little brother's problems."

"Stop, stop, stop," said Benson. "Anyone who doesn't vote for this near-perfect creature should not report for future meetings."

"Vote for your own canoe, Truman," retorted Rita Dorsett

firmly. "But I must say I am moderately surprised that any young lady could win your ringing endorsement."

"Hands, please," interrupted the Dean. All eleven shot up.

"Unanimous. Next is Sophie Roosevelt, the black girl who has had her ups and downs academically, socially, and emotionally. The product of what appears to be a midddle-class family; strong paternal influence; president of the student body of a powerful prep school; wrote her essay on the exchange trip to Japan; the girl whose school wrote so completely and sensitively about her moods, her uncertainties. And let's remember Lois Ruffin's reminder that our black pool is down somewhat this year."

"Yes, I think we need this girl. She can survive here if we keep an eye on her," Lois Ruffin said calmly but with precision.

"I still question the match of this girl and Oldebrick," said Benson quietly.

"Votes?" probed the Dean. After a good many quick glances at one another, five hands went up.

"*Jesus!*" exploded Ms. Ruffin. "Does the college's commitment mean *anything* to this group?"

"Yes, it does," said Truman Benson explicitly. "And I trust we'll be looking at other black applicants who are perhaps more stable and accomplished than this one. And perhaps more deserving—in several senses of the word."

The air was a little heavy, and the Dean moved on, "John Westerhall, the boy with the traffic light, is next. Remember: large suburban high school, Exeter summer school, president of the senior class, academic record that consistently improved, tons of letters from the town fathers praising him, dreary SATs, pre-law, strong interview impression here."

Without much hesitation, every hand shot up. And everyone seemed surprised to see everyone else in favor. There were a few smiles. Westerhall, despite iffy statistics, had convinced even Norton Taylor. And Taylor smiled.

"Unanimous. Now we move to Ken Jacobson. Bright, bright, bright: A record and sky-high SATs, super course-load in an above-average high school; strongly bent toward pre-med; disciplined athletic involvement in soccer and track; probably interested in the Ivies; and the one whom Sid Goldstein panned the hell out of in the interview. Who's for Ken?"

Again, hesitation. Finally, six hands went up and stayed up. Three admissions staff members were voting against, and so did Mr. Chin and Butch Lassiter.

"You're kidding," said the Dean sternly, and he paused a short while. "*Six?* Well, it is inappropriate for me to question votes of this Committee, but I do fail to see the everlasting flaw in this young man. Yes, he is intense. One might say he's obnoxious in his youthful, myopic goal orientation. But he's bright if not brilliant, and he's disciplined, accomplished, and even balanced, as demonstrated by his earnestness in athletics. With all the painful paranoia that Oldebrick carries because the Ivies and a few similar colleges seem to stay slightly ahead of us, how can we shut the door on this super-talented fellow? Again I ask: Do you have to be nice to be necessary at Oldebrick? I'm surprised by this vote, and frankly, disappointed. But so be it." The Dean looked down, tense.

Again a hesitation around the table.

"You make me feel more than a little guilty, Dean," said Mr. Chin, barely audible. "You undoubtedly suffer more than we in comments people make about the quality of the students here. But, you see, I agree with Adam McDermott in what he said about Oldebrick and its unique 'flavor' of community. If I wanted to be part of a college which prided itself in having student-technicians who grind it out for four years, I would not remain here. Yes, I want bright students in my classroom. But I want young people with a little compassion even more. I will not vote for Ken Jacobson, knowing that he wants Yale or Princeton anyway and would probably be happier at one of those places."

The Dean was visibly perturbed—his upper lip always stiffened when he was tense, and it was nearly frozen now. He flipped through the pages of Jacobson's folder rather mournfully, as though he were saying goodbye to a friend. Then he continued.

"Our next candidate is Ann Baker of Dallas, the young lady who is dying for Oldebrick, applied Early Decision and didn't make it, took Level 3 courses with adequate results, is an eques-

trienne and a cheerleader, and the gal who brings strong backing
from one of our most powerful alumni organizations."

"She's as drab as an overcast day in Newark," offered Benson. "Let's vote."

"All right, how many favor Ann Baker?" This time, there
was no indecision. Only two hands went up.

"Ann is already out. And because she musters so little enthusiasm among us, and because I know the phones will be
ringing like crazy if we put her on the waiting list, my impulse
is to reject her. Any objections?" There were none.

"If my rough tally is correct, you have just voted in Diane
Perkins, John Westerhall, and Mimi Becholdt. Mimi has one
more vote than our friend Jacobson. Also, if my tally is correct,
the eleven of us cast forty-two votes. If each of us had voted
for half the candidates, there would have been a total of thirty-
three votes for the six candidates.

"So now I must give you a terse little warning. If you want
Oldebrick to be more selective, hold back on your 'heart' votes.
And please remember to look at the forest rather than just the
trees: In forming our microcosm class, so far you have elimi-
nated our minority representation, you have said to hell with
the wishes of monied alumni, and you have axed one of the two
best scholars of the group—because you felt he wasn't a nice
enough fellow for our warm community. I don't mean to rap
knuckles here, but do be aware of the consequences of your
votes tonight in terms of the structuring of the class."

"Golly, are you going to keep badgering us all week over
Ken Jacobson?" asked Butch Lassiter. "I'm one of those who
voted too many times because I thought most of these kids were
pretty good material. I don't feel any more strongly *for* Mimi
Becholdt than I feel *against* Ken Jacobson. In view of that, I'm
withdrawing my vote in favor of Mimi so that she and Ken will
be tied. We can squeak in one more freshman, can't we? We
may lose Ken to the Ivies anyway."

"And we may lose Mimi to someone, too," said the Dean.
"I just don't feel it is fair to second-guess where these kids might
end up going to college. They applied to Oldebrick in good
faith, so let's vote on them in good faith. We know we're going

to lose half of our admittees to other good colleges—that's a given. Let's not try to guess at this point which kids we might lose.

"Because the week will be even more turbulent if I start allowing vote-swapping, withdrawing, et cetera, I think we'd best say firmly right now that once a hand is up, the vote sticks. And there will be no second-thought additions to votes. Let's go with our hunches at this late stage, or we'll never finish. We all know this is not an exact science . . . Thank God."

"However, so that I can sleep tonight, and because I didn't lay down the law regarding vote changes until just now, and because I think you made a real mistake on Jacobson, I'm going to let Butch's change of mind on Mimi stand. That means that Mimi and Ken both get into the class. And we'll just have to get tougher as we move along."

There was an exchange of uneasy glances around the table, as if people were wondering if the Dean was not being a bit high-handed. But his decision stood, and no one commented.

"In a more cosmic sense, let's consider what we've done in terms of overall selectivity. Tonight we admitted four out of six (with one pending), or 75 percent, of our applicants. Most private colleges in America would be thrillled to admit all seven. It is estimated that a strong majority of private colleges will open next September with empty beds.

"Some so-called 'selective' private colleges in America today would be in a position to turn down only one or perhaps two of the candidates we reviewed this evening. Here are the names of some fine institutions that have admitted two-thirds to three-quarters of their candidates during the last few years: Alfred, Bryn Mawr, Dickinson, Hampshire, Skidmore, University of Rochester, Hobart-William Smith—and even Oldebrick a few years ago, when we went through some sparse times due to image problems. Now we and a few other colleges are in the position of admitting approximately half our candidates: Bates, Hamilton, Haverford, Lehigh, Mt. Holyoke, RPI, Smith, Trinity, and Wellesley.

"If we were admitting only one-third of our applicant pool, consider the pain of selection. That would have meant, in tonight's exercise, that both Mimi and Ken would have slipped down to the waiting list. We'd have ended up taking only Diane Perkins and John Westerhall—one near-perfect student, one dynamic person. A very small number of colleges in America are in the position of admitting approximately one-third of the applicant pool. Among them: Colgate, Cornell, Holy Cross, Middlebury, MIT, Penn, Swarthmore, Tufts, and Wesleyan of Connecticut.

"Some of our faculty, as you know, want us to have top Ivy selectivity. I'd rather be the Director of Admissions than the Director of Rejections, so I don't aspire to admitting one kid out of four or five applicants. But Amherst, Bowdoin, Brown, Columbia, Dartmouth, Duke, Harvard/Radcliffe, Princeton, Stanford, Williams, and Yale do just that. If we were to get into that fortunate (or unfortunate?) position, we'd have to make a choice between Diane and John. Just for fun, let's see what you as a committee would do. Everyone can vote only once. How many would go for Diane Perkins?"

With surprisingly little hesitation, nine hands were stretched high. Only Butch Lassiter and Truman Benson abstained.

Truman nodded approvingly at Butch, grabbed the last Danish, and left.

They were all in their seats at nine the next morning.

# 2.

# The Candidate Looks at the College

Now that you have audited what happens at the end of the line, it is time to make enlightened choices at the beginning. Your first project is to settle on a list of colleges that seem a good match for you. Remember: There are probably several "right" colleges, not just one.

If you remain constantly suspicious of popular myths about private colleges, you will be off to an enlightened start. Let's look at a few of the most common misconceptions.

### Myth I, NAME: "THE MORE PRESTIGIOUS THE COLLEGE, THE BETTER THE COLLEGE"

On climbing down from the chapel pulpit of an old-boy-gone-coed prep school in Boston (having made a Sunday evening chapel talk which I was instructed should be "uplifting but not religious"), I was ushered to the rear of the Gothic structure by an impressive senior girl. Since it was mid-April, I asked how she had fared in college admissions returns.

"Gloriously," she exuded. "I'm so lucky: Trinity, Pomona, Duke, and Yale all admitted me. It is nearly embarrassing."

"Good grief," exuded I. "How could one possibly decide by the May 1st deadline which of those giants to attend?"

"It couldn't be easier," she stated firmly. "Yale is Yale, and I must go."

Miss Cup Runneth Over went on to say that her intended college had, to her dismay, reinstated formal proms, was located in a city which she defined as "the pits," and was reputed to be a bit less warm in accommodating women than men. But Yale is Yale, and she must go.

The higher a college's position in the popular pecking order, the more likely it is that an admitted student will ultimately pick it, regardless of compelling reasons to go elsewhere.

Penn recently paid over $75,000 to a New York public relations firm to come up with a dramatic new viewbook to be sent to candidates and parents who request information. Their prospectus is informative, honest, comprehensive though concise, and appealing to the eye. It is intended to be an "incentive piece" to prompt students to read the full catalog and visit the campus for a tour and interview. But no matter how appetizing the new Penn viewbook and catalog, no matter how tantalizing that picturebook-campus and role-model student tour guide, Penn knows that if Johnny Marks is admitted to one of the few institutions reputed to be slightly *more* prestigious, off he'll go— reinstated proms, urban blight, and anticipated cool receptions or not.

At this point, parents must enter our discussion, with emphasis on mothers. Mothers are very important to the college selection process. They may be quiet, but they are always there. We in the Admissions Office are aware of their background presence, and grateful for it, and surely the candidates are, too. It is often the mother who has or takes the time to read the college viewbooks so she can tell the family over dinner how College H differs from college Y. It is usually the mother who calls the Admissions Office to arrange for the tour and interview and asks for the names of the cleanest and least expensive motels in the area. It is often the mother who asks the student tour guide the gritty questions about drugs and sex on campus and the percentage of pre-meds admitted to medical school last year.

But regrettably, Mom sometimes just can't stay in the background. Too often, to the embarrassment of the applicant, it is the mother who, having been invited with father into the admissions officer's quarters after the candidates's interview, can't refrain from saying: "Did you remember to tell him that you were just elected to the Spanish Honor Society, that you were the first girl to be substitute manager of the boys' soccer team, and that you raised more money than any other high school student for our 'Save Union Station' drive?" Mothers are *almost* always a blessing to the college admissions process.

And there is Dad. Fathers seem to dwell a little heavily on what the associates at the office or the boss's wife say about St. Tom's U. versus St. Jim's. We in Admissions can't help wondering at times which has priority with the dads: a good match between offspring and college, or finding the institutional banner that will fly highest during the business lunch.

Unfortunately, both mothers and fathers impose old college images on new college candidates. (Imagine the havoc that has ensued in the homes of young *men* aspiring to Vassar!) Parents are important to the college search, but they sometimes cannot resist stepping over the boundary of discreet influence. Going to college is Today with consequences for Tomorrow. Helpful as parents can be, Yesterday looms all too heavily in their minds when colleges are discussed. Parents, more than any other party, are guilty of perpetuating the prestige-equals-quality myth.

Guidance counselors and principals must share the guilt, however. Placement in "name" colleges becomes the badge of success for all too many schools, for the schools must answer to their public or private boards. How tempting it is to push a very talented Joe or Jane into Ivy, whether or not he/she will be happy there, in order to bolster next year's Where-They-Went-to-College profile and cool political heat.

The candidates themselves, of course, should not escape blame. Funny thing: High school juniors and seniors scrutinize colleges wonderfully well when deciding where to apply. One would think that the same careful scrutiny would be applied after letters of acceptance arrive. But no. When the options are finally at hand, fame of the name rules supreme. You just don't turn down Harvard to attend Princeton; you don't go to Mt. Holyoke if invited to Brown; you can't turn Williams down to attend Bucknell, or snub Smith to attend Wheaton. Some immovable force keeps the pecking order intact, much as we in Admissions try to alter it. Our failure to succeed is demonstrated most poignantly every late April when the thanks-but-I'm-going-else-where letters from admittees arrive. A sample or two from my recent files:

As indicated on the enclosed card, I shall not be attending Bowdoin in the fall. Instead, I will be at Harvard. I feel, however, that after all you and the College have done for me, more than a simple card is required. Your every assistance while I visited your college, your invitation to a second weekend on campus, the letter from a professor—all were overwhelming. Nowhere else, at any time, did I receive such attention. Unfortunately, despite all you have done for me and despite all the obvious attributes of Bowdoin, I cannot turn down Harvard. I have made this decision not because Harvard is necessarily better or greater than Bowdoin, but rather because my life-long dream has been to attend it. Until the letters arrived, reason within argued that a small, personal college would perhaps be better for me than a large one. But when those fateful envelopes were opened, emotion took control and I found myself unable to reject my desire of so long. Sadly, I say goodbye.

From a Vassar fan held prisoner by his brother at Princeton:

I am writing this letter to you from my brother's dormitory room at Princeton. My decision to attend Princeton has been downright anguishing. It was only this weekend that I felt I could actually enjoy the college experience at this Eastern Establishment. For the first time I have found it electric and stimulating! These adjectives I always knew applied to Vassar. The Vassar people I met—be they students, faculty, or administrators—were all amiable, the kind with whom I'd like to be associated. Yet Princeton, perhaps only because of its fame, has always held a "trump card." Sorry.

The Ivy League (Brown, Columbia, Cornell, Dartmouth, Harvard, Penn, Princeton, and Yale), the once-upon-a-time Seven Sisters (Barnard, Bryn Mawr, Mt. Holyoke, Radcliffe, Smith, Vassar, and Wellesley), the Little Ivies (Amherst, Bowdoin, Hamilton, Haverford, Middlebury, Swarthmore, Trinity, Tufts, Wesleyan of Connecticut, and Williams), a few scattered notables outside New England (Bucknell, Carnegie-Mellon, Carleton, Colgate, Colorado College, Davidson, Duke, Georgetown, Johns Hopkins, Northwestern, Oberlin, Pomona, Rice, Stanford, University of Chicago, Washington University

of St. Louis), and Cal Tech and MIT—which seem to have
nations of their own—are difficult to turn down when invited,
although the pecking order *within* this group is severe. But one
must seriously consider the qualities of the good-but-not-quite-
so-famous. For example*:

Drew of New Jersey ranks above neighboring Princeton in the percentage of undergraduates who ultimately complete the Ph.D.

Bennington College (Vermont), although known for the arts, has
placed over 90 percent of its pre-meds in medical school during the
past several years. And although its dance and music programs are
reputed to be its best, Bennington's graduate roster of drama notables gains high marks also: Allan Arkin, Liz Swados (of "Nightclub
Cantata" and "Runaways" fame), John DeVries, and Carol Chan-
ning.

At Harvey Mudd College in California (where students wear T-
shirts that say "Harvey WHO?") more than half the entering freshmen ranked in the top ten students of their respective secondary
school classes in a recent year; the midway point in SATs among
freshmen in that same class was Verbal 610, Math 720. Several years
ago, Harvey Mudd's midway Math II Achievement score was 780.

Ten Washington University (Missouri) faculty members have won
the Nobel Prize, eight having done all or part of their research on
the WU campus. Also, the size and quality of WU's literary community is perhaps unrivalled in the United States. Its members,
virtually all of whom teach undergraduate courses annually, have
won the National Book Award, the Bollingen Prize, the Roethke
Award, the *Paris Review* Humor Prize, and both Guggenheim and
Rockefeller Foundation Awards.

Franklin and Marshall College (Pennsylvania) ranks first among
private colleges offering primarily undergraduate programs in the
percentage of graduates who earn the Ph.D. in geology, and second
in chemistry.

Graduates of Ohio Wesleyan include Dr. Frank Stanton, Branch
Rickey, Norman Vincent Peale, Trish Vandevere, Dr. Ralph Sock-
man, and Arthur Flemming.

Brandeis (Massachusetts), according to the American Association
for the Advancement of Science, ranks eighth in the nation in the
percentage of women Baccalaureate graduates who complete the
Ph.D., and sixteenth in the nation in the percentage of men (higher
than Amherst or Harvard).

*Examples provided by the colleges named.

Ripon College of Wisconsin has succeeded in placing 100 percent of its pre-law students in law schools during the last three years. And how many Ivies can say they graduated the hero of *Star Wars?* None. Harrison Ford graduated from Ripon, as did Spencer Tracy.

At recent count, over one dozen college and university presidents shared an important ingredient: they all were once administrators at Lawrence of Wisconsin. The list includes presidents of Brown, Duke, and Harvard.

The largest single gift to a college in the United States ($100 million) went to Emory University (Georgia) in 1979. Extraordinary expansion in facilities and programs are underway.

The general prestige of an institution may indeed denote quality, although images are often woefully dated and distorted. But remember, some of the average of the old schools may not be quite as good as the best of the newer schools. The prestige of an institution, although difficult to discount, need not point to the college for you.

## *Myth II,* LOCATION: "TO RETIRE TO THE OCEAN OR THE WOODS WITH MY BOOKS WOULD BE UTOPIA"

The location of a college is an important consideration indeed. But surf, sand, and sun, or mountains and glacial lakes hardly get at the core of what college is all about. It is easy to be miserable in the most beautiful college locale if one doesn't probe beneath surfaces and question one's own adaptability well ahead of time.

Private colleges—all private colleges—are eager to sell their produce today, and "packaging" becomes key. Promotion of activities available in the area of the campus has become important to the colleges' marketing campaigns.

I well remember arriving at Bowdoin in Maine in the late sixties to head Admissions. Here was a college of glorious tradition, founded in 1794, which had graduated Hawthorne and Longfellow and America's first undergraduate black (John B. Russwurm, in 1826). But for some reason, despite consistency of academic quality over the years, Bowdoin had slipped from national visibility and applications were declining. Part of the problem, it appeared, was the trend in the late sixties of teen-agers wanting a city college. To save the world one couldn't desert the city—only there did the ghettos call, only there were the visible podiums to demonstrate actively against America's wayward foreign policy. (Indeed, the extracurricular involve-ments of urban college students in that era helped change a nation.)

But trends and times change, too. Suddenly the Ecology movement came roaring in. "Our moment!" said Bowdoin and Williams and Middlebury and Dartmouth, for in the eyes of the young, saving the environment became an option to serving the downtrodden people.

We at Bowdoin lost no time providing collegiate music for that bandwagon. The sensitive, studious young man on the cover of the viewbook was dismissed in favor of pictorial displays that would impress Audubon: quaint fishing villages with (endan-gered) sparkling waters, magnificent sunsets, (endangered) ver-dant forests, and shots of backpacking extravaganzas. And it worked. Applications to the Bowdoins of the nation (we were clearly not alone in our newfound campaign and glory) soared; meanwhile, there was a decline in applications to urban uni-versities, which were suddenly labeled "troubled." (Granted, educational innovations at Bowdoin and other rural colleges in the early seventies helped to boost their stock, but locale seemed to deserve top honors for the turn-around.)

Bowdoin was honest in accompanying the descriptions of its academic offerings with pictures of the wonders of coastal Maine; the pine trees and the rocky shoreline and the incomparable sunsets were all there. But, just as Uncle Sam instructed the nicotine salesmen to put a warning on the label, so might some-one have gotten to us at the colleges. Kids should be warned that an idyllic natural location is not a "natural" for all.

Who wouldn't want to go to Bowdoin after seeing the campus on a sunlit, foliage-drenched Saturday afternoon in mid-Oct-ober? Who wouldn't be captured by the seals bobbing two miles away at the shore? Nature-starved high schoolers from Man-hattan and Boston and Los Angeles fell for it in droves. And after settling in, many were utterly happy there. But others found that four years without a subway, without "culture" beyond the campus, without the anonymity and freedom that tall buildings and crowded streets provide, was a strikingly different experience than the weekend visit.

True, one could argue that Manhattan kids need Maine and that Maine kids need Manhattan during those broadening college years. But academic adjustment and accomplishment through hard work may prove enough of a challenge without also risking a completely foreign locale. To each his own, of course, but teenagers must seriously examine their ability to adapt to dramatically different surroundings before being won over by the lush brochures put out by both country *and* city colleges.

As a postscript, I can't resist commenting that Miss Cup Runneth Over's description of New Haven as "the pits" seems a trifle unfair. True, New Haven, Poughkeepsie, Middletown, Connecticut, and Durham, North Carolina are not the garden spots of America. But they, and many other unattractive minor cities, are big enough and interesting enough to offer a quality relief from the campus. They are diverse enough to provide an arena for volunteer work that is both meaningful and, because the towns are small, visible; and they are all within proximity of unpaved areas of woods and grass and water and fresh air. The facade of ugly/urban cannot be overlooked, but some college locales tout versatility beyond looks—and some of the prettiest are limited indeed.

### *Myth III,* SIZE: "THE SMALLER THE COLLEGE, THE MORE PERSONAL THE EDUCATION"

Granted, everyone knows everyone in a tiny school, but is this stimulating, or is this boring? The communal comforts of the small college are clearly what some institutions push in justifying a hefty price tag.

Becoming a friend of both fellow student and professor can truly promote a warm learning environment. But surely there is a case to be made for the educational value of a diverse student body, which assures that a student will be exposed to cultural and lifestyle differences. At some point the notion "I like Reserve because everyone knows my name here" becomes a bit vapid: Reserve may be shortchanging this student in offering such limited exposure. Little places that do not structure diversity (by choice, or because they have too few applications) can be stifling in their rigidity and lack of differences. And larger places can be surprisingly personal as one moves from small group to small group: at least there is choice.

The diversity of the student body is only one aspect of the question of large v. small college. A more important issue is the faculty's accessibility to the individual student.

A favorite question of college candidates today is "What is your college's faculty/student ratio?" We admissions officers are always ready with a pat and persuasive answer, but often we fudge. Most colleges include the following in their ratio figures: faculty members on sabbatical leaves; administrators who are technically part of the faculty but who teach little (if at all); and "nonacademic" faculty members such as full-time coaches or music librarians. A more penetrating question would be "How many students in your college's average class?"

At many institutions today, including some of the famous ones, the faculty has been "frozen" due to financial constraints. This means the size of the faculty, by administrative decree, must remain constant until the financial crunch eases. If a faculty member is to be added to one academic department, one must be removed from another department to keep the total number of faculty the same. Obviously, political conflicts rage on a campus when this happens. Meanwhile, a faculty freeze is often accompanied by a "natural growth" in the student body (more tuition-paying students means looser purse strings), so individual classes grow larger.

At liberal arts colleges where the add-and-subtract method of accommodating the faculty freeze is too painful to be exploited, some departments remain underenrolled (Physics and Art History are common examples today), while others bulge with students (Business and Biology are two obvious examples in this era). Often an institution just cannot keep up with fads among students, as academic vogues rise and fall without fair warning. Students aspiring to the business world were subject to peer harassment in the late sixties; now the Economics and Business Administration classrooms are flooded.

Any college, large or small, can become "personal" if a student hits it off well with a particular faculty member. Oddly enough (given all the talk by college candidates), students often don't take the initiative. They settle instead on counting noses in a given classroom. If one is to use this method in determining the "personalness" of a college, careful prodding must be done. Neither the gross size of the college nor the faculty/student ratio necessarily provide accurate insight into the faculty/student ratio within a given department during a given term.

Should one really care how large the class will be if John Kenneth Galbraith is willing to teach undergraduates at Harvard? At many institutions there is "a course you *must* take before you leave here," popular because of a particular professor rather than because of the subject matter. That class is usually big. And when basic terms and concepts are being transmitted in Sociology I or Biology I, does it matter whether the professor is close enough to touch?

If one is paying an exorbitant price, however, one would seem to earn the right to assured attention. To get at the core of the matter, ask an admissions office how many freshman advisees a professor has at his college; ask if the person who lectures and conducts discussion in all courses is the same person who grades the papers; ask how often a typical professor eats with the students, or whether there is a separate faculty lunchroom; ask whether full professors teach freshman courses; ask whether the famous names at a famous institution teach undergraduates at all!

Big v. small college? There is no pat answer to this important question. What one gains at a large school because of the diversity of courses offered and people assembled, one may lose in feeling a member of an impersonal, fragmented community. But "personal" has many faces, and counting noses will not alone suffice.

### Myth IV, MAJOR: "ANY STRONG LIBERAL ARTS COLLEGE WILL BE GOOD IN MY FIELD"

Wrong, wrong, wrong. Take my recent college, Vassar, for example. Rumor has it that Vassar is superb in Art. That rumor is partially correct. Vassar has a superb undergraduate Art History Department. But Studio Art? The facilities and the breadth of the program are inadequate, compared to some of the competition. Photography? Vassar doesn't consider it a discipline worthy of formal academic credit.

Rumored general strengths can be deceptive, and the candidate must investigate below surfaces. Often, even at a liberal arts college, a specialized faculty within an academic department gains strength and fame and "settles in," unwilling or unable to shift departmental emphases with shifting times, needs, and demands. A "good" Music Department may not be uniformly excellent in theory and performance, and some of the best music departments may not accredit jazz or electronic music. Does an institution's Math Department bend toward the theoretical or the practical? Does the Psychology Department bend toward the Experimental or the Clinical? *Which* languages does Middlebury teach well?

However, before you become too immersed in researching the subtle shades of a major at specific colleges, a reminder is in order. Most of the selective, private colleges of the nation hold fast to the traditional liberal arts program ("which trains you for nothing but prepares you for everything," Bill Wilson, ex-Dean of Admissions at Amherst, said frequently). Mt. Holyoke College states the liberal arts philosophy in an admissions publication:

Mount Holyoke is committed to the liberal arts and the principles of philosophy such an education symbolizes. The liberal arts college maintains that the search for knowledge and with knowledge, compassionate understanding, is a central and not a peripheral human activity. It specifically provides the tools of mental inquiry and tries to reveal their variety, their inner logic, and their relatedness. It seeks to develop individuals committed to humane values, capable of rejecting oversimplifications of ideology or method, and liberated from narrow definitions of themselves and others and of human problems in general. It is an education that is evaluative, not merely factual and descriptive.

These are utopian ideals, and rightly so, but the world of a college that seeks to live by them is nevertheless a real and rigorous world—a world where a life of a particular sort is intensely lived: a life of the mind above all, and of individual and joint endeavor.

Liberal arts colleges realize that students often—and quite honestly—change their minds about their academic major after sampling the great smorgasbord of courses in the freshman and sophomore years, the "general studies" segment of the traditional liberal arts colleges' four-year format. Usually secondary school students have had in-depth exposure only to basic disciplines: English, History, Physical Science, Mathematics, Foreign Language. A freshman year introductory course in Anthropology or BioPsychology or Asian Studies or Computer Math can whet appetites and open new, exciting vistas. At most colleges, it is not unusual for as many as two-thirds of all freshmen to change their minds regarding a major after exposure to new disciplines during the first two college years.

Many liberal arts institutions are so supportive of investigation and change regarding the college major that they view applicants who appear determined to specialize in a particular area with some suspicion. The most common example on the current scene is the student who is hell-bent on being pre-medical. Almost all selective colleges today lament their unrealistically high percentage of "pre-meds." Many of these students have not even tasted an advanced course in biology or calculus in secondary school before making their plans.

Proud of its quality offerings in a diverse range of topics and disciplines, a liberal arts institution wants a student to investigate broadly: That is the meat of the liberal arts educational philosophy. Since a change in one's academic major is likely, one might feel that a large institution would be 'safest' due to its wide spectrum of courses and majors. There is some merit to this argument, but the smaller institutions today have a comeback.

Realizing their relative deficiency in the number of courses and majors offered, small colleges tap each other's resources so that an individual student can gain from two, or perhaps several, colleges' offerings during the undergraduate journey. Colleges in the same city allow and encourage cross registrations with each other. Twelve colleges in the Northeast* are involved

*Amherst, Bowdoin, Connecticut, Dartmouth, Mt. Holyoke, Smith, Trinity, Vassar, Wellesley, Wesleyan, Wheaton, and Williams.

in a formal exchange program through which a junior from one college can attend any of the other eleven colleges for a semester or a full year and return to his home college for the senior year. (Students on financial aid can usually carry their home-college scholarships with them to the other institution!)

Also, smaller colleges offer broad opportunities for independent study (the college budget permitting) for the student whose needs cannot be met through standard curricular offerings. And smaller colleges are generous in allowing students to "create" years for credit abroad or at other American universities that have specialized programs.

One must remember that enrolling at a college today, unlike a generation ago, does not necessarily mean four years of staying put. Not only is moving around possible, but good institutions encourage it. And if one settles on a major which the original college is ill-equipped to offer, a transfer is a possibility. As most colleges have grown more accommodating to mobility, they have simultaneously adjusted to the possibility of students' permanently leaving mid-stream. Transfer students from other institutions then fill the holes. As a result, there is heavy transfer traffic these days. (See Appendix, Chart I.)

All good colleges are not good in all fields. The candidate must analyze the quality of a specific institution's offerings, realizing all the while that immersion in liberal arts may well lead him to change his major field, if not also his college.

## Myth V, SOCIAL TYPE: "SINGLE-SEX COLLEGES ARE DEAD"

For men, it is so: The all-male academic bastion has nearly fallen. Harvard and Yale and Williams and Dartmouth and all their macho friends, including West Point, are now admitting (welcoming?—some questions remain) women. When Amherst and Washington and Lee opened their gates to freshman women, an era of exclusive education in America, primarily in the Northeast, passed. (A few noteworthy all-male remnants can still be found. Wabash College of Indiana, for example, continues to be for-men-only, but this is probably because a major endower attached strings to a fortune.) Today, men must count on going to college with women.

For women, there are options. And they are worth considering. Throughout America there are healthy private women's colleges: California has Mills and Scripps; the deep South has Sweetbriar, Randolph-Macon, Hollins; the Northeast has Chatham and Wheaton, plus the prominent and still-selective Seven Sister remnants—Smith, Mt. Holyoke, and Wellesley. (Other Sisters in the Northeast are now so cozy with men's institutions that they don't qualify for the all-women's college list: Barnard, the muted Siamese twin of Columbia; Bryn Mawr, the morosely academic live-in mate of Haverford; and Radcliffe, once the fabled and closeted mistress of Harvard, now wife. Vassar now has roughly equivalent numbers of men and women, much to the consternation of its old sorority.)

Until women are given an equal place in the American social and economic framework, educating them separately is warranted, say the proponents of all-women's colleges. The recent President of Smith College, Jill Conway, argues the position convincingly:

There are three major pedagogical reasons why women benefit from undergraduate study in an all-female student body. First, women students in such an environment are free to choose their area of academic specialization without reference to sex stereotyping. Thus, women's colleges have historically produced a disproportionate number of women who have gone on to achieve the doctorate in mathematics and science, and today they graduate many more majors in economics and political science than their coeducational equivalents.

Secondly, undergraduates have always been thought to learn more when exposed to a civilized and humane environment that gives them insight into themselves through access to the experience of their peers. Similarly, it is clear that women in a single-sex student body build a network of friendships with other talented women that is a source of support throughout their lives and a powerful force for the creation of female identity. For natural and self-evident reasons, the bonding of the young in coeducational settings tends to be pairing across sex lines. In fact, there is some evidence that friendships among women are inhibited in coeducational environments.

Finally, women in a single-sex—and thus self-governing—student body take on managerial and leadership roles in greater numbers and on different terms than is possible in society at large. In the running of an all-female student world, women see themselves as part of the solution of problems rather than as part of the enduring problem of female subordination.

The chief weakness of feminist thought has been to see liberation for women as freedom to adopt male styles of action and traditionally male occupations without penalty. However, this tends to downgrade or ignore the importance of nurturing the young and to oversimplify the complex social arrangements we need in order to come to terms with human generativity.

The difference between the coeducational college and the all-female institution is that, at the women's college, she does this in a world in which she is in charge instead of one where she may feel the need to win acceptance.

Ms. Conway does have opponents. One is Philip Jordan, the President of Kenyon College (and past Dean of Connecticut College, once all female, now coeducational):

Women's colleges nourished confidence and ambition in their students by freeing them from crosscurrents created by male peers and by providing examples to follow in the mature women who taught and oversaw them. But now that male bastions have fallen, the case for separating women is weak.

Why should women need a collegiate interlude of separatism before re-entering a society where, in graduate school or on the job, women work and compete with men? . . . Able young women today need no special treatment, just treatment and opportunity equal to that given to men.

Women's colleges were founded in response to the restrictive social attitudes of the last century. They flourished and did their job well. Now it is time for the next step: to take full advantage, for the good of both men and women, of the new freedoms that women are winning. This can best be done by educating men and women together, not apart.

The coed v. women's college debate has subtleties deserving more than a passing glance. For example, "coed" often means male domination (reflective of the nation as a whole) with women present: the big social events center around men's athletic contests, men's fraternity parties, etc. Oddly, however, women frequently do not complain about this problem at the "coed" institutions most guilty of remaining macho.

When traditional male colleges began going coed in the late sixties (along with the visible beginnings of the national women's rights movement), high school girls complained bitterly that these colleges had established quotas limiting the number of women admitted during the "transitional years." And often their cries were justified. But where were those same voices, once the women were admitted and enrolled? At Bowdoin, the "early women" were hesitant to join our battle for an expanded female enrollment: The smaller their number at the college, the more "select" they seemed to feel, and the more visible and celebrated their pioneer group. One wondered who was truly more conservative at that time in the campaign for a more equitable admissions policy: the cantankerous old board of trustees, or the girls-just-arrived.

Women's colleges do seem to have a higher transfer-out rate than coed institutions. Some feminists have said that this simply confirms the male domination of society as a whole: College women meet men and transfer to their institutions. Regardless, the single-sex college for women is a strong and popular option today and should be seriously considered.

## *Myth VI*, COST: "THE IVY-TYPE COLLEGES ARE NOW FOR THE RICH AND THE POOR: THE MIDDLE CLASS HAS BEEN SQUEEZED OUT"

History confirms old notions regarding the rich. The old elitist private colleges of the nation catered for years to the blue-bloods. Much as the Ivies and Seven Sisters and all their cousins brag about their institutions' open doors, there is little evidence to suggest that the doors have been unlocked for long. We thought the blue-jeaned scruffy hippies of the late sixties all looked alike? Take a look sometime at a Smith or Yale yearbook of the forties or fifties. For every headband and unwashed lock hiding a saddened face of the early seventies was a circle-pin and blonde coif over endless, well-gened blue eyes three and four decades ago.

For a long time those who attended the elitist colleges were, quite simply, those who could pay. But concurrent with zooming prices came a sense of conscience regarding equal access for all classes and races to the best and/or most established of American universities. Partly due to student pressures during the turbulent late sixties, literally all prestigious private institutions now support ambitious affirmative-action programs, with priority for disadvantaged minorities.

So visible have the programs for the disadvantaged become that the second segment of our "myth" is understandable: "Olde Ivy U. has paid the new poor to share the library and the football stadium with the old rich." True, both of these groups are highly visible in Cambridge, Palo Alto, Hanover, and other Ivyish hometowns. But it is unfair to say that the group in between has fallen between stools.

Is the middle class being squeezed out of Olde Ivy? No, say some convincing authorities. One of the nation's most astute education editors, Gene I. Maeroff of *The New York Times*, wrote:

> A report by the Bureau of the Census has challenged the contention that the Federal Government should reorient its programs of college aid so as to provide more help for the children of middle-income families. Speculation has been widespread among educators and public officials that the sons and daughters of middle-income families have been "squeezed out" of higher education because of their inability to meet its high cost.
>
> Although the proportion of college-enrolled children from families with incomes of $8,525 to $17,050 fell sharply from 1967 to 1973, it has increased in recent years, the Census Bureau report said. Data show that, overall, enrollment rates were not different in 1976 than they were in 1967, the report said. The trend of declining enrollment of middle-income students has reversed and returned to the higher levels.

The College Entrance Examination Board confirmed Mr. Maeroff's report by adding the encouraging note that middle-income families do indeed often qualify for financial aid, making attendance at highly selective private institutions more possible than many think.

Selective private colleges today are eager to construct a freshman "classful of differences." Doing so obviously requires committing significant financial aid for those who cannot make it on their own. A sampling:

## PERCENTAGE OF STUDENTS ON FINANCIAL AID
(from the colleges' own resources)

| | |
|---|---|
| Amherst (Mass.) | 44% |
| Bates (Me.) | 40% |
| Dickinson | 45% |
| Earlham (Ind.) | 65% |
| Mt. Holyoke (Mass.) | 46% |
| Ohio Wesleyan | 44% |
| Princeton (N.J.) | 43% |
| Vanderbilt (Tenn.) | 36% |
| Wellesley (Mass.) | 43% |

Although there is a recurrence in America of the "no-need" or "merit" scholarship (primarily at institutions nervous about filling their beds), nearly all of the most prestigious colleges use their considerable resources in financial aid only to assist those who have proved financial need. While there may be some favoritism shown in the *admission* of an athlete, a minority student or a legacy (see Chapter Three), there is negligible favoritism in the awarding of financial aid. Again, financial assistance at the highly selective private colleges is offered on the basis of proved financial need.*

Private colleges are expensive today—but they always have been. The candidate and the family will have to decide if the quality of education, the "name," the somewhat more personal atmosphere, and "the tradition" all add up to a value two to three times the price of the public institutions. (Public colleges also are quietly sneaking up the scale of cost and can, if a student is applying from out of state, be more expensive than some private colleges.)

Although the price tag for a year at an Ivyish school seems exorbitant today, the economists tell us that in relative terms (considering the diminished buying power of the dollar and

*The Ivyish colleges have essentially identical policies and practices regarding scholarships, loans, jobs, and financial aid application procedures. The Middlebury statement, succinct and comprehensive, is typical of a wide range of private institutions. See Appendix II.

escalating salary scales), it is no more expensive to attend an elitist institution now than it was in the mid-fififties, when many of today's candidates' parents did attend. A lingering question, however, is whether today's parents will be willing to sacrifice as much for their children's education as previous generations of parents did. Purchasing the second home, the third car, and the boat by credit complicates this sacrifice, no matter how generous the mood or the spirit.

## IN SUMMARY

Now that you are armed to debunk all private college admissions myths circulating among your nervous classmates or your mother's telephone grapevine or your father's commuter train, it is time to take some steps on your own:

1. See the school guidance counselor *early* (fall of the junior year, at latest) to talk candidly about where your secondary school record puts you vis-a-vis "selective level" of college to be considered. You may feel the school counselor is out of touch (rarely true) or has little time for you (often true— the whole nation seems to be defeating bond issues on education, and members of the counseling staff are frequently the first to be laid off, adding to each individual counselor's load). But a friendly overture by you will demonstrate your interest, and you will almost always receive sympathetic advice. You may be disheartened by straight talk from the counselor, but remember: he/she has passed through hundreds of college acceptance and rejection notices in recent years and has as good a handle as anyone on which college requires what level of accomplishment.
2. Write directly to colleges that interest you for informative materials. The literature in the high school Guidance Office is often out of date or in someone else's hands, so procure your own. Private colleges today are hungry for your inquiry and will respond with more "good news" than

you may wish to consume. A simple postcard requesting viewbook and application will suffice. (Full catalogs, which are available in your school library, are rarely sent; they often cost the college over $3.00 apiece today.)

3. *Study* the materials you are sent. The pictures can be entertaining (and are designed to create a mood), but hard prose is what you must absorb. Pay particular attention to profiles of the freshman class. Most selective institutions make these available today (but alas, not all the Ivies), and they are helpful indeed in charting one's chances for admission. For example, you can test yourself on every scale of the exhaustive freshman class profile published annually by Bowdoin College. Are you a "long shot," or are you a rather sure bet for Bowdoin next year? An astute reading of the following tables should bring you closer to the answer. *(See pages 105–106.)*

4. Talk with hometown friends about the institutions that seriously interest you. Current undergraduates returning for Thanksgiving, Christmas, spring, or summer vacations will provide the most accurate insights. Get their names from the guidance offices of neighboring high schools by phoning and asking, "Who from your school enrolled at SMU, Tulane, or Northwestern during the last couple of years?" Also, chats with local alumni can be helpful, if one is good at selective listening. Too often the alums romanticize "bright college years" and tell you about the college they attended rather than about the college that exists today. A few alumni, however, in each major city are well trained by their institutions just for the purpose of talking to you. On the whole, they know their college oday and will be happy to share their knowledge. Write the college directly to see who your local representative is.

5. Visit the colleges that interest you most. Perhaps the best idea would be to "sample" campuses during the summer months following your junior year in high school. Admissions officers are at ease during the summer, so this is also a good time for an exploratory interview. But the meaty visit can come in the fall of your senior year, when you

return to the two or three campuses that top your list. If possible, go on a Friday and attend a few classes, take your sleeping bag and stay overnight in an undergraduate's room (the Admissions Office will help you arange this), and test the atmosphere on campus outside the classroom on Saturday. *Always* sit down for half an hour or so in the Student Union and ask several undergrads, independent of each other, "What's wrong with this place?" The answers will provide a healthy balance to all the pap in the slick admissions literature you receive.

6. Seek an interview at the Admissions Office. This can be anytime: summer after the junior year, fall or winter of senior year. In summer you will receive a royal welcome because the crowds haven't descended yet. In the fall or winter you may miss the admissions officers altogether because they're visiting your school at home; if you do catch one on campus, the interview will be a bit rushed because crowds are waiting in the outer lobby. Whenever you're planning to go, write or call a couple of weeks in advance for an appointment. (Most private college admissions offices are open 9 to 5 weekdays, 9 to noon Saturdays, and all offer student-conducted tours before or after the interview.) The interview is important for two reasons: a.) your unanswered questions about the college can be cleared up at this time (although the tour guide or the students you meet in the Union may be more able to help you find answers); and b.) you can present your case for admission in conversation, which (regrettably) is often considerably more effective than the case for admission you will present in writing. Students talk better than they write today, so most enhance their chances for admission via the interview.

7. Apply to a "long-shot" or two, a couple of "sure bets," and at least one "safety." Which colleges fit the preceding definitions must be decided by the counselor, candidate, and parents together, not by anyone of these parties alone. Often college admissions officers will help you with these personal definitions if you can muster the courage to ask.

## BOWDOIN COLLEGE CLASS OF 1988

Admissions Data
Entering Freshmen: 405
  233 men, 172 women
Completed Applications: 3,009
  1,655 men, 1,354 women
Applicants Accepted: 856 (28.4%)
  472 men (28.5%)
  384 women (28.4%)
Schools with Candidates: 1,226
Schools Represented in Class: 271
Interviews on Campus: 2,882

Secondary Schools Visited: 324
Early Decision Applicants: 340
  182 men, 158 women
Early Decision Acceptances:
  122; 70 men, 52 women
% of Class Admitted via
  E.D.): 30.1
% of Public School Students
  in Class: 53.5
% of Independent School
  Students in Class: 46.5

### Range of CEEB-SAT Scores/Mathematics

| Score | No. Applied | % Accepted | No. in Ent. Class | % of Ent. Class |
|---|---|---|---|---|
| Not Submitted | 1,225 | 19.9 | 157 | 38.8 |
| 750–800 | 47 | 72.3 | 11 | 2.7 |
| 700–749 | 213 | 57.3 | 33 | 8.2 |
| 650–699 | 358 | 47.5 | 67 | 16.5 |
| 600–649 | 411 | 33.8 | 60 | 14.8 |
| 550–599 | 330 | 23.3 | 32 | 7.9 |
| 500–549 | 255 | 20.0 | 35 | 8.6 |
| 450–499 | 113 | 15.0 | 10 | 2.5 |
| 400–449 | 44 | 4.5 | 0 | 0.0 |
| 350–399 | 11 | 0.0 | 0 | 0.0 |
| 300–349 | 2 | 0.0 | 0 | 0.0 |
| 250–299 | 0 | 0.0 | 0 | 0.0 |
| 200–249 | 0 | 0.0 | 0 | 0.0 |
| TOTAL | 3,009 | | 405 | 100.0 |

## Range of CEEB-SAT Scores/Verbal

| Score | No. Applied | % Accepted | No. in Ent. Class | % of Ent. Class |
|---|---|---|---|---|
| Not Submitted | 1,225 | 19.9 | 157 | 38.8 |
| 750–800 | 7 | 85.7 | 2 | 0.5 |
| 700–749 | 85 | 76.5 | 15 | 3.7 |
| 650–699 | 222 | 57.7 | 44 | 10.9 |
| 600–649 | 394 | 49.2 | 71 | 17.5 |
| 550–599 | 432 | 29.6 | 65 | 16.0 |
| 500–549 | 325 | 17.5 | 30 | 7.4 |
| 450–499 | 180 | 13.9 | 16 | 4.0 |
| 400–449 | 89 | 10.1 | 5 | 1.2 |
| 350–399 | 32 | 0.0 | 0 | 0.0 |
| 300–349 | 13 | 0.0 | 0 | 0.0 |
| 250–299 | 2 | 0.0 | 0 | 0.0 |
| 200–249 | 3 | 0.0 | 0 | 0.0 |
| TOTAL | 3,009 | | 405 | 100.0 |

| Residence of Applicants | No. Applied | % Accepted | % Ent. Class |
|---|---|---|---|
| New England | 1,651 | 24.6 | 52.3 |
| Middle Atlantic | 646 | 33.1 | 23.7 |
| South | 123 | 35.8 | 5.2 |
| Midwest | 235 | 39.2 | 10.1 |
| West | 194 | 33.0 | 5.0 |
| Foreign | 160 | 23.1 | 3.7 |

## Rank in class by Decile/Public Schools

| | No. Applied | % Accepted | No. in Ent. Class | % of Matriculants |
|---|---|---|---|---|
| Top decile | 729 | 46.1 | 150 | 68.8 |
| 2nd decile | 335 | 20.0 | 40 | 18.3 |
| 3rd decile | 165 | 6.1 | 6 | 2.8 |
| 4th decile | 86 | 7.0 | 3 | 1.4 |
| 5th decile | 34 | 0.0 | 0 | 0.0 |
| 6th decile | 23 | 0.0 | 0 | 0.0 |
| 7th decile | 12 | 0.0 | 0 | 0.0 |
| 8th decile | 3 | 0.0 | 0 | 0.0 |
| 9th decile | 3 | 0.0 | 0 | 0.0 |
| Bottom decile | 2 | 0.0 | 0 | 0.0 |
| Not available | 221 | 19.0 | 19 | 8.7 |
| Total | 1,613 | | 218 | 100.0 |

43.6 percent of entering graduates stood in the top 5 percent of their classes.
47.7 percent of entering graduates stood in the top 5 percent of their ranked classes.

Rank in Class by Decile/Independent Schools

| | No. Applied | % Accepted | No. in Ent. Class | % of Matriculants |
|---|---|---|---|---|
| Top decile | 184 | 54.3 | 37 | 19.8 |
| 2nd decile | 171 | 32.7 | 33 | 17.6 |
| 3rd decile | 113 | 29.2 | 20 | 10.7 |
| 4th decile | 91 | 15.4 | 8 | 4.3 |
| 5th decile | 42 | 14.3 | 5 | 2.7 |
| 6th decile | 36 | 0.0 | 0 | 0.0 |
| 7th decile | 25 | 8.0 | 2 | 1.1 |
| 8th decile | 9 | 0.0 | 0 | 0.0 |
| 9th decile | 6 | 0.0 | 0 | 0.0 |
| Bottom decile | 2 | 0.0 | 0 | 0.0 |
| Not Available | 717 | 25.7 | 82 | 43.8 |
| TOTAL | 1,396 | | 187 | 100.0 |

8.0 percent of entering graduates stood in the top 5 percent of their classes.
14.3 percent of entering graduates stood in the top 5 percent of their ranked classes.

8. Spend time, effort, and imagination on the application. Remember, you're nearing the point of entry into your adult life. Why limit your options by postponing a serious application effort in favor of one more cheerleading practice, one more Decoration Planning Committee meeting? After seventeen years of thoughtful involvement and accomplishment, you have something to record and to present. The colleges are eager to review it. The highly selective colleges today have a wealth of B+ averages and 560 Verbal scores, but too few genuinely interesting candidates. Show the colleges how truly exceptional you are!

# 3.

# The College Looks at the Candidate

## STRUCTURING THE CLASSFUL OF DIFFERENCES

As suggested in Chapter Two, neither the exorbitant price tag at Harvard nor the availability of fine public university training at half to one-third that price have discouraged a horde of candidates and parents from courting the old, elitist institutions just to "try" for what is regarded as the summit of undergraduate academe. Competition of the Class of 1990 bears this out. *(See page 110.)*

Whether one makes Ivy or not, the tired old question of "Who gets in?" is important to discuss. What is true at the top is basically true throughout the order of private colleges, with all requirements being increasingly relaxed the further one descends the scale of selectivity. So, what are the most selective colleges looking for (with implications for their less choosey cousins)? Is it what you know or whom you know? Is there some special talent one must possess to earn a place at Brown?

The lavish catalogs and we tweedy admissions officers are frustratingly evasive. Of course, the higher the College Board scores and the higher the grade average, the better the chances for admission. But what of the nebulous "personal evaluation"? More to the point, how is it that Ann Alexander, in the top 10 percent of her class with 600 SATs, president of the student council and chairman of the Community Drug Abuse Program, is passed over in favor of that popular but not particularly academic boy from the same school whose height, weight, and strength seem to be his most impressive statistics?

Highly selective colleges do not judge all applicants by means of a uniform standard. Consciously or (in some cases) subconsciously they admit five (or more) freshman divisions, using a separate norm for each category, and then lump the composite together as a "class" (usually deemed "best ever"). This means that applicants compete against each other within categories, not against all other candidates judged by a single admissions standard. The Merit Scholar, the extraordinarily talented violinist, the Stanford alumnus' son, the nifty all-round kid, and the black are not going to nudge one another out of the running: They're competing against others of like interest and talent for that particular group's fair share of the class.

There are at least five categories that must emerge intact as each highly selective college structures and completes its freshman class.

1. *The Intellects.* The faculty of every college complains about the intellectual shortcomings of the student body. All professors want scholars who are polished at entry and will chase ideas with discipline and creativity thereafter. And admissions officers listen to the faculty. As a result, superior intellectual competence is uniformly admitted, even if the applicant isn't lovable, the future "human contribution" is in doubt, and the alumni couldn't care less if this one gets in. If a student has opted to take every tough course the school offers (particularly if the school is known to be demanding), has emerged with a near-perfect record, and has exceptional intellectual power as demonstrated by standardized tests (proving that the good grades are no accident), that student is almost invariably admitted. But there aren't enough "perfect" students around to fill even the most selective colleges' classes. Even if there were, a few would be passed by to make way for other types of candidates the elite college wants, needs, and always gets.

## CLASS OF 1986

| College | Percent Accepted in Declining Order of Selectivity | Number of Applicants | Number Accepted | Desired Class Size |
|---|---|---|---|---|
| Harvard | 16% | 13,614 | 2,177 | 1,600 |
| Stanford | 16% | 15,612 | 2,524 | 1,611 |
| Princeton | 17% | 12,220 | 2,128 | 1,150 |
| Yale | 19% | 11,737 | 2,182 | 1,275 |
| Brown | 20% | 13,707 | 2,674 | 1,375 |
| Dartmouth | 20% | 9,503 | 1,875 | 1,030 |
| Amherst | 22% | 4,400 | 958 | 429 |
| Bowdoin | 23% | 3,555 | 805 | 375 |
| Williams | 26% | 4,686 | 1,204 | 508 |
| Columbia | 28% | 6,570 | 1,834 | 792 |
| Georgetown | 28% | 9,727 | 2,712 | 1,369 |
| Middlebury | 30% | 3,890 | 1,172 | 500 |
| Cornell | 30% | 19,848 | 6,053 | 2,964 |
| Swarthmore | 32% | 2,590 | 834 | 325 |
| Duke | 32% | 10,296 | 3,380 | 1,403 |
| M.I.T. | 33% | 5,748 | 1,884 | 1,025 |
| Holy Cross | 33% | 4,861 | 1,587 | 620 |
| Rice | 33% | 3,000 | 1,000 | 506 |
| Tufts | 33% | 10,004 | 3,337 | 1,150 |
| Cal. Tech | 34% | 1,267 | 431 | 194 |
| Univ. of Penn. | 37% | 12,801 | 4,686 | 2,220 |
| Lafayette | 38% | 4,682 | 1,761 | 530 |
| Wesleyan | 39% | 4,365 | 1,714 | 705 |
| Haverford | 39% | 1,917 | 744 | 275 |
| Colgate | 40% | 5,498 | 2,220 | 690 |
| Trinity | 40% | 3,388 | 1,368 | 450 |
| Bates | 42% | 2,807 | 1,174 | 409 |
| Bucknell | 43% | 6,279 | 2,706 | 820 |
| Colby | 44% | 3,173 | 1,402 | 450 |
| Vassar | 45% | 4,001 | 1,793 | 610 |
| Hamilton | 45% | 3,094 | 1,401 | 430 |

2. *The Special Talent Category.* Every Bowdoin freshman class has a super hockey goalie. Hockey happens to be the crucial sport at Bowdoin (where the Maine winters are long). A good goalie does not compete against the 3,580 candidates for the 375 freshman slots. He competes against the two or three other hockey goalies applying, in the hope that he'll be judged the most likely of this little subgroup to keep the puck out of the nets and, somehow, survive the academic rigors of Bowdoin. Each year Harvard will get its offensive and defensive lines in order, Penn will end up with a roster of minor sports celebrities, Princeton will get its distance free-styler, and Amherst its fullback. Now and then an expert oboist or vocalist or sculptor will squeak through the "special talent" door, but on the whole it is athlete against athlete. Forget the high rank and the high CEEBs: Academic survival is what counts here, and the official rationale is in support of those winning teams that (reportedly) boost morale on campus and, more important (reportedly) lure the alumni to dig a bit deeper into their supportive pockets.

3. *The Family Category.* The public fills the coffers of the public university system. The private system counts on alumni to play the same role, rather more voluntarily. Many alumni are happy to do so in gratitude for good college years. Nevertheless, the college constantly floats inducements: gala reunions, winning teams, and perhaps most important, the "edge" a son or daughter is promised in the admissions process. Most private institutions are generous in admitting alumni sons and daughters—at some, the percentage of legacies admitted is twice as high as for all candidates. The same applies to more removed relatives (grandsons, nieces, sisters, et cetera) if the alumnus/a has given generously of his or her time or money to Alma Mater.

At some institutions the "family" extends beyond alumni. Harvard, for example, is good to hometown candidates from Greater Boston. On the whole, however, the Family Category relates to the alumni; and the closer the alumni tie, the stronger the favoritism in admissions. Legacies compete against legacies to claim a segment of the class. For example, according to a published letter from then-president Kingman Brewster to all alumni, at least 20 percent of each class at Yale is carefully "targeted" for legacies. "It's a tricky area," said Yale's Alumni Chairman of the Committee on Undergraduate Admissions in the alumni magazine. "How much is too much? Certainly we're cognizant that it's easy to backfire into a club mentality, a cozy relationship that involves dual standards. On the other hand, I don't think we should feel self-conscious when talking about the need for a higher percentage of alumni children. We recognize in very cold, practical terms that Yale has no automatic claim on the future. It exists partly on the strength of the emotional support that it gets from a loyal and enthusiastic community of people."

4. *The Social Conscience Category*. Because the elitist institutions of the nation were dominated for so long by children of the Protestant establishment, most of these colleges in recent years have tried to make good their debt to society. Great progress has been made, particularly in accommodating blacks. Many of the highly selective colleges had their social consciences stirred by student demands in the late sixties and resolved to make the percentage of blacks in each entering class comparable to the percentage of blacks in the nation's population (about 11 percent). Some institutions, Wesleyan of Connecticut for example, have come close to realizing this goal, thanks to ample resources and energetic recruitment. "The motivation quotient" is the vital criterion in judging applicants in this category, and often a student—because of inadequate secondary schooling and a lack of incentive from family and society—will be judged more on potential than on accomplishment. The size and quality of the minority-applicant pool dictates how flexible the admissions standard will become. But a respectable minority representation (now branching well beyond blacks) is an essential component of the prestige college's class today.

5. *The All-American Kid Category*. This is the tough one. Most well-meaning and generally accomplished candidates fall into this huge group. They don't wear special labels

or make special claims on a segment of the class. They usually don't have organized lobbyists hovering around the admissions office via phone or engraved letterhead. They're just the good kids who are decent but not outstanding as students, who help in a significant way to run the school and/or the community, and who have the intelligence and common sense necessary to someday help the community and the nation keep moving along at a good pace and in the right direction.

The prestige college is swamped with them . . . and the admissions office is remorseful that more cannot be accommodated. Although most of the faculty are less than enthusiastic about this "type," the alumni will like them, particularly if they're good family friends or relatives. Meanwhile, the admissions officers meet dozens and dozens of them on the road and in office interviews, knowing full well that only a small percentage can be taken.

If an applicant falls by default into category 5, he must be a very special person to win a place. For one thing, he is competing with hundreds of others in this division. Furthermore, other categories have more clout in claiming representation in the freshman class. Now and then, accidental factors such as a candidate's wealth or his geographic location (most selective colleges want broad geographic representation) can give a candidate a boost.

Remember: Many of the applicants who fall into categories 1, 2, 3, and 4 are also well intentioned, upright, and affable, so it isn't that the "good kids" are being overlooked altogether. Although only a small percentage of applicants from the "good kid" group is admitted, the number is large—usually the majority of a prestigious college's freshman class.

Admissions categories vary in importance according to the institution. The female-oriented colleges are less preoccupied with athletes than the male-oriented colleges. Oberlin, Swarthmore, and University of Chicago seem to reserve more of the class for Category 1, the high-powered intellects, than other prestigious institutions do, large or small. And some colleges have other requirements. Those that have gone coed often have a "target" for the newly admitted sex, members of which are forced to fight among themselves for the limited number of seats available.

A few institutions will readily admit that the category method (perhaps less rigidly adhered to than I have suggested here) is indeed the way a class is born. Many institutions are reluctant to make that confession publicly, and some colleges may not themselves realize that their long and tortuous candidate-against-candidate review eventually results in a class that might have emerged more easily through systematic category eliminations. A college simply can't apply a uniform standard of "academic and personal excellence" and end up accidentally with an adequate showing of legacy students and minorities, with a basketball team, and with geographic distribution.

Whitney Griswold, the late president of Yale, once said, "The admissions office is the umbilical cord of the university." If the undergraduate college has many purposes (an arena for training the mind, a national instrument for social access and change, an internal vehicle for self-survival), the Admissions Office must make certain the human material is there so that the institution can go about its variety of chores and reach its manifold goals. Diversity—by design—is essential to each incoming and outgoing class.*

## JUGGLING THE SPECIFIC FACTORS

No matter how closely specific colleges follow the "Categories" method of selection to achieve class diversity (usually the more selective the college, the more closely the method is followed), most private colleges agree on what components are basic to a fair evaluation of the candidate. These are: appraisal of the degree of difficulty of the student's high school courseload, school grades and class rank (incorporating a guesstimate of the quality

*This section of the book, a description of the categorization process in undergraduate admissions, appeared in similar form in the March 1978 issue of *Harper's Magazine*. Readers might be interested in responses from admissions professionals regarding Mr. Moll's "category" theory. See Appendix III.

of the secondary school), standardized test scores (the College Boards or a substitute battery of tests such as the ACTs†), the application essay, the interview, the depth of extracurricular involvement and achievement, the student's employment record, and recommendations from school authorities and teachers. Individual colleges differ somewhat in the weight accorded these factors in the selection process.

But almost all selective colleges make two general evaluations of the candidate: 1. an academic evaluation, and 2. a personal evaluation. Of course, college A may give more weight to one of these areas than college B, but the two evaluations are almost always made. Let's probe these zones somewhat more carefully, knowing (as every admissions officer can attest) that the boundary between them is difficult to draw.

## THE ACADEMIC EVALUATION

### Courseload: How Demanding?

A's in Glee Club and Hygiene aren't as interesting to selective colleges as B's in Advanced Placement History and Calculus. Before a college records the grade point average (GPA) of a given applicant, an analysis is always made of the degree of difficulty of the courseload. Obviously this is not an exact science, but colleges usually can spot the student who has ducked the tougher courses to avoid getting lower grades. Colleges today, as in the past, are most comfortable with the "basic disciplines." Admissions officers are impressed by applicants who have done well in the most difficult courses offered within the "core curriculum" of a given secondary school.

Most selective private colleges have a liberal arts orientation and will expose new students to a wide range of curricular offerings before asking the student to choose a major discipline (usually by the beginning of the third year). They feel, consequently, that the job of the elementary and the secondary schools is to prepare young people in "the basics," leaving peripheral disciplines and frills for later. This concept obviously created

†American College Testing Program, headquartered in Iowa.

tension in the early seventies, as elementary and secondary schools introduced "experiential" education and attempted to provoke greater student interest by allowing free choice in curriculum. The result was often a much heavier concentration in the humanities, social sciences, and the arts, with a minimum of exposure to the sciences, math, foreign languages, and tedious English grammar. But as linguistic skills among teenagers declined, national College Board averages fell, and college faculties complained that they were having to teach remedial grammar when they were hired to teach Shakespeare. "Back to basics!" became the cry.

To be certain, the "back-to-basics" movement in the lower schools draws nods of approval at the colleges. And the Admissions Offices follow suit. A sampling of the high school course of studies recommended in college catalogs:

Duke: To be a strong candidate for admission, an applicant should present a solid program of college-preparatory courses in secondary school, normally including four years of English, at least three of mathematics, natural science, a foreign language, and two years of history. Students are encouraged to enroll in advanced-level work in as many of these areas as possible.

M.I.T. expects that its applicants will have taken the broadest, most rigorous program available to them in high school. Ideal preparation for study would include English (four years) history/social studies (two or more years), mathematics through trigonometry or beyond (four years), laboratory sciences (biology, chemistry, and physics), and a foreign language. Interested students whose high school program does not match this in every detail are also urged to apply, since the selection of an entering class with broad interests will be guided as well by the quality of the applicant's work, by special strengths, and by apparent promise on grounds of intellect, character, and particular goals.

Wellesley does not require a fixed plan of secondary school courses as preparation for its program of studies. However, entering students normally have completed four years of strong college preparatory studies in secondary school. Adequate preparation includes training in clear and coherent writing and in interpreting literature, training in the principles of mathematics (usually a minimum of three years), competence in at least one foreign language, ancient or modern (usually achieved through three or four years of study), and experience in at least one laboratory science and in history.

Students planning to concentrate in mathematics, in premedical studies, or in the natural sciences are urged to elect additional courses in mathematics and science in secondary school. Students planning to concentrate in language or literature are urged to study a modern foreign language and Latin or Greek before they enter college.

There are often exceptions to the preparation suggested here, and the Board will consider an applicant whose educational background varies from this general description.

The best rule of thumb is for the candidate to take a balanced program of the most demanding courses his or her secondary school offers. No college will quarrel with that; to the contrary, applicants are given bonus points for their willingness to pursue the toughest possible curriculum despite the risk of getting slightly lower grades.

Regrettably, schools do not always adequately explain "levels" of various courses on candidates' transcripts. This is difficult to do, of course, since two teachers in the same department can be decidedly different in "degree of difficulty." But it seems only fair to the motivated candidate for the school to designate Advanced Placement (AP) courses and honors level courses on the transcript. Most schools do, but not all. Would that all schools were as specific in defining course levels as New Trier High School East, in Illinois. Each course on the transcript is accompanied by a level designation:

5 = Advanced Placement
4 = Superior or Honors
3 = Above Average
2 = Average
1 = Below Average

There are too few New Triers, so the candidate must check with his school guidance office to make certain that advanced courses are pointed out to colleges on the transcript. If the designations are not made clear by the school, the candidate himself must get the message to the college: this is probably best accomplished in the application essay. Some bright, well-motivated students today are hurt by the absence of course-level descriptions on the school report.

Another problem of communications regarding courseload is the college's ignorance of what substance lurks behind an exotic secondary school course title. Too often, even the best of schools do not adequately define what a course title means, and sometimes unintelligible abbreviations are used on computer printouts. Perhaps the vogue of school course titles that "sell rather than tell" is passing, but there still is a problem. What *is* the subject matter of a course called "Animal Behavior"? Is the student in Biology, Psychology, or Physical Ed.? Here is the transcript sent recently by a school-within-a-school, no explanations attached:

|  |  | Credit | No Credit |
|---|---|---|---|
| Phase I | Life Boat (Social Studies) | X |  |
| Sept.-Nov. | Acting | X |  |
|  | American Novel | X |  |
|  | Disease (Science) | X |  |
|  | The First Nine Months | X |  |
|  | Advanced Geometry | X |  |
|  | Behavior | X |  |
| Phase II |  |  |  |
| Nov.-Jan. | Waves (Science) | X |  |
|  | The American Experience (Social Studies) | X |  |
|  | Comic Fiction | X |  |
|  | Let's Explore | X |  |
|  | Law in Our Society | X |  |
|  | Pottery | X |  |

And from one of America's more distinguished suburban high schools, in Massachusetts, came these two senior courseloads not long ago:

| Candidate A. | Candidate B. |
|---|---|
| Resistance | Psychology in Literature |
| Short Story | Fantasy |
| Sociology | American Scene |
| Jewelry | Personal Math |
| Tennis | Sociology |
|  | Vocal Performance |

A realtor-uncle of mine told me that there were three things to remember in buying a house: "Location, location, location." As selective colleges approach the academic evaluation of a candidate for admission, there are three overriding considerations: "Courseload, courseload, courseload." A bit of an overstatement perhaps, but the high school student who has opted for the roughest possible courseload demonstrates (often quite unconsciously) the motivation that colleges equate with the drive to learn and to succeed. Given the luxury to choose among candidates, a college will nod to the "B" record in the honors courses much more readily than to the "A" record in fluff. And the colleges can almost always tell the difference.

## Grades: A = Honors = Mastery = What?

"The past is the best prologue to the future." Every admissions officer believes that, so every candidate must stand on his record. Presupposing that the courseload is balanced and demanding, a college applicant's high school grades become the most important factor in the admissions folder.

A consistently strong record is, of course, the best. But the most recent grades interest the admissions office the most. Grades of the junior year and first semester of senior year carry greatest weight.

Colleges will be humanly forgiving if made aware of interim handicaps and distractions that hurt the GPA—health problems, family problems, school problems, financial problems, love-life problems. But any candidate can come up with excuses for not performing along the way, and admissions officers grow weary of hearing "I'd have done better if. . . ." If Princeton has five candidates for every place in the class, why shouldn't they go for the one who has consistently performed and has overcome whatever obstacles were placed in the way?

Admissions officers are aware of the impact of environment on performance. Candidates for any selective college come, of course, from a variety of environments. Ironically, it is probably slightly to a candidate's disadvantage to come from an advantaged background. If a youngster is the offspring of well educated parentage, has been carefully guided to make the most of top-level courses at a college-oriented high school or private school, has been exposed to world-and-local-affairs discussions around the dinner table for seventeen years, and has been constantly reminded of the advantages that come to those who reach higher levels of education, *shouldn't* he be expected to have produced somewhat more in the classroom than a working-class candidate who works after school to help make family ends meet, attends a mediocre high school where the minority aspire to higher education, and is habitually subjected to "time to get married and settle down" talk?

Private colleges do look at a candidate in terms of where he has been, where he hopes to go, and at what pace and with what resolve he seems to be traveling. And we know that some bright kids find academic incentive late. We are sympathetic— to a point. But direction and discipline must be evident by the time of college entry. Again: the more recent the achievement, the more important it becomes.

After the student comes up with the grades, the college must interpret them. This is no mean trick. There is no consistent pattern of grading in America's school system today. If the colleges were to vote, the A to F system would probably win out, or the traditional 0 to 100. Colleges find these systems easiest to cope with, partly because they are most familiar with them. But today, one transcript might record a 1-to-7 system, the next a Pass/Fail system, and the next a High Honors/Honors/Pass/ Low Pass/Fail system. One huge high school in Brooklyn gives M's (Mastery) to nearly all comers in all courses, and some schools don't grade at all, much to the dismay of most college admissions offices.

Some admissions offices try to convert all grading schemes into one system in order to uniformly compare one candidate with another. But most colleges just try to cope with what the high school sends—if the grading code is hazy, more weight is usually assigned to that uniform quantifier, the standardized test scores.

"Is a candidate at a disadvantage in the admissions deliberations if his school does not have a (somewhat) traditional grading system?" Some responses from Admissions Directors:

Allegheny (Pennsylvania): No, provided sufficient descriptive information is available to allow for an accurate translation of the record.

Bates(Maine): Yes.

Boston College (Massachusetts): No problem, as long as the substitute system is not all sparkle with little substance.

Brandeis (Massachusetts): Reading reams of teacher statements and self-evaluations sent as substitutes for grades can be frustrating and may cause an admissions committee to miss the essence of a student—ironically, quite the contrary of what is intended in nontraditional grading programs.

Earlham (Indiana): It is more difficult for us to figure out just what a person has done, but we'll work with anything we're sent.

Franklin and Marshall (Pennsylvania): In most cases, yes. We try to deal with nontraditional systems, but there always seems to be a psychological block on the part of the readers.

Hampshire (Massachusetts): Definitely not.

Harvard (Massachusetts): Grades are a form of communication. If they're missing, we need a superb substitute. If the substitute is a string of adjectives, we need a point of reference: whom is this student compared to? Also, we have to know the school well enough to believe what they're saying. Credibility in the absence of grades becomes crucial.

Lafayette (Pennsylvania): Perhaps in a small way, but this is not intentional on our part unless the grading system is simply unfathomable.

Lewis and Clark (Oregon): If forced to guess, we don't always guess right.

Manhattan (New York): Yes. We're suspicious of the many nontraditional systems.

Mr. Holyoke (Massachusetts): Sometimes.

Ripon (Wisconsin): Yes.

St. Lawrence (New York): Yes.

Smith (Massachusetts): In some cases, if the system is difficult to interpret, we may have to weigh test scores more heavily than normal.

Princeton (New Jersey): If schools explain their system adequately, there is no problem.

Williams (Massachusetts): Yes, unless the write-ups are superb.

Judging from these responses, a student's position in the selection process is rarely, if ever, enhanced by his school's sending a nontraditional set of grades. The larger issue, however, is whether the college can interpret a non-traditional grading system correctly. Once again, the candidate must make certain that the secondary school is defining his classroom accomplishments intelligibly—if not, the student must do so himself.

### Class Rank: Cold, Crass, and Valuable

How difficult is it to get an "A" at Central High? The admissions office really doesn't know if a student's grade point average (GPA) is not put in context with the averages of other students from the same school. Class rank is, in a way, a crass and cold appraisal of a student's accomplishments, but it is an important ingredient in the college admissions process. Colleges not only like to receive rank in order to make a specific GPA more intelligible, but they also want it because validity studies have indicated again and again that class rank is one of the most valuable predictors of college success. The few quantifiers that seem to work are in demand, and class rank is one of them.

The smaller the secondary school, of course, the more unfair class ranking may be. Richard Cashwell, Dean of Admissions at the University of North Carolina (Chapel Hill), once said that he would forever wear the scar of having ranked in the lower half of his high school class—he graduated second in a class of two from a one-room school. In large schools, shades of percentages can keep a student from ranking in the upper half or upper third or upper fifth of his class. But performance is performance, and the colleges need to know rank in order to place a given GPA in context.

Some high schools avoid the dangers of precise ranking by "grouping" students in less arbitrary categories. The Loomis Chaffee School's (Connecticut) grade distribution chart is a sound substitute for class rank in a competitive preparatory school where students do not greatly differ from one another in ability and performance. *(See page 124.)*

How much importance do private colleges place on class rank? The question was posed this way: "Are students whose schools do not rank at a disadvantage in your admissions deliberations?" A potpourri of answers from the Admissions Directors:

Bennington (Vermont): No.

Brandeis (Massachusetts): Although we do consider and eventually admit a good many nonranked students, it is more difficult to judge the student's response to the level of competition in his school setting if rank is not provided.

Bucknell (Pennsylvania): I think so. Schools who do not rank require the admissions office to make judgments of a candidates's relative strengths that the school is in a better position to make.

Carroll (Wisconsin): In comprehensive high schools, yes. In private schools, from which we normally receive adequate profile information, no.

Denison (Ohio): Not really. We are at a disadvantage, but they are not.

Duke (North Carolina): The absense of rank from top prep schools does not concern us. Familiarity breeds confidence and we grow quite familiar with many of the schools because of their large number of applications to Duke. Prep schools have a way of defining course level and grade patterns rather effectively. The absence of rank from public high schools, however, may work to the detriment of the candidate. If forced to guess what a grade point average might mean in a given school's context—a school which has not had many applications to Duke, for example—we may guess in error. The less familiar we are with the school, the more we need their class rank.

Franklin and Marshall (Pennsylvania): From small private schools, no problem. From big high schools, it could hurt. However, we always try to compensate to the advantage of the student.

Kenyon (Ohio): Sometimes. It depends on the other supporting materials the school sends.

Manhattan (New York): Not consciously, but probably unconsciously.

Ohio Wesleyan: Yes, but probably not as much at my college as at the more selective colleges with all those applications to process.

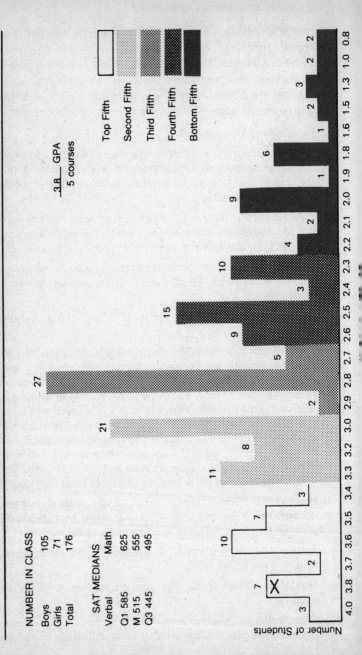

THE LOOMIS CHAFFEE SCHOOL
Windsor, Connecticut 06095
CLASS OF 1979 - GRADE POINT AVERAGE, 1ST TRIMESTER SENIOR YEAR

NUMBER IN CLASS
Boys    105
Girls    71
Total   176

SAT MEDIANS
        Verbal   Math
Q1       585     625
M        515     555
Q3       445     495

Top Fifth
Second Fifth
Third Fifth
Fourth Fifth
Bottom Fifth

3.8  GPA
5 courses

Number of Students

Princeton (New Jersey): They can be, unless the school is one we know and one which gives other means of distinguishing among students (charts of grade distribution, etc.).

St. Lawrence (New York): Yes.

Smith (Massachusetts): Although rank is extremely helpful, we try not to penalize the student for the school's system.

University of Richmond (Virginia): Lack of rank forces us to place a heavy emphasis on standardized Achievement Test scores because we are not able to establish peer-group relationship within a graduating class. Unfortunately, "A's" and "B's" do not always mean superior achievement. If we cannot get a comparative statistic from the high school, we are forced to resort to some other method.

Wellesley (Massachusetts): No.

Williams (Massachusetts): Yes.

The college Admissions Office's interpretation of the quality of an "A" or a "B" is assisted not only by a school's providing rank-in-class, but also by the school's providing a profile of the socio-economic background of its students, its college placement record, its curricular offerings, and the range of student ability. Would that every transcript was accompanied by a profile as comprehensive and helpful as that of New Rochelle High School (New York). (See pages 127–28.)

One of the inherent qualities of the American system of education is variety, we are told again and again. And it probably is so. But when trying to judge applicants' past perfomance and future potential, we, in the selective colleges, feel most comfortable with traditional quantifiers—precise grades and precise rank—fleshed out with appropriate write-ups from teachers and counselors. Neither type of information can stand alone.

### Those Detestable Tests

Recently I walked into a St. Grottlesex-type school for my college's scheduled "information session" with juniors and seniors. My delight in being told by the guidance counselor that there was great interest in my institution was softened considerably by the way he introduced his candidates. I was handed a list that went something like this:

| Jane Ackerman | V | 540 | M | 510 |
| Joann Knowlton | V | 610 | M | 630 |
| Abe Feldman | V | 580 | M | 600 |
| Liz Smith | V | 620 | M | 560 |

In a "personal" school touting individualized education, kids were being defined as SAT scores! An extreme instance perhaps, but this was not the first time I'd had the experience. No wonder candidates feel their scores are tattooed on their foreheads and it is their fate to wander through life muttering at every turn, "I am a 510."

And colleges are just as bad, if not worse, in overemphasizing standardized test scores. At Seven Sister and Ivy League gatherings there is far too much informal talk of what this and that institution's College Board averages are this year compared to last, implying a conclusive qualitative comparison of the two classes. College faculties talk endlessly about the College Board signposts—rarely of range, too often of the mean or the median, erroneously defining an entire new freshman class by the middle score.

Ironically, it is the College Entrance Examination Board that keeps warning schools and colleges and kids and counselors and parents against such extremes of emphasis. The Board reminds us all that the test scores are intended as a *supplement* to other important data, and "if properly used," can become an important interpretive tool, benefiting both applicant and institution. Of course they're right. But the problem is that no other single means of appraisal is so uniform—high school grade patterns differ from school to school, and class ranks are computed by different means, if at all. So, by default, College Board (or ACT) scores become a universal language for defining the quality of a candidate or the quality of a college's freshman class. Until other methods of candidate evaluation become more consistent, we'll probably all continue to be guilty of overemphasizing test scores.

Approximately one million high school students take the College Board's three hour SAT (Scholastic Aptitude Test) each year as a requirement for college admission. Those who are

CITY SCHOOL DISTRICT OF NEW ROCHELLE, NEW YORK

# NEW ROCHELLE HIGH SCHOOL

265 CLOVE ROAD, NEW ROCHELLE, NEW YORK 10801

(914) 632-9000

James R. Gaddy, Ph.D., Principal             Donald Baughman, Asst. Principal
Linda E. Kelly, Associate Principal     Marvin Bookbinder, Coord. of Guidance

## 1985-86 PROFILE

### Accreditation
Regents of the State of New York
Middle States Association of Colleges
& Secondary Schools

### Community
New Rochelle is an "urbanized
suburban" city of 71,000 located
northeast of New York City in
Westchester County. Residents are
primarily business commuters.

### School
A comprehensive school, New Rochelle High School serves the city of New
Rochelle. The per pupil cost is more than $7,000. The enrollment is 1986
with a qualified senior class of 550 students. These pupils have earned
the units of credit required by the end of their junior year. One hundred
sixty-four members comprise the high school's professional staff. Organized
as a school-within-a-school, the three house units have their own administrative and guidance staffs and contain a cross-section of students, grades
10, 11, 12.

### Class of 1985 - 552 Students

| | |
|---|---|
| 4-year colleges | 54% |
| 2-year colleges | 11% |
| Business Schools | 4% |
| Tech.&Vocational Schools | 3% |
| Employment | 20% |
| Armed Services | 3% |
| Other Plans | 4% |
| | 100% |

### Graduation Requirements

| | |
|---|---|
| English | 4 units |
| Social Studies | 4 units |
| Mathematics | 1 unit |
| Science | 1 unit |
| Health | 0.5 unit |
| Phys.Education(4 years) | 2 units |
| Electives (chosen to prepare for college entrance, business or occupational careers) | 7.5 units |

### Rank in Class
Computed at the end of junior year, class rank is based on the subjects
taken and grades received since 9th grade. Numerical grades are weighted
to reflect degree of academic difficulty: Honors and Advanced Placement
courses 1.1; Regents courses 1.05; Basic courses 1.0. 528 students are
ranked out of a senior class of 550 eligible. Approximate ranks are
given to 22 students who recently transferred from other schools or who
are accelerated.

H....Honors Course
AP...Advanced Placement Course

Determination of Credits
1   Unit: course meets daily for full yr.
1/2 Unit: semester course meets daily;
          full year course meets 2 or 3
          times a week

## Academic Highlights

Major Programs: Over one hundred and eighty courses are offered in three
program areas: college preparatory, business education, occupational
education. Within the college preparatory field, three choices are open
to students depending on ability and interest: Honors/Advanced Placement,
Academic (Regents sequence), and Comprehensive.

Honors Courses
American History,
English III, Latin IV
French II, III, IV
Math X, XI, XII,
PSSC Physics
Spanish II, III, IV

Advanced Placement Courses
American History, Art, Biology
Calculus AB, BC, Chemistry
Computer Science, English, European
History, French, Latin, Music
Physics
Spanish

Extended Day School: An educational alternative for students whose needs
cannot be met in a traditional day school environment; full-time extended
day students may work during the day and continue their education in the
evening. Students who leave high school prematurely may resume their
education in order to receive a high school diploma. Students who attend
the traditional day school may use the resources of this program on a
part-time basis for remediation or acceleration.

Foreign Study: In cooperation with the Council on International Educational
Exchange (CIEE), the high school sponsors annually school-to-school student
exchange programs with partner schools in France, Israel, and Italy. Students
spend three weeks in the exchange country living with local families and
studying at the "linked" school.

## Recommendation of Students

Description of applicants and their achievements, helpful to both students
and colleges, are provided. Students are recommended for admission based
on the premise that they are entitled to such support in the competition
for admission. When additional information is desired, you may contact
the Guidance Department.

seeking entry at the more selective colleges are also required
to take three one-hour Achievement tests—usually the English
Composition test and two of the thirteen others offered by CEEB.
Schools and colleges recommend that candidates take the Preliminary SAT (PSAT) in the fall of the junior year of secondary
school; this test also serves as the initial qualifier for the prestigious National Merit Scholarship. Between spring of the junior
year and winter of the senior year the candidate will take the
SAT at least once, often as many as three times. He will also
take three Achievement tests at one or more sittings.

Considering the importance of the College Board tests, there
should be clear agreement on what they are. But definitions
remain a little fuzzy.

A recent president of the College Board wrote:

It might be useful to consider what the SAT is and what it does.
First, let me suggest what the SAT is *not*. It was not designed as a
measure of a *school's* performance and should not be used for that
purpose. To single out the schools as being responsible for the current
decline in scores, for example, is unwarranted, unfair, and scientif-
ically unfounded.

Secondly, the SAT is not a measure of some innate and unchanging
quality that somehow mystically categorizes people. It does not gauge
the worth of a human being, or his or her capacity to function well
or creatively in society.

What, then, *is* the SAT? *It is a measure of developed verbal and
mathematic reasoning and ability*. It measures those abilities that are
most commonly needed for academic performance in colleges and
universities. Therefore, how students perform on the SAT is a useful
and well-validated indicator of how they might do in one college or
another. It is intended to supplement the school record and other
information about the student in assessing competence to do college
work.

It is a uniform measure of the same mental tasks, expressed on a
common scale for all students. Thus, it operates as a "leveling agent,"
or if you will, a democratizing agent, cutting across differences in
local customs and conditions, and affording admissions officers help
in the assessment of the *academic* potential of students in relation
to the differing academic demands of institutions.

One point of continual popular confusion is whether the SAT
reveals a student's endowed capacity of intelligence (one more

IQ test?) or whether, more like the Achievement Tests, it reveals what one has *learned*. The College Board president's definition, note, emphasizes "*developed* abilities. . . ." the president of the Educational Testing Service (ETS authors the SAT and the Achievements) underscores that:

> The SAT's describe *developed* ability at a given point in time. The test describes present capability—the scores say nothing about native potential.

In "Guide to the Admissions Testing Program," the College Board defines the tests perhaps most clearly to guidance counselors and admissions officers:

> *Aptitude* tests are predictive measures of the intellectual abilities needed to perform academic tasks well. The SAT is an aptitude test which measures reasoning abilities that tend to develop slowly over the student's entire life, outside as well as inside the classroom. SAT scores are used to predict students' first-year academic performance in college.
>
> *Achievement* tests are curriculum based; they are designed to measure the results of study in specific subject matter areas. Achievement tests are generally designed to assess outcomes of courses that students have taken recently and are used to predict academic performance and for course placement.

Interpretation is as much a problem as definition. Often candidates and parents ask what the median SAT score of a given college's freshman class is, and mistake the median figure for the bottom line of that class. When Colgate says that its SAT Verbal median of accepted candidates is 600, it means one-half the admittees are below that score. But so frequently the reaction is, "Oh, if I don't have around a 620, I don't have a prayer of getting into Colgate!"

To prevent this common misconception, some colleges now avoid releasing means and medians of SAT and Achievement scores. Following are examples of SAT range at four institutions for the class of 1990. They are plotted somewhat differently, but all are helpful as a counseling tool for the student who wants to predict his or her chances at a particular institution. *(See pages 131–33.)*

# DUKE

## ADMISSION STATUS BY VERBAL AND MATH SAT

| Verbal | of Arts and Sciences | | | School of Engineering | | | Both Colleges | | |
|---|---|---|---|---|---|---|---|---|---|
| | Applied | Accepted | Entering | Applied | Accepted | Entering | Applied | Accepted | Entering |
| 750–800 | 112 | 97 | 23 | 18 | 17 | 4 | 130 | 114 | 27 |
| 700–749 | 431 | 319 | 87 | 79 | 65 | 17 | 510 | 384 | 104 |
| 650–699 | 975 | 631 | 212 | 164 | 106 | 41 | 1139 | 737 | 253 |
| 600–649 | 1697 | 908 | 379 | 319 | 151 | 75 | 2016 | 1059 | 454 |
| 550–599 | 1750 | 547 | 282 | 358 | 100 | 45 | 2108 | 647 | 327 |
| Below 550 | 2476 | 376 | 210 | 508 | 50 | 21 | 2984 | 426 | 231 |
| Not Given or ACT Only | 179 | 12 | 6 | 27 | 1 | 1 | 206 | 13 | 7 |
| Total | 7620 | 2890 | 1199 | 1473 | 490 | 204 | 9093 | 3380 | 1403 |
| **Math** | | | | | | | | | |
| 750–800 | 356 | 283 | 71 | 214 | 142 | 47 | 570 | 425 | 118 |
| 700–749 | 1104 | 693 | 235 | 396 | 187 | 72 | 1500 | 880 | 307 |
| 650–699 | 1786 | 828 | 360 | 393 | 116 | 65 | 2179 | 944 | 425 |
| 600–649 | 1793 | 620 | 278 | 249 | 42 | 19 | 2042 | 662 | 297 |
| 550–599 | 1204 | 277 | 151 | 100 | 1 | 0 | 1304 | 278 | 151 |
| Below 550 | 1199 | 177 | 98 | 94 | 1 | 0 | 1293 | 178 | 98 |
| Not Given or ACT Only | 178 | 12 | 6 | 27 | 1 | 1 | 205 | 13 | 7 |
| Total | 7620 | 2890 | 1199 | 1473 | 490 | 204 | 9093 | 3380 | 1403 |

# M I T

## SCHOLASTIC APTITUDE TEST

| Range of Scores | Verbal | | | | Math | | | |
|---|---|---|---|---|---|---|---|---|
| | # Applicants | # Admitted | % Admitted | # in Class | # Applicants | # Admitted | % Admitted | # in Class |
| 750–800 | 175 | 115 | 66% | 50 | 1517 | 833 | 55% | 438 |
| 700–740 | 679 | 319 | 47% | 197 | 1989 | 756 | 38% | 439 |
| 650–690 | 1127 | 530 | 47% | 296 | 1047 | 220 | 21% | 155 |
| 600–640 | 1130 | 418 | 37% | 257 | 562 | 56 | 10% | 34 |
| 550–590 | 962 | 230 | 24% | 141 | 261 | 16 | 6% | 10 |
| 500–540 | 700 | 126 | 18% | 93 | 104 | 3 | 3% | 1 |
| Below 500 | 841 | 59 | 7% | 43 | 80 | 0 | 0% | 0 |

## ACHIEVEMENT TESTS
### English Composition or History

| Range of Scores | # Applicants | # Admitted | % Admitted | # in Class |
|---|---|---|---|---|
| 750–800 | 166 | 121 | 73% | 56 |
| 700–740 | 673 | 424 | 63% | 206 |
| 650–690 | 1084 | 542 | 50% | 310 |
| 600–640 | 1068 | 374 | 35% | 232 |
| 550–590 | 903 | 208 | 23% | 121 |
| 500–540 | 703 | 127 | 18% | 88 |
| Below 500 | 792 | 71 | 9% | 54 |

## S C R I P P S (Class of 1990)

### SCHOLASTIC APPITUDE TEST

|  | Verbal | | Math | |
|---|---|---|---|---|
|  | % Applied | % Accepted | % Applied | % Accepted |
| 750–800 | 2 | 1% | 0 | 0 |
| 700–749 | 3 | 2% | 3 | 2% |
| 650–699 | 7 | 4% | 4 | 2% |
| 600–649 | 14 | 9% | 27 | 17% |
| 550–599 | 37 | 23% | 33 | 20% |
| 500–549 | 36 | 22% | 44 | 27% |
| 450–499 | 35 | 21% | 29 | 18% |
| 400–449 | 24 | 15% | 13 | 8% |
| Below 400 | 4 | 2% | 9 | 5% |
| NA | 2 | 1% | 2 | 1% |

## O B E R L I N

### SCHOLASTIC APTITUDE TEST (FRESHMEN ONLY)

|  | Verbal | | | Math | | |
|---|---|---|---|---|---|---|
|  | % Applied | % Accepted | % Enrolled | % Applied | % Accepted | % Enrolled |
| Over 760 | 2.3 | 3.2 | 2.3 | 2.3 | 3.2 | 1.7 |
| 710–750 | 8.8 | 11.5 | 8.0 | 11.5 | 15.3 | 10.7 |
| 660–700 | 19.1 | 22.8 | 19.8 | 18.6 | 23 | 21.5 |
| 610–650 | 21.7 | 23.5 | 23.5 | 21.6 | 23.1 | 22.6 |
| 560–600 | 18.8 | 17.8 | 20.9 | 21.2 | 19.8 | 22.5 |
| 510–550 | 13.9 | 11.3 | 13.2 | 12.1 | 9.1 | 11.6 |
| 460–500 | 7.9 | 5.4 | 5.8 | 6.4 | 3.8 | 5.6 |
| 410–450 | 4.7 | 2.7 | 4.1 | 4.0 | 2.2 | 3.0 |
| Below 400 | 2.8 | 1.8 | 2.4 | 2.3 | .5 | .8 |
| Mean | 600 | 619 | 605 | 608 | 631 | 614 |
| Median | 610 | 630 | 611 | 615 | 638 | 619 |

Granted, everyone laments overemphasis of SATs in college admissions talk. But just how important are these tests? Private colleges rarely place as much importance on test scores as on the degree of difficulty of the high school courseload and the grades and class rank attained. Many institutions talk about the Board scores as "confirming other data."

Fred Jewett, former Dean of Admissions at Harvard, says Board scores become a priority consideration for his Committee if they fall *over* 750 or *under* 550; if they fall somewhere between, the scores fade in importance because that range is "normal" for Harvard. Of course, some colleges have a reputation for being a bit more conscious of Board scores than others—Amherst and Wellesley and Penn are names frequently mentioned—but no institution will admit or reject a student on the basis of very high or very low scores alone.

As indicated earlier, an "A" record is harder to achieve in some high schools than in others, so test scores provide a leveling factor. Following a thorough appraisal of a candidate's secondary school record, test scores enter the picture as confirming evidence. If something seems out of line, some hard questions will be asked. For example, if a young man has 700 SATs, and a middling school performance, yellow flags fly, and the admissions officer digs a bit more deeply for comments regarding motivation—maybe he will call the school to discuss the situation with counselors or teachers.

At the other end of the spectrum, the applicant with very low scores and high grades will come under similiar scrutiny. Is there grade inflation at this school? Did we thoroughly check this student's courseload? In a more demanding academic milieu, will he have any "stretch" left? Was there some reason for such a poor performance on the tests?—Dyslexia? Sickness on the day of the test? Might a foreign language be spoken at home?

Clearly SATs (or their substitutes), although given slightly different weights from one college to the next, are an important part of the candidate's resume because colleges seem satisfied with the tests' predictive powers. Even at maverick Bowdoin, one of the handful of highly selective colleges where submission of standardized test scores is optional, a memo from a Chemistry professor to the chairman of the Faculty Admissions Committee said:

I would like to make clear a few points which might be open to misinterpretation. In no way do I favor a return to the strong emphasis on SATs which may have characterized admissions policy at highly selective colleges in the past. But I do feel that the score is a useful number and that it should be required of all applicants. My classes, and the College as a whole, are better places as a result of the presence of some students with low scores, but let us not kid ourselves any longer by saying these same students have been accepted because of potential to do science. We need students who can merely survive in science while they make a real contribution to college life in another area, but we also need students who will be *distinguished* in science. Those accepted because science is a strong suit should have significant potential as indicated by their SATs and Achievements and a well-defined interest in science which is more than skin deep (more than "I would like to be a doctor"). There will certainly be special cases where the SAT is not a meaningful measure of potential to do science, but I think they will be rare indeed.

Although the SATs seem most often to be the topic of popular discussion, many colleges look at the Achievement tests, the one hour tests of knowledge in specific areas, with as great or even greater interest. A letter to Vassar from the Research Division of CEEB said:

A memorandum regarding aspects of the Vassar validity study is enclosed. Finding that the CEEB Achievement average tends to be a better predictor of Vassar grade average than the SATs has been a fairly consistent result of validity studies conducted at similar colleges the past ten years or so.

Students and parents always have a raft of questions regarding standardized testing—and no wonder, since the test scores are correctly rumored to be important in the admissions program but are an "agent removed," some external force that one cannot easily address or have control over. Actually, CEEB and ACT have an answer to every question, just for the asking. Write:

College Entrance Examination Board
45 Columbus Avenue
New York, N.Y. 10023–6917
            or
American College Testing Program
Box 168
Iowa City, Iowa 52240 (319)337–1332

Let's quickly discuss what you always wanted to know about standardized tests but perhaps had no one to ask. The following information has been culled from recent CEEB literature:

1. *How and when do I learn my scores?* Within six weeks after a test date, a student will be sent his scores with more-than-adequate comparative percentile rankings, explanations, etc. Within five weeks of each test date, the colleges that the student has designated will receive the test scores.

2. *Are the tests getting harder?* Through a complicated equating process, a given score today indicates the same level of mathematical or verbal ability as it did years ago.

3. *Is the SAT really predictive of how I'll do in college?* In most validity studies made to date, the validity for the high school record is higher than the validity for either the SAT Verbal or the SAT Mathematical sections alone. On the other hand, the validity of the *combination* of tests and high school record is considerably higher than that of high school record alone.

4. *How can what I know become such a precise number?* Test scores should be viewed as approximate rather than exact, using a range of about 60 points. For example, if a student's "true" score is 500, chances are two out of three that the score he or she will actually make on the SAT will be between 470 and 530.

5. *Do I have a good chance of improving my score if I repeat the test?* For those students whose scores change when they repeat the test, 65 percent have score increases, while 35 percent have score decreases. The average score increase is only 15 points.

6. *If I take the SAT several times, which score will a college use?* Most selective colleges will use your highest scores. Some will use your latest scores; some will use an average of all scores.

7. *If I can't answer a test question, should I guess?* Scores are based on the number of questions a student answers correctly, minus a fraction of the number answered incorrectly: This insures that there is no advantage to random guessing.

8. *Should I prepare for the tests with a "coach"?* The abilities measured by the SAT develop over a student's entire academic life, so coaching can do little or nothing to raise the student's scores. Students not familiar with timed, standardized testing, however, may benefit from exposure to the format of the test. (Today, when a student registers for the SAT, he or she will receive a complete SAT and a Test of Standard Written English to be used for practice.)

9. *What if I'm nervous or really tired the day of the test?* Anxiety and/or fatigue rarely cause significant increases or decreases in a student's test performance.

10. *Are the tests culturally biased?* Results from studies of minority and low-income students indicate that test scores can be useful to predict freshman grade point averages for black or other disadvantaged minorities. The Educational Testing Service reports that the SAT predicts college performance as accurately for blacks as it does for whites. (Since the mid-1960s, the Educational Testing Service has included passages by black authors in the reading comprehension segments of its tests.) It is agreed, however, that test scores are less significant than such factors as strong motivation and maturity of purpose in the admission of some students.

11. *Are the tests valid predictors for the handicapped?* Although the total number of physically or visually handicapped students who have taken special editions of the SAT is relatively small, limited data indicate that their test scores predict college performance about as well as the scores of the general population do.

## THE PERSONAL EVALUATION

### The College Essay: A Procrastinator's Dream

Surely there is no assignment known to man that is postponed longer than the application essay. Suddenly the college candidate is no longer reporting grades, birthplace, or lists of brothers and sisters and activities and addresses and dates. Instead he is asked to fill an ominously large space with "what is important to me."

Regrettably, most do it poorly.

Most probably do it poorly simply because they postpone the task for so long, and suddenly have to dash off the essay the Sunday evening before the application deadline. For some reason, applicants don't seem to take this assignment as seriously as a term paper. And that is too bad.

The application essay is the candidate's chance to take the admissions situation into his own hands and emphasize to the college "what *is* important about me." Enough of the colleges' terse little questions, with just enough space provided for terse little responses. Here is the free-for-all section of the application, which students could use joyfully, imaginatively, provocatively, and politically if only they would seize the initiative in their oft-stated plea: "I want to be treated like more than just a number in the admissions process."

Too often, when the essay finally gets written, it has a distinct ring of "what I think they want to hear" rather than "what I want to say." Too often the essay simply puts into prose what already has been stated in the application: a list of activities in sentence form. And that is drab, very drab.

A 17-year-old doesn't have to be first cellist of the County Youth Symphony or all-state halfback to have something interesting to talk about. Every kid who has passed through the teenage years has something worthwhile to say. And we admissions officers listen. In fact, a near-reject can be pulled from the "out" drawer if the essay is sterling—it happens often.

Some colleges go so far as to give the application essay top billing in importance for all candidates. The Harvard Dean of Admissions reports that the essay gets a moderate weighting in his college's admissions process, unless it is particularly good or particularly bad, in which case it becomes important. Dean Jewett also says that his Committee often does not receive enough information about a candidate and that the essay therefore takes on added importance. Jewett urges candidates to tell their story, whatever it happens to be, with care, and to develop strong points thoughtfully and persuasively. He cautions, however, that fake interests and involvements are usually caught by admissions committees: "Things that are fake clank," he says.

What do colleges hope to learn through the application essay? First, whether or not the applicant can put a sentence together. There is a linguistic skills scare today, so the colleges are extremely interested in students' ability to write: the essay, the English grades, the comments of the English teacher, the SAT Verbal and the English Achievement test scores all contribute to a college's appraisal of the student's ability to communicate. The essay provides a piece of the puzzle, even though admissions officers realize that some application essays have been rather carefully screened by a parent, a sister, an English teacher, or a college advisor. (Because of this screening, a handful of institutions require that the candidate submit a graded paper from a high school course in addition to the application essay. Not only does the college receive a rather typical sample of the applicant's in-school writing, but also a grade, plus a teacher's criticisms.)

As important as it is to learn how well a student writes, the admissions office also wants to learn what a student has to say about him or herself when given a free hand. Colleges fully realize that most application questions are perfunctory, information-gathering necessities. In a way, then, only the essay allows an admissions officer to have a personal conversation with an applicant—if the applicant will allow that to happen. Too few do.

There are no specific rules on writing the application essay. But there are a few general guidelines to be seriously considered. Despite the fact that the essay is not an admissions committee's conclusive insight into a student's ability to write, the applicant should be certain that the essay is not bogged down with dreadful spelling and illegible handwriting. The length of the essay should concur with what has been requested (during the late winter "reading period" admissions officers have thousands of pieces of paper to pursue and simply can't—and won't— read beyond a reasonable length). The essay should say something that the rest of the application doesn't say, or at least should elaborate on something another segment of the application barely suggests: a talent, an interest, thoughts on a world or local problem, a personal accomplishment.

The subtleties of a candidate can be captured nicely in the essay. One of the best essays I remember was by a young man who wrote "On Always Placing Last in Cross-Country." With articulate humor, he convinced the Admissions Committee, through tales of arduous running, that he could survive the toughest required academic course and could be counted on to "travel the extra mile."

Perhaps it is best at this point to display a few real-life examples. First, an extreme example of—of what? not caring? not spending the time? not thinking? not drying out? not being serious about the application? Tragically, this essay was submitted to a highly selective college along with a very decent set of grades, adequate test scores, and glowing school recommendations:

> well if you want to know me better, I guess I should write about my favorite subject, myself. Now your probably thinking I'm conceded or a little zany but not conceded. I'm always looking for new people and places to discover, thats why I love working at McDonalds. I try to do everything in my power to make the customers smile, especially when they're grouches. I have 1001 different facial expressions and more actions to go along with them. I love nature and any type of athletic competition fascinates me, especially hockey. Playing a nice and hard game of tennis is my idea of fun. Cooking is one of my favorite hobbies, besides what else do you do on rainy days. I have two brothers who I try all my new recipes on. Last time I looked they were still alive. I'm a very logical person, at least that's what all the horoscopes and handwriting analysis say, and I plan what I should do every week on Sunday and about Wednesday something turns up and all my plans are wrecked. That's life! I would love to go to _____ College because I love your location, the college campus, the interest taken in the classes, and it seems the people there are more concerned with learning than getting messed up with something else. I always try to live for the future because you should 'think only of the past as its remembrances give you pleasure" (Jane Austen). That, by the way, is my favorite saying. Ha! Ha! I didn't exceed 500 words!!!!!!!!!

So much for the down side. Now let's look at a few essays that have struck admissions officers in selective colleges as successful in conveying individuality, maturity, and sensitivity.

### A.

I am 5'9" with a stocky build. My main facial feature is a set of red mutton chops and a matching crop of hair. My hair style is not the only anachronism attributed to me: I prefer folk music to rock, and an acoustic guitar to an electric. I identify myself as a realistic optimist. I still live under the fable that man is basically good, and over a period of time each will reach his potential.

No one could ever say that I am afraid of work or that I actively search it out. I am a poor chess player, looking forward to little improvement, and tennis is a fun game for others.

My family experience has taught me how to deal with people. I am the second oldest of four children, the other three being females. Harriet, who is attending Yale, has visions of a Supreme Court appointment; Frances has a collection of almost all the clothes in the world; and Aurenna wants to be a fullback.

There is an urge in me to express myself in music and art: I have written poetry and have composed songs. I am a member of a few school choirs and perform occasionally with my guitar. My guitar gets the applause. Besides music and writing, I backpack, hike, camp, and canoe for recreation. I am also into photography and leathercraft. I keep mending my shoes. Another pastime I have is reading. I have an extensive collection of books ranging from Shakespeare to Doonesbury. If anything, they are a constructive vice.

I am going to college to learn. There are many things both academic and social that I am curious about. Through my studies I hope to find something I could base a profession on. But it is simply College that attracts me, where many find knowledge that before was not theirs.
                                                            —Wade Komisar

### B.

I believe there should be a nominal or no-cost neutering program for dogs and cats to curb the proliferation of strays. I don't believe in a mandatory retirement age. Some program of consulting work should be worked out for those who wish to remain in their fields but who wish to cut down the work hours. I think it should probably be a lot more difficult to get married than it is. Perhaps at the time of applying for a license a period of time should have to elapse during which classes or counseling would be required. I believe in a liberal arts education and that these institutions should be distinct from vocational schools. Vocational schools should have their images upgraded. They are necessary and no less noble than colleges, just different. We don't have enough skilled artisans—just amateurs. People wander into professions like carpentry, plumbing, etc. Efficient apprenticeship programs could be worked out.

Why can't mental health agencies advise the public to seek a twice yearly checkup, very much the way dental societies do? I believe in a close-knit family. I believe we lost out when the extended family was sacrificed in the cause of a mobile society. I find the world divides itself in two camps on the question of how supportive a family should be. There are those who say that too much support fosters weakness and dependency. Then there are those who say that there is no such thing as too much loving and caring. Put me down for number 2.

Let's hear it for cloudy days. Days that allow us to stay indoors to read, go through old letters, and experiment with nail polish without guilt.

I'm against: generation gaps, working for grades, smoking in public, perfume in restaurants, too many rules, too few rules, boots for strolling, designers' monograms on clothes, haircuts that have names, food additives, exercise that requires counting, cabs that are hard to climb into, mindless TV for children, mindless TV for adults, and department store prices.

I'm for: zip codes, daily garbage pickup, brevity, the N.Y. Times, Rudolph Nureyev, Chinese food, Woody Allen, the diversity of New York, boots for riding horses, cats, comfortable shoes, James Herriot, anything Irish, shorter school days, more career exposure in school, fresh bread, and modified vegetarianism.

—Jessica Miller

### C.

Life has a dual nature and I have experienced both sides. There have been times of bliss as well as times of grief and I have found that each can have value if only understood. I have grown up in Harlem where many times the understanding has been harsh, but the merit still remains. Perhaps ostracism at the hands of my peers (caused by my light skin-color and West Indian background) was a terribly rugged road through childhood, but just how valuable are the lessons of self-communication and individuality? Is it not essential to learn that one can not always be what others may want him to be, or more importantly, that he doesn't have to? Despite the numerous attempts, I have never been separated from my sense of self, never the victim of egotistical homicide; each attempt induces palingenesis.

Intermediate School 201 was always known as the school without windows, simply because it was one of the first buildings designed not to have any. It was in this architectural "wonder" that I experienced my first encounter with the universe of sound and emotion that I feel lies dormant in every mind—the art of poetry. Although encouragement came from many sources, my own beginnings were largely due to the impression left upon me by poetess Sonia Sanchez and the few but still treasured words she wrote for me quite some time ago: "To Brother Carlos, keep on being Black and together; Black love, Sister Sonia Sanchez." Many years later, as I look back on that experience and my entire junior high school career, I realize that I.S. 201 had many more windows than we thought.

Although I had been exposed to a great many ideas while still going to school in Harlem, I was nonetheless ill-prepared for the kaleidoscope of diverse peoples and experiences I have encountered in my more recent years. Ours is not a universe of one; many stars are shining and in Stuyvesant High School the glow can be ofttimes overpowering. But I have found that if I view each person as an individual, many lights will be broken down into colors of realism and sincerity that my eyes can accept. As president of the Black Students' League, or as a former member of Stuyvesant's Acting Class, my experiences have also been many and varied, but each is the same in one aspect: whether an experience is "good" or "bad" it is still unique and every moment should be savored. "The pedigree of honey does not concern the bee; a clover anytime, to him, is aristocracy."* I accept each moment, each event and every individual as rare, for in actuality they are.

There is much that I would like to do in life, and my only restrictions, I believe, are whatever limitations I place on myself or allow to be placed on me. My major goal is to contribute as much as I know I will make use of, via programs such as the Archbishop's Leadership Project, a highly selective group which for the past ten years has sought to develop the leadership potential of young Black men. However, my most important aspiration is to move ever closer to erasing the phrase "I wish I had" from my vocabulary.

—Carlos Griffith

### D.
### Reflections on North High

A look back at six years of schooling at North High evokes many fond memories: padded bras of seventh grade, spin-the-bottle games of eighth grade, football games, homecoming parades, carnivals, sweet sixteens . . . so many things. Tennessee Williams wrote in *The Glass Menagerie*, "In memory, everything seems to happen to music." How very true of my high school years! Only good times remain vivid in my thoughts. All the rest has been erased. Junior high tragedies have matured into senior high jokes. I was in love sixty-two times, and I nearly died thirty-four times. As I turn the pages of high school back, I feel like an onlooker watching the development of a stranger, certainly not myself. North High is a large part of me, for it has been the center of my life for nearly six years. I remember the years with a warm smile.

Since North is a junior/senior high school, the students can be described as nothing less than mottled. As scared little seventh graders, we were overshadowed by the seniors: as seniors, we are tormented by seventh graders rushing to their next class.

Like most high schools, North houses the standard stereotypes: "fags", "greasers", "jocks", "heads", and "nothings". I was always

*Emily Dickinson.

classified as a "fag" because I was taking honor courses and usually did my homework. I will never forget one Friday evening at a local movie theater. A classmate of mine, with whom I was never particularly friendly, was there. He approached me and asked: "What are you doing here? I always assumed that honors kids stayed home on weekends to study." My only reaction was a satirical laugh.

Socializing in the school parking lot with a can of beer in one hand and a cigarette in the other are the earmarks of the "greaser". Any involvement with learning experiences or school activities totally disgusts this individual. I remember one particular week when several of the "greasers" smashed seven windows, one following another. The administration solved the problem by replacing them with plexiglass.

The standard "jock" of North is not necessarily involved with sports. "Hanging out" after school near the gymnasium is the basic criterion. His athletic ability and participation are secondary.

The enlightened sect of the school is the "heads", also known as the "druggies". Their intelligence is far above that of the other students (so they think), hence they shun the high school learning system.

Finally, there are the "nothings". These people are not accepted in any of the groups. They simply exist as parasites, and spend their time doing nothing.

The result of such a pluralistic society is conflict. This is not only limited to high schools, for it must exist in any heterogeneous community. A constant battle rages between the "greasers" and the "heads". One group has even sent a petition around the school in hopes of eliminating the other. The "fags" envy the "jocks", and the "jocks" resent the "fags". Unfortunately, these differences often eclipse in violence.

Nobody likes to be categorized. None of the standard high school stereotypes are flattering. Individuals cannot be pigeonholed, except in the eyes of others. However, they are an undisputed part of our society. The youth is a mere reflection of the adult world.

Apathy best pinpoints the flavor of North High. It is a schoolwide dance when six tickets are sold. It is a grade meeting when the president and the vice-president are the only attenders. It is a school newspaper when the editors are forced to write all of the articles. This feeling of apathy seems to be a trend across the country. Again, the high school emerges as a microcosm echoing the modern society.

Many times through the years I have felt like I belonged in a movie, a <u>Gidget</u> movie perhaps. I have seen the things I have lived through portrayed so many times on the screen. My high school reality became movie fantasy. One particular day highlights my memory: the day of the annual float parade and homecoming game. End October, a chilly afternoon with a crisp wind, all of North High was buzzing with excitement. The band was playing, the cheerleaders were shouting, the students were adding the final touches to their floats.

I drove the principal's car in the parade, and watched everything from the rear view mirror. The Queen of North, with a bouquet of roses resting on her lap, waved to the crowd. The batons twirled high, the trumpets roared, the floats lost bits and pieces on route. Families anxiously awaited the parade. Wrapped in autumn sweaters with rosy cheeks and cheery smiles, they picnicked on front stoops as the parade marched by. The women had pink curlers in their hair. The men stopped raking the leaves and leaned upon the poles of the rakes. The kids followed the parade on their bicycles, thinking about the days when they could finally go to the high school. Little dogs with floppy ears tried to keep up with their little masters. Certain patriotic citizens placed their hand over their hearts as the American flag proudly sailed by.

After the parade, red-nosed kids sipped hot chocolate while the adults drank coffee. Bundled in blankets with shakers in hands, the crowd cheered the football team to victory. With thirty seconds left to play, North won the game by a slim margin. The entire day belonged in a Norman Rockwell painting, but then again, what else should high school be?                    —Leslie Gell

Now and then, real-life secondary school tales can be conveyed with great humor. But only now and then . . .

### E.

I've taken many different courses throughout my high school career, but many were just "typical". Last year, however, I took an advanced Biology program. Advanced Bio at my school is a lab-oriented course requiring patience and manual dexterity.

During the year our class dissected four specimens: a fetal pig, a bull frog, a pigeon and a cat. In each specimen we studied only a few systems, but in the cat we studied them all. Each presented special challenges.

People knew I was enrolled in Advance Bio and would cringe when I sat next to them on the bus. It wasn't me—it was my fetal pig. My favorite perfume became "Formalin No. 5". Probably the worst experience I had was with my cat: three dogs chased me home once when my specimen was still under my arm. One girl's dog ate her cat's arms, so another student loaned her his specimen's arms. Another student ended up with two left feet on his skeleton until someone came up with a cat skeleton that had two right feet. One guy used Krazy Glue to hold his cat's arteries together. Granted, these were not a surgeon's techniques, but they did help us survive Advanced Bio.

I'll always remember that course . . .

And now and then a candidate will get into a topic that conveys a bit more than was perhaps intended:

*F.*

The summer of my junior year was the most educational and exciting I have spent. I was employed in New York, in the offices of Penthouse, Ltd. Here I worked with the staff photographer of *Penthouse, Viva,* and *Penthouse Photo World* magazines. Working here I almost gained a professional's knowledge. During the course of the summer I had contact with many famous and influential people. I feel that my knowledge gained from this experience will benefit me as much, if not more, than any formal education I have acquired as of yet, and I can truly say that I will not forget that to which I was exposed.

The application essay (some colleges will ask for more than one) should be done thoughtfully, personally, imaginatively, and with equal shares of seriousness and daring. Your record is your record . . . but the essay can add a refreshing and vital dimension to your college candidacy.

### The College Interview: Tell and Sell

"Every candidate should leave here having *enjoyed* the interview; at the same time, every candidate should leave here having been *challenged* by the interview," my boss in the Yale Admissions Office told me some years ago. And I've been passing that word along to my own staff members ever since. Most admissions colleagues at other institutions would perceive the interview similarly: a serious but friendly, informal conversation between college representative and prospective student.

The interview and the application essay create equally good opportunities for high school seniors to personalize, explain, and perhaps even dramatize their candidacy for college. And because young people today have been trained and encouraged to speak up, to express their feelings and their differences, the interview comes easily for most. It almost always serves to strengthen the student's chances for admission.

Selective private colleges do not, on the whole, accord the same weight to the interview as to the actual in-school record. But at some institutions where there are far more superior in-school records than there are places in the class, the interview can make a big difference (particularly at the smaller colleges). At the other end of the spectrum, a few institutions use the interview solely as a mechanism for transmitting information about the college and the interviewer's impressions of the candidate are not even recorded: Stanford and the University of Pennsylvania, for example. At most selective colleges the interview serves two purposes: 1. to reveal personal strengths of the candidate that perhaps have not been transmitted adequately through other channels of the admission process, and 2. to answer lingering questions about the institution that the candidate has not found answered satisfactorily in the college's literature or through other contacts.

The interview should not be perceived as a "test." To the contrary, the admissions officer (or faculty member or undergraduate or alumnus/a) will make every effort to create a friendly, relaxed atmosphere so that the applicant can feel as natural as possible. There is tension, of course, but the astute interviewer will seek to defuse the charged atmosphere. Also, the astute interviewer will try to pass the initiative to the candidate as quickly as possible. And the astute candidate will seize that opportunity and run with it.

The applicant should not come to the interview unprepared. Basic information about the college should be mastered before this personal meeting. The viewbook and/or catalog, the back-home guidance counselor and local alumni, and the pre-interview campus tour can help. Nothing antagonizes an interviewer more than a candidate's pulling out a long list of questions beginning with "Are you coed?" and "What is the size of your student body?" The list approach is particularly annoying if the student is more interested in getting to the next question than in absorbing the answer to the last. Probing and thoughtful questions, of course, *are* appropriate: "Do you envision major campus renovations or expansion in the near future?" "Do classes for freshmen tend to be considerably larger than classes for juniors and seniors?" "Are there tensions on this campus between men and women? Between blacks and whites?" "What happens here on weekends—do students tend to stay or leave?" "What are the major complaints of students here?" "Is your library crowded?" Questions should be prompted by a yearning to know rather than a yearning to impress: The interviewer can almost always guess the intent, and "staged" inquiries frequently backfire.

For his or her part, the interviewer will ask questions with the intent of simply getting to know the applicant better. True, some interviewers can be Bores Supreme and can only muster discussions of your grades, your scores, your activities, your home, your summers, and why-do-you-want-to-go-to-this-college. But the drab interviewer is an exception. Most would truly like to know the applicant, and will work at reaching that goal.

Initial let's-get-relaxed chatter proceeds to more serious discussion if and when the interviewer feels the candidate will be comfortable switching gears, or if the candidate himself turns in a new direction. John Hoy, in *Choosing a College* (Dell, 1967), compiled a helpful, representative list of questions the candidate might be asked at the selective college's interview. A sampling:

1. Do you have contemporary heroes? historical heroes?
2. If I visited your school for a few days, what would I find is your role in the school community? What would your teachers say were your greatest strengths as a person, as a student; likewise, what about your shortcomings or weaknesses?
3. What kind of self-development do you wish to see in yourself in the next four years?
4. What do you feel is the most important weak point you would like to overcome in the next four years?
5. What is the most significant contribution you've made to your school?
6. What will be the "good life" for you twenty years from now?
7. Where and when do you find yourself most stimulated intellectually?

8. If our roles were reversed, what would you like to know about me so that you could make an intelligent and fair decision on my application for admission or, better still, on my competence as your interviewer?

9. In a sentence or two, what points about yourself would you like to leave with me so that I can present your strongest side to our committee on admissions?

10. What books or articles have made a lasting impression on your way of thinking? Have you read deeply into any one author or field?

11. What events would you deem crucial in your life thus far?

12. What pressures do you feel operating on you in society to conform? Describe ways in which you and your friends "go your own way."

13. Describe some things that you have really become indignant over in the past year.

14. What do you feel sets you apart as an individual in your school?

15. If I could hand you my telephone and let you talk to any one person living, to whom would you like to talk? Why?

16. If I said you had $10,000 and a year to spend between high school and college, how would you spend the money and time?

17. Have you ever thought of not going to college? What would you do?

18. What have you read, seen, or heard about [Oldebrick] College that you don't like? What rumors can I confirm or deny?

19. If you were chosen as the new principal in your high school, what would be your first move?

20. Is there anything you'd like to toss into the interview as a parting comment?

The average college interview is 30 to 40 minutes—sometimes shorter, sometimes longer if the two people enjoy talking with each other. Usually the admissions officer will request the candidate to come into his/her office alone for the interview, and then ask the parents to come in for a few minutes at the end to see if they have any questions. These last few minutes can be a bit tense if either parent insists that the entire interview be reenacted to make certain all the bases have been covered. (Important as parents are to the college search, the interview should be the candidate's.)

Today, there are any number of "official" interviewers for colleges. The bulk of on-campus interviews at private colleges are handled by professional admissions officers, but now and then a faculty member will be called to substitute. And it is popular today to hire a few outstanding undergraduate seniors to interview on campus, particularly in the fall when admissions officers are away from campus, recruiting nationwide in the secondary schools. Often these "senior interviewers" do the best job: They can convey news of the college in a credible manner, and they are adept at getting the candidate to talk about himself. Also, because becoming a "senior interviewer" is such a campus honor, the undergrads take the job quite seriously, write extensive interview reports, and even follow up on some candidates with encouraging letters. Some of the most satisfied candidates have had college seniors as interviewers, unpopular though this may be with a few parents (particularly fathers), who feel the teenager may not have been exposed to the "power base." In actuality, all campus interview reports are considered with equal weight, no matter who interviewed.

Alumni interview in their hometowns for nearly all private institutions, and on the whole they do a superb job, considering the fact they are often years out of Alma Mater and miles away. Indeed, keeping alumni interviewers in touch with the changing college is a major challenge for the admissions office. But alumni who volunteer as interviewers usually take the job seriously (with some embarrassing exceptions). They return to campus for seminars, often at their own expense, and spend hours visiting local high schools and candidates' homes to spread the word. For the candidate who lives quite a distance from the college of his or her choice, the alumnus/a (usually) provides a happy and responsible substitute for dealing with the Admissions Office directly.

Students undoubtedly wonder what goes into the file after an interview has been completed. Interview reports are usually not lengthy, and they rarely repeat all that has been or will be listed in the way of courses and activities on the application. High points of the personal impression are recorded along with any information that the interviewer feels might not otherwise be known to the Admissions Committee.

A typical report from the Vassar files:

Roxanne could be described as a "low-keyed bohemian—or a moderate individualist." This I gather from her gypsy jaunty dress and her description of clashes she has had with the Journalism staff, who, she says, fail to give her articles bylines. She's not afraid to be herself nor to speak her mind freely, though she's not a full-fledged maverick. Roxanne is not highly provocative or scintillating personally, but certainly has a lot going for her academically, having pushed herself in curriculum and in activities (She's ARISTA president, a jock, etc.) I'd say Roxanne is a moderately accomplished, fairly solid applicant, although not quite strong enough in any zone to transcend The Big Middle.

Reference to "jaunty dress" in the above passage surely begs the question of the importance of appearance. Granted, the interview should be a "natural" occasion. At the same time, it is an event. And one usually dresses up to events: interviewers do, and candidates should also. Coats and ties or heels are not necessary, but a comfortable "up" appearance is appropriate and most welcome. The tattered-jean look doesn't quite make it today.

In sum, the interview can be enjoyable, not to mention highly informative, and in many cases, just plain profitable. Every candidate should try it.

## The Extracurricular Whirl

There is one more regrettable myth afloat that was not mentioned in Chapter Two. It goes something like this: The more activities, clubs, sports, and busy-busy things the candidate can mention on his or her application, the more the college will be impressed. Actually, the opposite is closer to the truth.

If a teenager gives priority to learning, in addition to fulfilling his responsibilities in the home, there isn't time left for joining everything. A student who takes the more demanding courses and does well in them must often pass up the temptation of high school Americana, boosting all the teams, helping raise money for the drug center, and being in the front lines of club after club. The longer the list of school and community activities, the more suspicious colleges will become that a superficial joiner is at hand, popping from place to place, responsibly involved in very little.

Back in the late innocent fifties, when I was working at Yale, we talked about filling the class with "well-rounded men." Yale and its brothers and sisters are still looking for a healthy roster of Category 5 types, but the "well-rounded" theory has been altered somewhat. Now most highly selective colleges are looking for a well-rounded class—a class of different types of individuals, some quite lopsided and some involved in a variety of things, but deeply involved. The feeling is that a classful of well-rounded kids who are mirror images of each other would be a dull class indeed.

Often, some of the most mature and accomplished young people are those who have given enormous time to one extracurricular endeavor, at the expense of others. The Yale Dean of Admissions, Worth David, addresses that point nicely:

> One of the most compelling characteristics that a candidate can bring to the admissions committee is the demonstrated capacity to do something superbly. If it's obvious that a youngster has thrown an enormous amount of energy into some worthwhile activity, that helps his case. It might not necessarily be an activity which is available at Yale. For example, there's the Midwesterner who does a superb job with the 4-H Club. But some kind of demonstration of the willingness and the ability to commit oneself to a worthwhile activity is a very compelling argument for admission.

Today the emphasis in the extracurricular zone is "depth," not "breadth." He plays ball—is he disciplined, improving, *good?* She paints—has she sought the best instruction in the area? Does she show? Is she *promising?*

Don't fret. Obviously, every teenager can't have the One Big Talent. But every student can, at 17, be aware of his or her own strengths and talents and find appropriate outlets. The youth of the early seventies left many marks on this nation— one was the healthful notion that teenagers think, get involved, and can move responsibly. That legacy makes Betty Boop the cheerleader look a little pale today.

Let's not forget the young person who has to work every waking hour when not in school, and who consequently must leave blank the extracurricular slots on the application. Not only can employment demonstrate extraordinary discipline, it also can stimulate one's ambition to learn. Some of the young people who have had to work rather than join clubs or teams or bands are the most mature around, and Admissions Committees would like to hear from more of them.

There can be no precise "how to" on impressing the Admissions Committee with the extracurricular record. What's done is done. Certainly the candidate should not whirl to a few club meetings in the last weeks before filing an application just to be able to list another activity. Depth of involvement is central today—a sense of caring, contributing, and yes, achieving.

## On Chasing Recommendations

Some few years ago, parents of a college candidate in Connecticut demanded to see what the high school guidance counselor had written about their son, surmising that a less-than-glowing recommendation had surely been the reason for the boy's rejection by selective Bates College of Maine. That inconspicuous court case ultimately led to the now-famous Buckley Amendment, which became law in 1974. The moral (and political) concept behind the Buckley Amendment made sense at the time and perhaps still does: the right of a student and/or his parents (until the youngster reaches age 18) to know what is in the student's file—statistical data, counselors' and teachers' reports, etc. The amendment ordered high schools and colleges to open their files at the request of an enrolled youngster or the parent.

The night before the Buckley Amendment became law, I remember heading to the Harpswell, Maine town dump—the most beautiful dump in the world, tucked in a series of Atlantic islands near Bowdoin College—to burn all interview reports, school recommendations, and teacher recommendations of the then-enrolled Bowdoin students for fear that students would storm the Dean's Office the next day to prepare suit against the counselor or interviewer who had once said "Jane is bright, but a trifle dull." As I entertained the gulls with my frenzied offerings to the fire gods, at more mechanized institutions the shredding machines were hard at work. At Yale they were finding remote holes for storage in the underground archives. With colleges' legal counsels hustling to invent interpretations of the new law (often at odds with each other), the schools and colleges eventually learned to cope with the amendment, though they had quite mixed emotions.

Why "mixed emotions"? We all agreed that the students and their parents had, to some responsible degree, "the right to know"—but *everything?* The immediate consequence of the amendment was to curb distinctly what schools, particularly the public ones, were willing to tell. The fear of libel ran so deep immediately following the enactment of the "The Privacy Act" that counselors and teachers and principals just decided it was safer to keep their mouths shut regarding candidates. "We must let the numbers speak for themselves," was a common response. And that was directly contrary to the way the private colleges were accustomed to going about their admissions business.

If one admits "by the numbers," meaning judging each candidate by a formula (giving appropriate weights to Grade Point Average, class rank, and standardized test scores), there obviously can be little room for the student who does B work in tough courses, for the classic late bloomer whose awful first two years are offset by two fine "come alive" years, for the kid who may flunk math but is a genius in foreign language, for the student whose grades have been affected by bad health or family problems, for the nifty kid (scholar or not) who might turn out to be one of those rare leaders of men.

It simply would not be fair to say that all schools stopped sending balanced, sensitive, insightful reports on candidates when the Buckley Amendment became law. But many, if not most, watered down their comments considerably in order to water down their risk. On the whole, the private schools ran less scared than the public. (I don't know why, as the "private" status would be irrelevant, I'm told, in court.)

In short, college admissions officers are told less about the human dimension of the candidate today (and consequently the application essay and interview become all the more important). Here are three rather typical public high school counselor reports on candidates to one Ivy college:

Constance Jameth is an outstanding high school senior. She is a good student as well as being very active in school and in the community. She is a varsity player on the tennis team. Swimming is her favorite sport and she belongs to the AAU at the local junior college. She competed in the Junior Olympics. She also likes to ski and surf.

Constance is very interested in Art and has won awards for her ability. She plays the piano and works part-time. Other activities at school have been her membership in the Service Club, C.S.F., and Ski Club.

She is a very personable and attractive young lady who has set her goals toward art. She is an independent worker who seems to have lots of self-discipline.

Possessing superior academic potential, Robert Krakus has performed very well in academic work in high school. He impresses me as a very sincere, dedicated student who has a wide range of interests.

Not only has Robert been a good student academically; he has also been very active in extracurricular activities in the school and community. He was selected by AFS to spend last summer in Paraguay, worked on the yearbook staff, and participated in a tutoring program.

Robert has impressed me as a conscientious student and is a strong candidate for college admission.

Melinda Jacobs is, in my opinion, a multi-talented young lady who is applying to a number of excellent academic schools. She is capable of academic success in those institutions receiving this recommendation.

This young lady has constantly followed a solid college preparatory course of study, including a number of honors courses.

Feedback from her teachers indicate positive contributing in all of her classes even though in Physics this year she is having some difficulty.

I am highly supportive of Melinda's application to your fine institution.

One can't blame the public school counselors for reporting only the obvious. First, they are enormously overworked. Having 300 students to advise is considered a "small load" these days. College counseling is only a segment of their responsibility: Class scheduling, discipline problems, and career counseling are all part of their job. And budget cuts often mean the elimination of a counselor rather than of other school officers or teachers. Some counselors probably welcomed the Buckley Amendment because they felt uneasy making personal judgments: Their heavy student load meant not knowing individual students well. In many ways, the cards are stacked against the public school counselors. So, considering the odds, counselors do a good job (some much better than others).

As a result of public school counselors' saying less to the colleges about specific candidates, the colleges have turned to the high school teacher. This is obviously unfair. The teacher is also overworked and underpaid—and here come the colleges king perspicacious comments on each and every kid. Generally, however, teachers tell us more than counselors—they're uninhibited, they know the students better, they have seen them in the environment the college cares most about, and they write rather well (particularly the English teachers). We in the colleges feel guilty asking teachers for student appraisals—but frankly we don't know where else to turn, and most teachers are unbelievably cooperative.

Following is a rather typical Teacher's Report submitted on the Common Application form (which teachers love since a single report can be photo-copied and sent to as many as 100 cooperating colleges). *(See pages 157–58.)*

I am reluctant to draw a firm line between the public schools and the private schools regarding college recommendations. But I must: the private schools win, hands down. There are obviously some bold exceptions on either side of the boundary: but *most* private school principals, college advisors, and teachers go the extra mile to inform colleges about the candidate beyond the obvious. Yes, some risks are taken and some highly subjective judgments are made, but almost always to the benefit of the candidate. Consider the following superb counselor recommendations from four private day schools:

*I.*

### School Recommendation for Cassandra Hopewell

Cassie is probably brilliant and certainly exasperating. The brilliance is literary, and Cassie's gifts are dazzling. Intuitive and instinctive, she makes quick leaps of insight. Her mind cannot be described as analytical in its methods, but she achieves results that go far beyond what her methodical contemporaries can manage. Her Class XI Eng-

nes Scott • Allegheny • American University • Antioch • Bard College • Bates • Beloit • Bennington • Boston College • Boston University
wdoin • Brandeis • Bucknell • Carleton • Case Western Reserve • University of Chicago • Clark • Coe • Colby • Colby-Sawyer • Colgate
lorado College • Connecticut College • Denison • University of Denver • Dickinson • Drew • Earlham • Eckerd • Elmira • Emory • Fairfield • Fisk
rdham • Franklin and Marshall • Furman • Gettysburg • Goucher • Hamilton • Hampshire • Hartwick • Haverford • Hobart • Hood
lamazoo • Kenyon • Knox                                                                          Lafayette • Lawrence • Lehigh
wis and Clark • Macalester    **COMMON APPLICATION**    Manhattan • Manhattanville • Mills
unt Holyoke • Muhlenberg                                                    Newcomb College • New York University
erlin • Occidental • Ohio Wesleyan • Pitzer • Pomona • University of Puget Sound • Randolph Macon Woman's College • University of Redlands • Reed
e • University of Richmond • Ripon • University of Rochester • Rollins • St. Lawrence • Salem • Sarah Lawrence • Scripps • Simmons • Skidmore
versity of the South • Stephens • Stetson • Susquehanna • Texas Christian University • Tulane • Union • Valparaiso • Vanderbilt • Vassar
shington College • Washington University • Washington and Lee • Wesleyan • Wheaton • Wheelock • Whitman • Willamette • William Smith • Williams

# TEACHER REFERENCE

udent name _____ Matthews, Bonnie _____
　　　　　　　　　　　Last　　　　　　　　　　　First　　　　　　　　　　Middle

dress _____ 323 S. Central Ave., Mason City, Iowa _____

hool Now Attending _____ North High School _____

e colleges and universities listed above encourage the use of this form. The accompanying instructions tell you how to complete the
py and file with any one or several of the colleges. Please type or print in black ink.

PLICANT:
Fill in the above information and give this form and a stamped envelope, addressed to each college to which you are applying that
uests a Teacher Reference, to a teacher who has taught you an academic subject.

ACHER:
The student named above is applying for admission to one or more Common Application group colleges. The Admissions Com-
ttees find candid evaluations helpful in choosing from among highly qualified candidates. We are primarily interested in whatever
u think is important about the applicant's academic and personal qualifications for college. Please submit your references promptly,
rticularly if the student is applying to a college as an early decision candidate. A photocopy of this reference form, or another re-
ence you may have prepared on behalf of this student is acceptable. You are encouraged to keep the original of this form in your
vate files for use should the student need additional recommendations. We are grateful for your assistance.

TINGS
Compared to other students in your school who are applying to selective colleges, check how you would rate the applicant in terms
academic skills and potential:

| No basis | | Below Average | Average | Good (above average) | Excellent (top 10%) | Outstanding (top 2-3%) | One of the top few encountered in my career |
|---|---|---|---|---|---|---|---|
| | Creative, original thought | | | | X | | |
| | Motivation | | | | X | | |
| | Independence, initiative | | | | X | | |
| | Intellectual ability | | | | X | | |
| | Academic achievement | | | X | | | |
| | Written expression of ideas | | | X | X | | |
| | Effective class discussion | | | | X | | |
| | Disciplined work habits | | | | | X | |
| | Potential for growth | | | | | | |
| | SUMMARY EVALUATION | | | | X | | |

(Please see reverse side)

**EVALUATION**

1. What are the first words which come to mind to describe the applicant?

        Open, dynamic, insightful, probing, concerned, interested

2. Academic Characteristics:

        Bonnie has not always shown her potential in terms of academic grades. ~~Perhaps~~

        this is because she has some difficulty expressing herself clearly, especially

        when she first writes or speaks. Her ideas and originality, however, are gratifyi

        She is able to make connections between ideas and areas of study – and is able to de
        with the figurative in creative ways. She is  truly a student and is interested :

3. Personal Characteristics:
                              study and growth.

        I can't praise Bonnie highly enough! She is a fine person who is going to make a
        wonderful contribution in whatever field she enters. She is always willing to wor
        to reach, to learn. She is full of ideas which are significant. In addition, she
        blossoming as a person now, taking in knowledge from her surroundings and making i
        part of herself.

**BACKGROUND INFORMATION**

How long have you known the applicant? ____3 years

Note any capacity in which you have known the applicant outside the classroom (advisor, family friend, etc): _____

List the courses you have taught, noting for each course the applicant's year in school (10th, 11th, 12th), the level of course difficul
(AP, elective), and the applicant's grade.  Sections of English II - B
                                        Sections in English IV - Psychology in Literature  B+
Please return to the appropriate admissions office(s) in the envelope(s) provided you by the applicant.  (challenging sectic

Secondary School _____North High School

School Address _____1717 Northern Boulevard, Mason City, Iowa

Name (print) _____Jane Euibler (Mrs.)

Position _____Instructor of English

Signature _____*Jane Euibler*_____ Date ____11/19/85

lish teacher wrote, "Cassie has a genuinely aesthetic sensibility and a creative imagination of awesome proportion." She is already a considerable stylist. Another English teacher comments, "She writes a marvelously baroque style which is truly delightful to read after the usual student prose; it is like coming upon a genuine oriental rug after miles and miles of indoor/outdoor carpeting." Cassie's gifts are not confined to the writing of prose. When she was in Class VIII, she won the Middle School Poetry Prize with an amazingly mature poem entitled "Wondering". Last year, her English teacher and her French teacher both marveled at her multilingual poem, written in imitation of T.S. Eliot. By her own account, in the fall of eleventh grade she had "started about seventeen novels and finished about seven volumes of journals." Much of her literary sophistication is the natural result of wide and constant reading. When Cassie applied to enter our fourth grade she was already reading <u>Jane Eyre,</u> and she has kept on at the same rate. She is the only student in years to have read all of Proust.

It is Cassie's attitude and methods that exasperate her teachers. She is a true intellectual for whose mill the world provides grist in abundance, but Cassie limits herself to a narrow group of subjects and will grind at no others. She is, for instance, mathematically gifted, and (rather against her will) she has often been fascinated by math. In the last analysis, however, she seems to have dismissed it as alien to her sensibility if not to her intellect. Even in those subjects to which she is attracted, Cassie shows little staying power. She balks at assignments that demand the patient construction of a thorough argument supported by evidence. As her American History and Literature teacher pointed out, "Her very facility with language occasionally hampers her ability to deal faithfully and fairly with a text." Her attraction to the bizarre and the peripheral vitiates her ability to confront a task of substance. As her current French teacher observed, "She remains a dilettante, juggling with ideas and titles, unable to analyze a text in depth or to write a complete, balanced essay." But what an inspired dilettante! It will surprise none of us if Cassie becomes a novelist or belletrist of peculiar power.

Just as Cassie has set herself apart from certain subjects, she has removed herself from the usual routines of school life. The punctuality of either her papers or her person is of small concern. She has found our gym requirements irksome, and in fact cut so many gym classes in tenth grade that she failed the course and was surprised to find herself making it up the following year. Startled surprise is Cassie's usual reaction to any reminder of her responsibility, and indeed the concept of personal responsibility does not seem to be part of her philosophical constitution. Vague and dreamy, she is immensely polite and charming, especially to adults, with whom she feels most comfortable. She has had little time for adolescence. Cassie's parents are immensely cultivated people who have made her a part of their very adult life. She loves the ballet and goes as often as possible. In eleventh grade she worked on weekends at the New York City Ballet in a routine but fascinating backstage job. Cassie has traveled widely and with discrimination. In the summer after tenth grade, she studied English art and architecture and Elizabethan literature at Lincoln College, Oxford, and then went on to study French at the Institut de Touraine in Tours. Cassie has a highly personal style which depends only partly on wardrobe, though her fashion sense is as baroque as her prose. Her tenth grade homeroom teacher observed, "Much of her style is a matter of playing roles, but she has instinct and taste as well. When she grows into and out of the attitudes she now assumes like poses, she will be a very formidable person indeed . . . Underneath a facade of enervated indifference and superiority, Cassie harbors a good heart and kind instincts." Cassie presently inhabits a small world in which these latter qualities are less valued than her great beauty, her style, and her responsiveness to any aesthetic pleasure. We hope the balance may some day be redressed. Our acquaintance with her has been fascinating.

## II.
### Headmaster's Recommendation on Justice Bayrock

At first glance the muscular young man who stares you right in the eye gives the impression of a tough teenager of his urban milieu. In a way, Justice Bayrock is just that if one allows for perhaps fifty points more IQ, a sensitive insight into himself and his world, and the kind of moral toughness which will, one day, sweep aside the epicene competition.

Indeed, Justice is a first-rate athlete: a varsity basketball and baseball star, accomplished swimmer, skier, etc. These are important to Justice, yet clearly subordinate to a more profound competitive sport of which he is increasingly aware: survival—moral, intellectual, and aesthetic—in a muddled society.

He brings rare skills to the business of survival. A natural mathematician and apt science student, Justice clearly intends to somehow put his talents at the service of an eventual career (economics? business? law?). A leader by instinct and training, his counselor positions have prepared him to deal with constant demands with dignity and authority.

There is, however, an emergent Justice who is less predictable. This is the sensitive observer of an urban milieu. The romantic buff of Black music, the catholic reader balancing science fiction against the philosophical flow of Garcia-Marquez, is no longer the uncomplicated, bright athlete/leader.

Justice is the most exciting kind of student one offers to college. He has absolute character, loyalty, and guts. He adds to that a growing sensitivity enhanced by a truly powerful intelligence. He is open and offers himself body and mind to his community. Vassar is the kind of environment which can reward the virility and energy which will make this young man be heard from in years to come.

III.

### Headmaster's Recommendation for Mary Douglas

Mary Douglas came to _____ in eleventh grade looking for a realistically demanding school after the warm, human, rather fuzzy little place that she had gone to in northern Vermont. She was poorly prepared, was often subdued by her argumentative, confident new classmates and the amount of work expected of her, but at the same time possessed some very real qualities she could build upon. She had good sense in the handling of any personal problems. She was straightforward, realistic, modest, naturally courteous. She rapidly won trust and respect in her new community and was given positions of responsibility—running a meal at our all-school country weekend, managing the dining hall—much sooner than the usual new student. As a senior Mary has been pleased by the expansion of her range of skills and confidence. Her writing has improved markedly—she wrote a couple of first-rate papers on Hamlet—and has, to her surprise, found herself interested in math and physics. She was an imaginative printmaker last year, has a worthwhile part in this month's performance of <u>Inherit the Wind,</u> is a fine athlete in tennis and soccer.

Mary's family is a complicated one but she is able to manage its turns and help steady her younger sister in difficult times. Grandfather was wealthy and Mr. Douglas used these resources to become a sculptor in every medium from plaster to auto parts. Her mother ("I get my talkativeness and liveliness from her") runs a daycare center near Cape Cod. Her step-father, whom Mary admires highly, started life as a street gang leader in Detroit, went to Harvard and became a marine biologist, and now helps to manage a humane reform school.

Mary's transcript is nothing special but I have a great deal of liking and respect for her. First of all, you can trust her: her sense of responsibility, kindness, resourcefulness, honesty. She is someone you'd be glad to have around in a rough situation. Secondly, she is growing and aware of this process of intellectual growth. She can see the difference between what she is able to do now and what she could do or be interested in twelve months ago. What Mary admires in her classmates, like their academic outreach, she will try to emulate without feeling she has to protect herself, or give up her own personal qualities. She trusts her ability to carry through on a commitment and knows she can be helpful to people. I would back her strongly.

## IV.

### School's Recommendation for John Downing III

_____ School very rarely accepts students after the 10th grade year, long after close friendships have been made and academic skills necessary to compete in a high-powered intellectual environment have been ingrained. Because John Downing felt so unchallenged by his previous schooling, he literally uprooted himself and talked his way into being admitted to _____ at the beginning of his junior year. The only child of quintessentially middle-class parents, John had led a sheltered, highly conventional existence.

John has written far more graphically and eloquently than can we about the great awakening he experienced at _____, but suffice it to say that this is a very different young man from the naive one that came to us last fall. It is to John's credit that he aspired to something more than a humdrum existence and he has taken maximum advantage of the educational and creative opportunities at _____. Exposing himself to a wide variety of new ideas, lifestyles, and priorities, John was encouraged to think and be his own man for the first time. As a result, he has unleashed his profound sense of the absurd and begun to develop his ample abilities (SAT: Verbal 670, Math 630).

John has paid the price for daring to open up his mind. His parents, particularly his father, claim that he has changed so much that they do not recognize him. His father feels threatened by John's increasingly liberal attitude and father and son barely communicate. John's mother realized that most of the changes that have occurred with John will ultimately be for the good, but she too finds it difficult to adjust to her son's orientation. Although John has found special satisfaction and interest in the theatre, he is firmly committed to the pursuit of an enriched and balanced liberal arts education. His solid grade point average becomes all the more impressive in light of the voluminous number of credits he accrued in an effort to make up for lost time. He has done his best work in English and Social Science.

John has become greatly enamored of English culture, almost to the point of being an Anglophile. His mannerisms and comportment could easily lead to being deemed an affectation, were it not for John's basic honesty and openness. A veritable afficionado of the English theatre, John has shared his expertise with the entire _____ community.

Last year he assumed a leading role in <u>The Real Inspector Hound</u> and this past fall directed an extremely well-received production of <u>Billy Liar</u>. "John's direction was remarkable in its humor and in its ability to create reality on stage," says _____ resident director of theatre operations who has presided over a series of award-winning productions. This spring he is undertaking a major independent project directing two of his classmates in <u>Sleuth</u>.

John also tried his hand at scriptwriting with an original play entitled <u>You Can't Have Chairs in the Audience</u>. It was patterned after the highly successful contemporary black comedy of Tom Stoppard and Joe Orton. "John has a good grasp of the English speech and manners as demonstrated by the dialogue," says his teacher. "John's wit is charming and his imagination stimulating. When he releases his unusual capabilities into more refined patterns, he will become an outstanding student. It has been a distinct pleasure to see John discover a decided talent for writing. He must continue to polish up his techniques as a writer of expository essays but he possesses great imagination and inventiveness which should be nurtured."

In sum, we are happy to have shaken up John Downing's world in a positive way. Although slightly offbeat at times, John has a firm grasp on where he is headed. Having responded so well to the academic and personal demands of a competitive liberal arts secondary school environment, John is looking for a similar experience in college. This is one young man who does not take education for granted. He knows the difference between being a student and merely going to school, and we feel confident that he will take maximum advantage of a quality college experience. He has added zest and life to our community, and we recommend him with affection.

Some schools, public and private, do an end run around the Buckley Amendment by showing the student a draft of his or her recommendation before it is sent to colleges. Ironically—but predictably, it seems to me—the student often feels the school authority has gilded the lily and asks for a more balanced, believable report. Kids today are candid and will often be disappointed with the counselor who is playing safe with the new law. Would that every school might incorporate this technique. It seems to work to the benefit of all parties.

With the complications today in reporting on students—the law, finding time when other responsibilities call, questioning whether one knows the student well enough to write a personal appraisal—it is a wonder we get as many good recommendations as we do. The college Admissions Office is grateful for them— and clearly the candidate who comes alive in the folder has an advantage over others.

Now and then, however, the recommending parties get carried away and we are challenged to defoliate the green prose or are treated to sheer comic relief. As a breather, let's consider a few recent examples:

. . . She can be trusted to not only exploit college like a stripminer, but to replace every bit of topsoil—fertilized as well.

. . . An able, yet somewhat inscrutable product of intellectually oriented and academically distinguished parents, Monty has quietly and resolutely carved out an interesting act of scholarly interests and personal pursuits. . . . His reluctance to become his own advocate may cause him to get lost in the shuffle of your high-powered applicant pool. But secure in his own abilities and eager to expose himself to a wide variety of experiences, Monty is slowly coming to the conclusion that it is decidedly in the best interests of the entire community for him to heighten his profile. Thus, his accomplishments at college will undoubtedly transcend his rather mediocre high school achievements.

. . . Other students may be brighter but I know no one but Jimmy who is clean to the bone.

. . . Joyce was driven to our school by the gnawings of hunger. She felt the offerings of her previous school could not satisfy the demands of her voracious academic appetite.

. . . Perhaps the finest, most glowing, most representative example of Ann's total personality and personhood is the emotionally demanding type of volunteer service she has performed at the local hospital. But the sphere and scope of Ann's constructive, productive endeavors encompass yet much more than her consuming occupation with service. There is scholarship. . . .

. . . As literary editor of the school magazine in her junior year, she salvaged it from distinction.

. . . He has been active—instrumentally so—in the losing campaign of a candidate for Congress.

. . . His parents are twice divorced and Alex lives with his mothers.

. . . Although Jennifer is under considerable pressure from her family to achieve high grades, she has resisted this pressure with a high degree of success.

. . . If June didn't have so much difficulty with tests and quizzes, her average would be an "A."

. . . Margaret is a student who has demonstrated her intentions to me.*

As stated or implied in other sections of this book, the student must bear considerable responsibility for all segments of his or her college application, and not just turn over sections to others (counselors and teachers), uncaring. A concerned student should ask what the major points of the recommendation will be, and whether or not the final report is to be shared. Often students can offer valuable suggestions for balancing recommendations, and those asked to recommend are usually grateful.

Also, it is within the realm of common sense, not to mention good manners, to ask if a particular teacher feels comfortable, has time, and is willing to write a sound recommendation for a student. This is not in the regular line of duty for a teacher, particularly in the public system, and should be considered no small favor, if it is done well. (By the way, some of the most convincing teachers' reports come from those who teach the most demanding courses, not from those popular ones who hand out the highest grades.)

Finally, a word about "other recommendations"—the ones from outside the school, particularly those unsolicited by the college.

Certainly a student's employer can say a great deal about the candidate—and usually employers say it well. This is a partic-

*Reprinted in part from an article by Mr. Moll in the *Wall Street Journal*, April 16, 1978.

ularly important ingredient in the application when the student has not been involved in school affairs. But the line stops there.

Rarely does the friend of the family (alumnus/a of the college included) add much but pressure to a candidate's folder by sending a "friendly, unsolicited" recommendation. These letters are almost always bare-boned summaries of what a student has done in and out of the classroom (we know all this), a celebration of the parents' importance to the community, and a "warm endorsement" of so-and-so, about whom the endorser generally knows very little. Lawyers and senators and rabbis and chief committeewomen don't add an ounce of punch to a candidate's folder because nine times out of ten they simply don't know the candidate well enough to comment. There are exceptions, of course, but I don't recall more than a handful in two decades.

# 4.

# Sell, Sell, Sell: Why Colleges *and* Students Must Flaunt Themselves

## THE COLLEGE

### Where Have All the Students Gone?

Not long ago in New Haven, the Alumni Association chairman of the Committee on Undergraduate Admissions said to a throng of Old Blues and other assembled Yale compatriots: "This whole issue of admissions takes on greater importance when you realize that there are now thousands of vacancies in American colleges, that the number of good schools is increasing, that many former 'cow colleges' are now distinguished universities, and that the number of high school graduates is declining. That spells competition. Anyone who assumes that Yale is somehow buoyed effortlessly on its reputation, or is immune to the pressures of the marketplace, had better take another look. Special efforts will have to be made to reach out and identify the first-class minds in this country and to interest them in Yale. It will have to be much more than a casual business of sitting back and waiting for the lucky to arrive somehow or other in New Haven."

If Yale is uneasy about the future, consider what unrest looms elsewhere. The New York State Education Department estimated quite publicly that two-thirds of the state's private colleges faced the possibility of going out of business by 1990. This conclusion was based on demographic studies predicting that the number of full-time undergraduates in the state would fall approximately 23 percent below current levels by 1990, primarily because of the declining birthrate.

"Ominous signs are all around," Boston's College Dean of Admission gloomily states in B.C.'s alumni magazine. "For one thing, the national birth rate has continued to plunge at a precipitate rate so that there will be significantly fewer 17-year-olds eligible for college in the late 1980s than there have been in recent years. Even more alarming is the perception among a growing number of young people today that, with escalating college costs and diminishing payoffs in terms of guaranteed career opportunities, a post-secondary education simply may not be worth the huge investment. Boston College, as a private university with almost total dependence on tuition income, is in a particularly vulnerable position. An unanticipated shortfall of little more than two percent of the undergraduate student body would result in an immediate $1 million operating deficit."

Private colleges fret imaginatively about what the escalating price of an undergraduate education will do to the applicant pool, whether a bleak job market will discourage students from attending college at all, and what effect the growing quality and prestige of the public university system will have on the private sector. But their primary concern is not one of conjecture at all: it is a fact that the number of 17-year-olds in the nation is declining. Granted, demographers differ on specifics, but the sharp downward trend is real. The number of potential college students in the near future will be depleted.

And there is more for the private colleges to worry about. Even though the percentage of 17-year-olds who decide to attend postsecondary institutions has climbed to a high of approximately 60 percent, the percentage opting for the private sector of education has dramatically decreased. According to Colorado's Education and Economic Systems, 47 percent of the students who attended college nationwide in 1953 were enrolled in private colleges or universities; three decades later, in 1983, that figure had dropped to 22.7 percent, and the percentage continues to descend.

So the private colleges are faced with a double-edged threat: a declining market of the traditional college-age group, and a declining percentage of that declining market who opt for the private sector of education.

Administrators and faculty within the private sector are now keeping a watchful eye on what the demographers come up with, hoping for an eventual return to the good news of the expansionist sixties. But the crystal ball gazers aren't predicting much to smile about yet. Humphrey Doermann, once Director of Admissions at Harvard and now head of the Bush Foundation of Minnesota, is one of the most respected gurus in the field. In a paper entitled "The Future Market for College Education," presented at a College Board symposium in 1976, Mr. Doermann said:

Following a century of expansion, higher education in the United States is about to enter at least a 15-year period of either no growth or shrinkage, depending on the projection assumptions one makes and upon the decisions made by federal and state governments concerning public policy in this sector. . . .

The number of high school graduates each year will begin to shrink: 15 percent by 1984, and 22+ percent by 1990. . . . The general pressures of steady or declining enrollment probably will place individual colleges and systems of colleges under strains they were not designed for. The principal casualty is most likely to be the capacity of these institutions to adapt and to preserve vitality. This appears almost certain unless the new conditions can be addressed soon with intelligent analysis, forbearance, and ingenuity.

During the 100 years prior to 1970, degree enrollment in colleges in the United States doubled approximately every 14 or 15 years. During the 1950s and 1960s the rate of expansion was even faster. Never has there been a long period of enrollment decline. Brief declines occurred only during the two world wars, the Korean War, and in 1933–34. Expectations, planning processes, federal and state budgeting mechanisms, and the administration of colleges and college systems have until recently all been built with an assumption of continued growth in enrollment. Some of these fundamental elements still are built that way, but for a time probably ought not to be.

Once we move beyond the next 20 years, the traditional forces of growth *may* take hold again. By then the population of 18-year-olds probably will expand, the number of high school graduates probably will grow again, and colleges will hire relatively large numbers of new faculty members to replace the retirees who were appointed during the sharp expansion of the 1960s. If the rest of the national economy is healthy, the first part of the 21st century should be a time of optimism for colleges. But the period from now until the mid-1990s looks different. . . . Whether we believe the no-growth projections, the sharp-decline projections, or something in between, colleges appear to face a decade or two of unprecedented stress, competition, and perhaps retrenchment.

Doermann, in his array of articles and books, has attempted to rather specifically predict the volume of young people at different levels of aptitude and income who would be available for college in future years. In his first book which caused educators to sit up and take notice, *Crosscurrents in College Admissions* (New York: Teachers College Press, 1968), he drew several broad and important conclusions which he now feels have stood the test of time:

1. The number of students prosperous enough to pay full tuition at private colleges and academically able enough to do satisfactory work at most of them is a relatively small portion of the total high school graduate population. The many colleges that plan to expand by enrolling more students of this kind will not succeed; the applicant pool is too small.
2. Colleges that attempt to raise tuition faster than family incomes rise and colleges wishing to raise dramatically the measured verbal aptitude of their entering students are likely to find these moves unexpectedly difficult unless they are also willing to decrease enrollment, or somehow are able to broaden and strengthen their applicant pool.

The chart on page 171 represents the type of specific demographic projection that has made Doermann and his colleagues somewhat ominous celebrities in academic circles. (Doermann invites the reader to note that in the high scoring SAT Verbal columns, the number of students increases as income levels increase. In the lowest score column, the reverse is true. The conclusion is not new: Measured verbal aptitude and family income are correlated.)

Although Humphrey Doermann suggests that colleges might

# Estimated Parental Contribution toward Applicant's Education, by SAT Average

| Parental Contribution | Plan to Apply for Financial Aid % | Below 350 % | 350-399 % | 400-449 % | 450-499 % | 500-549 % | 550-599 % | 600-649 % | 650 or over % | No SAT % | All Students % |
|---|---|---|---|---|---|---|---|---|---|---|---|
| $0 | 93.6 | 37.0 | 24.4 | 20.2 | 17.0 | 14.5 | 12.6 | 10.6 | 8.8 | 34.4 | 21.0 |
| $1–499 | 90.6 | 11.0 | 10.1 | 9.1 | 8.3 | 7.4 | 6.5 | 5.8 | 4.7 | 9.2 | 8.6 |
| $500–999 | 89.1 | 7.5 | 8.3 | 8.3 | 7.8 | 7.5 | 7.1 | 6.4 | 5.5 | 7.1 | 7.6 |
| $1,000–1,499 | 86.8 | 7.8 | 8.6 | 8.4 | 8.1 | 7.8 | 7.2 | 6.7 | 5.9 | 7.4 | 7.8 |
| $1,500–1,999 | 85.1 | 4.8 | 5.7 | 5.9 | 6.1 | 6.1 | 5.8 | 5.7 | 5.0 | 4.6 | 5.6 |
| $2,000–2,999 | 82.3 | 7.6 | 9.3 | 9.7 | 9.9 | 10.1 | 9.9 | 9.5 | 8.9 | 7.7 | 9.3 |
| $3,000–3,999 | 74.2 | 5.2 | 6.6 | 7.1 | 7.6 | 7.7 | 7.6 | 7.5 | 7.4 | 5.5 | 6.9 |
| $4,000–4,999 | 73.1 | 3.0 | 4.3 | 4.8 | 5.4 | 5.7 | 6.2 | 6.3 | 6.6 | 3.8 | 4.9 |
| $5,000–5,999 | 68.4 | 3.8 | 5.1 | 5.4 | 5.7 | 6.2 | 6.3 | 6.9 | 6.7 | 4.3 | 5.4 |
| $6,000–7,999 | 57.0 | 4.9 | 7.0 | 8.5 | 9.5 | 10.6 | 11.9 | 13.1 | 14.8 | 5.8 | 8.9 |
| $8,000–9,999 | 59.1 | 1.3 | 1.7 | 1.9 | 2.2 | 2.5 | 2.6 | 2.9 | 3.3 | 1.8 | 2.1 |
| $10,000—Over | 47.7 | 6.0 | 8.9 | 10.7 | 12.3 | 14.0 | 16.2 | 18.5 | 22.5 | 8.5 | 11.8 |
| Total | 77.3 | 100.0 | 100.0 | 100.0 | 100.0 | 100.0 | 100.0 | 100.0 | 100.0 | 100.0 | 100.0 |
| Number Responding | 897,034 | 115,815 | 105,608 | 130,473 | 129,855 | 110,924 | 77,225 | 44,422 | 29,112 | 47,844 | 791,278 |
| Number in Report | 1,052,351 | 168,615 | 142,352 | 170,341 | 166,253 | 140,119 | 96,690 | 55,916 | 37,079 | 74,986 | 1,052,351 |
| Mean Contribution | $2,730 | $2,190 | $2,970 | $3,370 | $3,720 | $4,050 | $4,410 | $4,820 | $5,380 | $2,660 | $3,510 |
| Median Contribution | $1,340 | $ 630 | $1,420 | $1,850 | $2,270 | $2,660 | $3,100 | $3,710 | $4,580 | $ 950 | $2,020 |
| Mean Income | $34,600 | $29,300 | $36,300 | $39,700 | $42,700 | $45,500 | $48,200 | $51,200 | $55,300 | $32,500 | $40,600 |
| Median Income | $28,600 | $22,600 | $29,100 | $31,800 | $33,900 | $36,000 | $38,400 | $41,000 | $44,500 | $24,700 | $32,200 |

*Calculated from 1984–85 Student Descriptive Questionnaires, The College Board

be able to broaden their market in future years by concentrating on four groups—recent high school graduates who have planned on college but have not decided where, high school graduates who might be encouraged to attend colleges, transfer students from two-year colleges, and adult part-time students of various kinds—his key message is fairly gloomy:

> The traditional market of high school graduates begins to shrink about 1978 and does not begin to recover until the 1990s. This shrinkage, in turn, will set up a new set of pressures and stresses to which U.S. colleges must respond somehow. How each one will respond will depend partly on what the college's purpose is, how it is governed and financially supported, what its competitive position is compared with similar colleges seeking the same students, and perhaps whether its location is in a region of growing or decreasing population. Most of these elements have been viewed by colleges as important fixed constants in their own planning. Under new pressures, many of these constants may instead become variables. Therefore, finally, a college's ability to adapt intelligently, quickly, and surefootedly probably will determine its quality and even its survival during the next 15 years to a far greater degree than was true during the past 30 years. . . . If colleges manage only to compete aggressively with each other for a larger share of a shrinking pool, the total system will be in disarray 15 years from now.

So the handwriting is on the wall: Many private colleges will not fill their beds due to a declining number of college-age young people in the nation; the cost of private education is forcing a significantly higher percentage of the college-bound to the public sector; and to make matters worse, young people are wondering, considering the woes of the job market, whether getting the college degree is really worth the investment of time and money after all.

True, the predictions of student (and financial) shortage at the colleges bode well for the individual student's chances of gaining admission—more on that later. But what are the colleges doing to prepare for or to offset lean times? In most cases, very little, except beefing up the admissions program to "compete" more effectively.

Directors of Admission submitted the following responses to this question: "As demographers predict significantly declining numbers of 17-year-olds and a declining percentage opting for private higher education, many colleges are responding with creative planning. What is your institution doing?"

Allegheny (Pennsylvania) is studying its entire admissions approach (from inquiry to enrollment) to make it more responsive to prospective student needs. Establishing broader visibility is one of the marketing strategies being employed, and this is being done in light of an image study which will indicate the way Allegheny is perceived by its different constituencies. No specific plans exist to cut back faculty, but that will be done if declining enrollment eventually requires it. The same thinking would apply to the size of the student body.

Furthermore, a more elaborate alumni-admissions program is being developed to deal with the enrollment issue.

Amherst (Massachusetts): No plans yet. We're still "fat," and the numbers continue to climb. But we're inwardly concerned. . . .

Boston College (Massachusetts) has instituted a program of enrollment management that integrates marketing, financial aid, student flow, demand, retention, and institutional research into one area for planning and control purposes.

Bowdoin (Maine): All of these decisions lie ahead of us.

Brandeis (Massachusetts): Other than the strengthening of our admissions program, no definite plans as of yet.

Bucknell (Pennsylvania): I honestly wish I could respond by saying that we are actively involved in creative planning. I can only hope that within the next two or three years answers to these questions will be forthcoming.

Colgate (New York): We are presently considering ways of responding to this challenge. No interesting tactics yet.

Denison (Ohio): We have formulated a marketing action plan. And tenured faculty positions are harder to come by. A faculty-student-administrative committee on the eighties is studying the matter of the size of the College and our current 14 to 1 student/faculty ratio.

Franklin and Marshall (Pennsylvania): We have been on a program for four years now to reduce the College by 25 students per year. It is possible we would bring the College size down from 2100 to about 1950 students.

Kenyon (Ohio): No plans for any reductions. We are hoping to be more aggressive in recruiting and marketing.

Lewis and Clark (Oregon): So far, we're just hoping to buck the trend. We have not had to be aggressive to meet our goals. More activity in selected target areas and groups will be one approach. No "retrenchment" here—it's a bad word.

Manhattan College (New York): Little is being planned here in terms of a decline, to be quite honest.

Manhattanville (New York): Unfortunately, we are like too many colleges in our projections—we're simply expecting to hold our own.

Ohio Wesleyan: Sadly, recent successes in admissions have created a new wave of apathy with regard to the need for long-range planning. We have recently developed a School of Nursing (to broaden our market), and have engaged in some new direct mail recruitment activity. But the already competitive Ohio picture will intensify until a few of us become extinct and the birthrate has stabilized.

Pomona (California): No plans of note. We anticipate little decline in the West.

Princeton (New Jersey): In the marketing area, we shall continue to try to strengthen our national network of alumni volunteers, since they are far more effective in recruitment matters than direct mailing and staff travelers (at least on a cost basis). No current plans to cut back either the faculty or student body—and certainly no plans to expand, either!

Ripon (Wisconsin): We are adding courses in fields that are more employment-oriented, and expect to move from a faculty-student ratio of 1/11 to 1/13.

St. John's (New Mexico): Nothing.

Scripps (California): First of all, the high-stepping Scripps admissions team, in lavish costumes of the period, is going to *scour* California. We shall wrest some souls from the U.C. system. And we're flirting with recruiting "non-traditional" and "resuming" students.

Stephens (Missouri): Broader use of alumnae in recruitment; use of faculty in recruitment; use of students in recruitment; more productive use of telephone for recruitment. There are also preparations to cut back faculty in specific departments.

Suffolk (Massachusetts): We have a hip pocket plan to function with 20% fewer students.

Susquehanna (Pennsylvania): Help! . . . The president wants to increase our total enrollment by 200!

Tulane (Louisiana): No cutbacks planned. We think our best strategy is to strive to improve and thereby increase our market penetration.

Vanderbilt (Tennessee): Expansion of mass mailings, increased secondary school visitations, increased use of alumni, a continuation of our Honors (no-need) Scholarships.

Most private colleges give the impression that they are indeed aware of the demographers' forecast of cloudy skies. But almost all seem to be saying: "The neighbor college will be affected before ours, and hopefully, ours won't be affected at all." That attitude and posture, of course, cannot be altered by the Admissions Office. If the president and trustees refuse to cope with a changing, perhaps negative situation, all the Admissions Director can do is to accelerate recruitment and enrollment activity to plug the dike.

So, imaginative and expensive college promotional activity flourishes now, despite the warnings of Humphrey Doermann: "If colleges finally manage only to compete aggressively with each other for a larger share of a shrinking pool, the total system will be in disarray 15 years from now." But Admissions Offices have little choice. . . .

Terms such as "marketing," "promotionals," and even "selling" are foreign to the admissions officer, who until recently shared the faculty image of slightly-disarranged-tweedy-but-warm-with-pipe. No longer! We all spend hours pondering which public campaign will not just tell, but sell. Many institutions today, including the most prestigious and selective, have hired the professionals of Madison Avenue to bolster their urgent campaigns. The result—as any student or parent can quickly see by scanning the bulletin board or conference table of the local school's guidance office—is a gorgeous array of viewbooks, catalogs, posters, films, slideshows, and giveaways ranging from Afro combs, distributed by the United States Military Academy, to dignified calendars circulated by Pomona of California.

Some of the promotional efforts seem alien to the academic community. Philip Kotler, a marketing expert who addressed a

CEEB gathering entitled "A Role for Marketing in College Admissions," offered these examples:

> One private college passed out promotional frisbees to students on spring break in Fort Lauderdale.
> A midwestern college sent first-contact letters to high school students—based solely on alumni recommendations—reading, "Congratulations! You've been accepted."
> A Kentucky university planned to release 103 balloons filled with scholarship offers, but canceled the plans because of adverse reaction.
> A college in Indiana offered undergraduate students rebates of $100 for each new student who actually enrolled—up to a limit of the student recruiter's total tuition. They discontinued the practice after criticism from colleges across the country.

Mr. Kotler's message to college administrators, most of whom could not be more unfamiliar with the tactics of the "marketplace," is that "marketing makes selling unnecessary—the better the marketing job, the less the need for hard selling." And he is probably right. Colleges have spent far too little time analyzing their own true strengths and weaknesses and systematically pinning down appropriate "markets." Kotler calls for "positioning" among colleges—that is, an institution should determine its own specific mission and publicize that uniqueness with objectivity, with a sense of timing, and with consistency of message. "If you try to appeal to everyone, you end up appealing to no one," he says.

But a good many private colleges are already feeling hunger pains, and haven't the time or money or expertise to undertake a sophisticated marketing analysis. Consequently, the rush is on. Even among institutions that are filling their beds—including the handful that do so with considerable ease—there is a growing interest in the complexities and benefits of "sales consciousness."

Experimentation has begun. At Yale, toll-free lines were installed in the Admissions Office from April 15 to May 1 so that an admitted student from Utah or Texas could pick up the phone and ask how Yale's housing situation or Philosophy Department compare to Harvard's. Elitist little Reed of Oregon has borrowed Madison Avenue lingo for its mailing to National Merit Semifinalists:

First and most important, Reed students are excited about learning and are committed to obtaining the best, genuinely liberal education possible. The fact that people come to Reed prepared to demand the most of themselves and their college is one reason Reed is often considered the finest liberal arts college in the West.

Second, they are attracted to a small, but diverse, community where people are valued for their individuality and where they are governed not by bureaucratic authority but by a clear sense of responsibility to each other.

Third, they relish the opportunity of living in a major city with a vital culture and an enlightened politics, a city which is, at the same time, only minutes away from some of the most varied, beautiful, and unspoiled country in the world.

Bryn Mawr, reputed to be one of the most academically demanding institutions in the country, sophisticates its sales pitch by quoting E. B. White (who happened to marry an alumna):

A Bryn Mawr girl is like a very beautiful waterfall whose flow is the result of some natural elevation of the mind and heart. She is *above* paperclips, above Kleenex, above jewels, above money. She spends a large part of each day *making* money, and then comes home and rises above it, allowing it to fall gently through the cracks and chinks of an imperfect world.

Smith and Wellesley hold gala open houses for admitted students on campus, and their alumnae do the same in private homes throughout the nation. Each college hopes, of course, to slightly outdo the other to win the young woman admitted to both institutions.

Some college open houses have become extravagantly expensive affairs. Rockford College of Illinois, for example, circulated the following invitation nationally to seniors who had scored very high on the SATs:

You are cordially invited to spend two days on the Rockford College campus at a CAMPUS PREVIEW. Rockford will provide meals and housing at no charge, and will provide 75% of your transportation expenses if you travel by air, bus, or train. Should you live within 125 miles and arrive by automobile, the college will reimburse your costs at a rate of 7½¢ per mile. You will receive your reimbursement check within 10 days following the CAMPUS PREVIEW.

Other institutions get right to the point and offer more than a low cost ride to the campus: they offer a free ride through the four undergraduate years. A recent mailing from Morris Harvey College in West Virginia to National Merit Finalists read:

> Each year Morris Harvey College honors academic excellence by granting a full tuition scholarship to Valedictorians, Salutatorians, and National Merit Finalists. . . . When we receive the enclosed prepaid reply card, I will forward to you a catalog and additional information on Morris Harvey College.

Now that there is open warfare among institutions to win a fair share of the diminishing candidate pool, abuses are bound to appear. The most obvious is the exaggeration of a particular college's strengths and advantages. When one is trying to win—in some cases, to survive—one is tempted to overstate. That is not new to Ford and AMC, but it is new to College, USA. Overstatement in private college promotions is common now, and it is obviously compromising to "academic tone."

Some admissions officers have addressed this regrettable development with considerable feeling. Richard Haines, Director of Admissions at Lafayette College of Pa., says in an open letter to secondary school counselors:

> A college, someone said a century and a half ago, is a "community of scholars engaged in the search for truth." Colleges still say that about themselves. How, then, can colleges justify the deceptive and misleading tactics so often now associated with their recruitment activities?
>
> It should surprise no one that students sometimes make poor college choices, considering the dazed state which must result when an adolescent mind collides with the powerful barrage of information and misinformation penned by publicists and poured forth by admissions officers. If it were accurate information alone, evaluation would be difficult. The intrusion of a vast store of misinformation makes the task of selection almost impossible.
>
> Some colleges have planted a veritable forest of fraud. Growing in it are such hardy perennials as glittering generalities, gross exaggerations and outdated statistics, which flourish alongside new

varieties such as trumped-up majors and "special programs" that sprout but never bloom. A recruiter will guide any willing student through the forest to the "one" college which merits all the superlatives he can command.

Disraeli said, "There are three kinds of lies: lies, damned lies, and statistics." Colleges are adept at the use of all three. Let me cite a current example of each. A lie: the brochure boasts that "admission to the College is competitive," while less readily available information reveals that 96% of all applicants are accepted. A damned lie (damned because it implicates others) statement in a two-year college catalog reading: "The following are some of the institutions to which graduates have transferred within the past few years," followed by a carefully culled list including Lafayette, which has no record of any transfers from that institution during the past decade. A statistic: an admissions officer's statement that "95% of our medical school applicants were placed last year," with no mention of the step-by-step screening process which weeds out well over half of the pre-meds before applications can be filed.

There will be honest mistakes made by every admissions officer. Colleges are so complex and conditions change so rapidly that no one can know everything about one institution. I'm concerned, though, about the *dishonest* mistakes, those made with intent to deceive. We need to discover them and eliminate them, in the interest of informed choices by students, and also to preserve the integrity of higher education as a whole.

Meanwhile, counselors, students, and parents should challenge suspicious statements emanating from colleges, remembering Artemus Ward's warning that "It ain't so much the things we don't know that get us into trouble. It's the things we know that ain't so."

The majority of private colleges, going about their recruitment business earnestly and honestly, are dismayed that a relatively small band of hungry institutions might cloud the ethical image for all. One salutary result of this scare has been the formation of the "Ethics Committee" (more formally entitled the Admissions Practices and Procedures Committee) of the National Association of College Admissions Counselors, a huge and influential professional organization that brings together admissions officers and guidance counselors for nationwide discussion and service. This Committee authored an important document several years ago entitled "The Statement of Principles of Good Practice" (see Appendix, p. 226), a Ten Commandment-type tablet that colleges and secondary schools can emulate. The statement was made "law" by the organization. There is also a no-nonsense monitoring system to check abuses.

Thanks largely to regional Ethics Committees—divisions of the national ACAC framework—the "Statement of Principles of Good Practice" has had some clout. Some local committees— the one in New England, for example—have issued severe warnings to colleges that abuse the guidelines stated in "Principles." One target has been the institution that admits a student early and demands a hefty deposit before the student has heard from other institutions (the most selective colleges inform by early April). "The Principles" states: A college must permit the candidate to choose without penalty (deposit) among offers of admission until he has heard from all colleges to which the candidate has applied, or until May 1." Secondary school counselors, college admissions personnel, and candidates can report abuses in the recruitment and enrollment process to their regional Ethics Committee and be assured of complete confidentiality.

The declining birthrate, the questionable value of the baccalaureate degree in the job market, and the high cost of higher education will obviously have an increasingly profound effect on the manner in which private colleges conduct their admissions operations. Some results are already obvious: the dazzling advertising campaigns, the no-need scholarships, the gala parties for admitted-but-not-yet-enrolled students, the hiring of professionals to accelerate the hoopla and make it more productive. Colleges, including the most selective, must ponder the future with grave concern. And they must sell.

Buyer, beware.


## THE STUDENT

We've come full circle now, touching on all key components of the undergraduate application process. It is time to remind the candidate and parents of the "basic concepts" listed 200 pages ago, when this exercise began. Hopefully, they mean even more now:

1. Most private colleges in America today, including some with rather prestigious names, are *not* highly selective; if they feel you can survive their program, you'll be admitted. High price, a declining number of college-age Americans, apprehension regarding the worth of a bachelor's degree in the job marketplace, and the growth and strength of the state university system nationwide have created this phenomenon.

2. Unfortunately, many colleges pose as being more selective than they really are. They feel good students will not be attracted to them if there is not an aura of selectivity at the front gate. But as a result of the hidden anxiety that the upcoming class may not be filled with the quantity and quality of students hoped for, the admissions office tends to overstate the qualities of the institution. So students and families must analyze a private college as carefully as they would analyze an automobile before buying it. Probing questions must be asked to confirm what is advertised and to check tone, performance and justification of price. "Test rides" must be made by visiting classes, libraries, Union buildings, campus art galleries, athletic facilities, laboratories and dorms. Hunches must be confirmed by talking with those who earlier decided in favor of the product.

3. A few private undergraduate institutions in America today are as highly selective as they ever have been, and a handful are even more selective. But not more than forty private colleges enjoy the luxury of admitting one out of two of their candidates, and not more than a half-dozen private colleges admit one out of five applicants. Aspiring kids and parents flock in droves to the latter little inner-circle, hoping to get a bit of the juicy and seemingly irresistible prestige. Even though fame-of-a-name is not always consistent with an Ivy college's quality, the hordes keep applying, not realizing (or caring?) that the academic program may be as good or better at a place considerably more accessible.

4. Nothing speaks louder than a strong high school record in the college admissions game. "Other considerations" are almost always secondary in importance to the degree of difficulty of a candidate's courseload, grades, class rank, recommendations from teachers and school officials, standardized test scores, and the depth of extracurricular involvement.

5. Given the (rare) highly selective college situation, and given an average candidate in that college's admissions competition, "other considerations" can indeed enter the picture, some of which the candidate can capitalize on. Who is admitted from the muddy-

middle of a selective college's applicant pool is partly a matter of chance, and the applicant has some control over "positioning" himself.

Given the gloomy demographic predictions that affect colleges imminently, high school juniors and seniors might be tempted to relax, knowing that private colleges will hustle to seek them out and admit them. Granted, private college admissions has changed from the seller's market of the mid-sixties to the buyer's market of today. But remember, a few colleges have never been more difficult to enter: Amherst and Brown and Harvard and Yale and Stanford and Bowdoin and Williams and Duke and Wesleyan and a handful of others. The very small openings at their front gates may widen with time, but for the moment the great majority of young people who want to get in are left standing outside.

It is human nature perhaps for the candidate and the family to try for whatever is most difficult to get. As long as one realizes that hardest-to-procure is not necessarily best, and not necessarily life v. death, then why *not* play the college admissions game? A strategy of good moves to attempt to win the most difficult victory can only serve to a put one in a better position for scoring "down" a few notches (where the education and environment may be as good or better than up top). So nothing is lost—indeed, a great deal is gained. Candor, introspection, imagination, energy, time, relaxation: all these are prerequisites to "playing the game" well.

Hopefully, I've passed along a few good tips to candidates in these chapters. Here now are the thoughts of my colleagues when asked, "What quick advice would you give a college candidate regarding 'selling' him/herself to the college of his/her choice?":

Amherst (Massachusetts): Relax and be totally candid. Know plenty about the college, and know even more about yourself.

Beloit (Wisconsin): Be realistic.

Bennington (Vermont): Oh goody, a chance to pontificate. Try to figure out what will be a good college or university for *you*—remember that there are several. Try not to base your decision to apply/enroll on whether or not your friend in Algebra II applied and was admitted or refused at Institution X.

Boston University (Massachusetts): Do your homework.

Bowdoin (Maine): You personable ones: arrange an interview! You with an edge, a special ability or a significant hobby: define these well to the admissions office!

Brandeis (Massachusetts): Shut off the TV. Read. Relax.

Case/Western Reserve (Ohio): Look carefully before you leap. View college selection as a major life decision.

Colgate (New York): 1. If you have a clear first choice, apply early decision. 2. Don't be so modest as to shield accomplishments. 3. Visit the campuses. 4. Present a strong record.

Denison (Ohio): Be yourself, and blow your horn.

Duke (North Carolina): Remember that the "sales job" doesn't start with the application process. And the "selling" is not directly to us, but through teachers and counselors to us. They can best measure and capture you, over a two to four year period of time.

Earlham (Indiana): Be open and forthright. Know the college well, and say why you are as appropriate a choice for them as they are for you. Address your weaknesses as well as your strengths.

Franklin and Marshall (Pennsylvania): Visit the college. Prepare a neat, clean, and concise application. Tell a college if it is clearly your first choice.

Hampshire (Massachusetts): Demonstrate energy, honesty, and a sense of humor. Show a high "aspiration index" regarding college. Don't allow yourself to be propped up by counselors or parents.

Harvard (Massachusetts): Through the application, the interview, etc., develop your strong points. Too often applicants just don't tell colleges enough about their exceptional accomplishments. But don't *fake* them. Be clever, but don't cross the fine line between clever and gimmicky.

Kenyon (Ohio): Present what you are with pride.

Knox (Illinois): Be honest, but warn the admissions officers first: this will help prevent trauma and shock.

Lafayette (Pennsylvania): 1. Seize the initiative. Don't let mommy or daddy take it from you. 2. Be neither too modest nor too boastful.

Rather, be factual and thorough. 3. Don't be afraid to be yourself. You want to get into a college which is appropriate for you, not for someone you're pretending to be.

Ohio Wesleyan: Your record must stand for itself. So relax. Enjoy the application routine. The same holds for the interview.

Mt. Holyoke (Massachusetts): Read.

Pomona (California): Do a competent, complete job on the application itself. Solicit recommendations *only* from those who know you well.

Princeton (New Jersey): A demonstration of energy is the key—in things academic, in things nonacademic. Beware, most of all, of being glib.

St. Lawrence (New York): There is no quick fix. The die is cast by the time the application is filed.

Scripps (California): Think of good questions. Ask them. Laugh in the interview. Do all the basic stuff: dress right and don't chew gum (unless you're an artist). Have thoughts about what you want, what you like, and what you are pretty sure of. Show some spunk. And write the application thoughtfully, properly, and with flair.

Stanford (California): Be yourself. Don't *try* to be what you think Stanford *wants* you to be. Where are the natural Huck Finn's in our applicant pool?

Tulane (Louisiana): Tell everything, good and bad. If the bad is revealed, an admissions officer might suggest senior year strategy to enhance your chances of admission.

Wabash (Indiana): As Tom Leherer used to sing, "Be prepared."

Perhaps, through all this meandering, through all this bombardment of definition and advice, you the reader have noticed that differences of opinion can surface among the authorities. That just underlines the fact that private college admissions, as hinted throughout, is not an exact science. Happily, formulas do not reign supreme in deciding whether John and/or Jane will be admitted to Oldebrick. Instead, people with biases and quirks and bad days and good days are (rather humbly, and very earnestly) "judging" other people, hoping to find the best possible match between institution and student. An uncomfortable task.

The Director of Admissions of Trinity College, Connecticut, expressed the human dimension from his side of the desk nicely:

> We don't define the shape of our ideal candidate, as if there were such a phenomenon, but instead try to stress the importance of selecting those who seem most ready to identify themselves as they really are. . . .
>
> Thus, the objective of the admissions policy is not most importantly defined in terms of good grades, of high College Board scores, of all-state tackle nominations or class presidencies, but by the selection of persons embodying the outward marks of an inner determination to live at their fullest capacities. It is all very, very subjective.

Absolutely every young person has some attribute worthy of Harvard's notice. Regrettably, too many feel that if Harvard doesn't notice, it's all over. The college admissions' decision can be harsh, largely because it is often the first judgment of finality handed to a teenager.

But no harm trying to "play the game" to claim a spot in the prestigious Winner's Circle. If you play, try your hardest. Do remember, however: There are deeper seas to conquer than a place in next year's freshman class at Oldebrick.

# Transfer Patterns, 1985

| College | Total Transfer Applicants | Total Transfer Offers | Transfer Matriculants |
|---|---|---|---|
| Amherst | 192 | 26 | 20 |
| Barnard | 290 | 178 | 103 |
| Bowdoin | 99 | 7 | 6 |
| Brown | 807 | 148 | 109 |
| Bucknell | 137 | 31 | 20 |
| Colgate | 179 | 55 | 31 |
| Columbia | 649 | 145 | 93 |
| Cornell | 2371 | 570 | 412 |
| Harvard/Radcliffe | 696 | 90 | 72 |
| MIT | 340 | 129 | 86 |
| Middlebury | 159 | 43 | 23 |
| Princeton | 381 | 21 | 12 |
| Smith | 203 | 137 | 103 |
| Swarthmore | 305 | 20 | 16 |
| Tufts | 457 | 50 | 30 |
| U. of Penn. | 1345 | 581 | 405 |
| Vassar | 194 | 63 | 30 |
| Wellesley | 110 | 19 | 14 |
| Wesleyan | 327 | 126 | 85 |
| Williams | 207 | 52 | 32 |
| Yale | 638 | 24 | 16 |

# Financial Aid Procedures: Middlebury College

## FINANCIAL AID AT MIDDLEBURY

Middlebury has made a firm commitment to enabling the most qualified students to enter the College regardless of a family's ability to meet the full cost of a Middlebury education. We believe that a student body that reflects the diversity of the larger society provides a livelier, richer education for all its participants. Especially in the most recent decade, the College has devoted a sizeable portion of its energies and resources to ensuring that the full need will be met of every admitted student seeking financial aid. In the past three years, no accepted student who has shown financial need has been denied the assistance to attend Middlebury, and fears that you and your family may not be able to afford the cost of a private education should not deter you from applying to the College. Admissions decisions do not include consideration of your family finances, and the admissions and financial aid decisions are wholly separate enterprises. Following are some figures and tables that will provide you with persuasive evidence of the scope of the Middlebury financial aid program.

- In 1983–84 over 45% of the students have received some form of financial aid, with a total in excess of $4.4 million from federal, state, college and private sources.
- In the fall of 1983 thirty-two percent (32%) of the Class of 1987 received grant assistance from Middlebury College.
- The average financial aid package (grant, loan and work) for all financial aid students at Middlebury was $7,750 in 1983–84, with awards ranging from $500 to $11,815.
- Over 60 percent of Middlebury students had on-campus jobs during 1983–84. Employment is readily available for *all* students, whether or not they receive other forms of financial assistance.
- Students receiving financial aid represent a wide range of income levels. The following two tables will give you data on the percentage of families in each category, with the figure for an average contribution to be placed in the context of the first table showing the wide distribution of awards within the various income levels.

**Average freshmen awards for financial aid at Middlebury College in 1983–84**

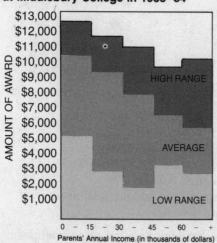

*Note:* The wide variation in awards from high to low within a given income category results from differing family circumstances.

| Parents' Total Income | % of Total Recipients | Average Parent Contribution Toward Total Educational Cost |
|---|---|---|
| $      0–11,999 | 11% | $   908 |
| $12,000–24,999 | 22% | $1,659 |
| $25,000–39,999 | 35% | $2,983 |
| $40,000 and up | 32% | $5,038 |

## COSTS

The Comprehensive Fee charged to Middlebury parents and students, in fact, pays slightly less than three quarters of the real annual cost of a Middlebury education. The rest is met by income from the College endowment, annual giving, and other outside sources.

The student budgets used to calculate need include the following:

|  | 1983–84 | 1984–85 |
|---|---|---|
| Billed by the College: |  |  |
| Comprehensive Fee (excludes sickness ins.) | $11,800 | $12,600 |
| Student Activity Fee | 60 | 60 |
|  | $11,860 | $12,660 |
|  |  |  |
| Additional Expenses: |  |  |
| Books and Supplies | 360 | 360 |
| Personal Expenses | 580 | 600 |
|  | 940 | 960 |
| Total | $12,800 | $13,620 |

Under certain circumstances, an allowance for travel expenses may be included in the budget.

### DETERMINING NEED
### BUDGET less FAMILY CONTRIBUTION
### equals NEED
#### How family contributions and financial need
#### are determined.

Middlebury is willing to share the financial responsibilities of attending college with you and your parents, but we expect the primary effort to pay for college to come from you and your family. The basic purpose of financial aid is to lessen the cost barriers that may prevent you from pursuing your educational goals. We view our role to be one of providing financial assistance to supplement—not to replace—what you and your family are expected to contribute to the cost of your college education. In order to evaluate your family's ability to contribute to your education, Middlebury—and most other colleges and universities—uses a nationally developed system called the Uniform Methodology. Employing a fairly subtle formula that takes into account the interrelationship of many variables, such as income, number of family members, assets, number of children in college—to name but a few—we are able to help assess what is a reasonable contribution from your family. Students applying for aid from Middlebury must submit a Financial Aid Form (FAF) to this central processor, the College Scholarship Service (CSS), which in turn sends us an analysis of your family financial information. (CSS does not award or deny aid.) Together with the tax return (a complete copy with all schedules), this provides us with a comprehensive picture of the family's financial strength.

Despite all the forms and documents, the aid process remains a very human one. The Director and the staff in Middlebury's Office of Financial Aid personally review each application and are responsive to individual circumstances. After a careful reading of all the information, we arrive at a figure that you and your parents are expected to contribute toward your educational expenses. This is called the *family contribution;* subtracted from the total budget (the cost of attendance), we then arrive at your *financial need*.

## PARENTAL CONTRIBUTION

Through the information on the Financial Aid Form and the parents' tax return (for dependent students) we arrive at an estimated *parental contribution*. Students from a wide range of income categories receive aid and Middlebury does not require a set minimum contribution or have an arbitrary income cutoff beyond which a student ought not apply for aid.

Children from families in which the parents are **divorced or separated** often present complex circumstances, and while you should bear in mind that we make every effort to accommodate to the financial realities of the new family units, the College is guided by the same principle underlying our financial aid policy for all students: to the extent they are deemed financially capable, parents are responsible for their children's college education. Divorce, separation or remarriage does not absolve either natural parent of this very basic obligation.

In the case of divorce, we require that each parent submit a Financial Aid Form (FAF) and a complete copy of the tax return. The *custodial* parent (i.e. the parent with whom you lived for the greater period of time during the past year) should submit the FAF to the College Scholarship Service (CSS) for processing. The non-custodial parent should submit the FAF (or the Divorced/Separated Parent's Statement) directly to Middlebury for review along with a complete copy of the tax return. The contribution from a non-custodial parent takes into account all circumstances—e.g. a new household, child support, alimony etc. Natural parents who are separated or divorced should not complete a FAF together even if they will be filing or have filed a joint federal income tax return for the base year period. If either parent has remarried, the FAF filed by that parent must contain all financial information for the new family unit—i.e. spouse, spouse's children, etc.

We are keenly aware of the sensitive nature of the information we ask for in the financial aid process; never more so than in the case of a divorce or separation. The confidence and the privacy of any documents submitted to us are assured.

## STUDENT CONTRIBUTION

Students receiving financial aid are expected to contribute to their education from their summer earnings, any savings and assets they may have and any other resources such as Social Security or Veteran's benefits.

A share of a student's past savings and assets is considered to be available for educational expenses. In order not wholly to deplete a student's assets, this percentage remains the same for each year in college. We include a standard summer earnings expectation as part of a student's resources even if you choose not to work. For freshmen entering in the Fall of 1984, that amount will be $950, for upperclass students it will be $1,050.

## THE FINANCIAL AID AWARD PACKAGE

After we have arrived at a determination of your need, we will develop a financial aid "package" that will enable you to meet the need shown through our analysis. The award will combine various forms of aid—grants, work, loan. The first portion of your financial aid will be in the form of *self-help* (loan and work), because Middlebury believes that students receiving assistance should be prepared to commit current and/or future earnings to their education during the academic year. A job during the academic year allows your current earnings to meet expenses; loans enable you to borrow from your own future income and to repay at a time when your earnings capacity will be higher. Both the job and loan are suggested however, not required. If you choose not to work on campus or to borrow, the self-help figure may be met through your own increased summer earnings or a larger family contribution. For the academic year 1984–1985 the self-help requirement is $2,800.

## JOBS

College departments hiring students are urged to give priority to financial aid recipients, but all students are eligible to apply for on-campus employment. In 1983–84 sixty-five percent (65%) of the undergraduates worked during the academic year earning a total of $530,000. The average earnings for a student on financial aid was $600. A smaller number of jobs involve off-campus work with non-profit municipal and social service agencies.

Many students are funded by the federal College Work-Study Program but many are also funded directly from Middlebury's own resources. In both instances wages are paid directly to the student, with most students using this money throughout the year to meet their personal expenses. While the College's resources are not unlimited, we make every reasonable effort to provide job opportunities to students who wish to work on campus during the academic year.

## LOANS

An educational loan with a low interest rate and deferred payment may be included as part of your financial aid award. The College reserves the right to indicate from what source the loan may be obtained.

### Guaranteed Student Loan

The eligibility criteria for this loan program changed substantially two years ago but since that time has remained unaltered. Currently, it permits the students of families with an adjusted gross income of $30,000 or less to borrow up to $2500 per year through commercial and private lenders. Students of families with an adjusted gross income of greater than $30,000 may still qualify for this loan but would have to undergo a needs test such as the Guaranteed Student Loan Needs Test or the College Scholarship Service's FAF. *(Students applying only for the Guaranteed Student Loan for the 1984–85 academic year will be required to submit a signed copy of page one of their parents' 1983 Federal Income Tax Form 1040.)* The maximum aggregate limit for undergraduate study is $12,500. These loans are guaranteed by the federal or state government. The interest rate of 9% (or 8% for new borrowers) is ordinarily subsidized by the federal government until repayment begins six months after the student ceases to be at least a half-time student. Several deferment provisions are available (e.g., for professional internships, service in the Armed Forces, Peace Corps, etc.). Repayment generally extends over a period of ten years with a minimum repayment of $600 per year. *The Office of Financial Aid must receive the application by August 1st or December 1st if the loan is to be applied to the fall or spring bills, respectively.*

### National Direct Student Loan

These loans are comprised of money from the federal government and from College funds. The loans are awarded on the basis of financial need. The College determines who will receive assistance from this source, with the loans generally given to those with the greatest need. Undergraduate students may borrow up to an aggregate total of $6,000 in a program leading to a baccalaureate degree. The interest rate is 5% and repayment must begin six months after the student ceases to be at least a half-time student. Minimum repayment is $30 per month for up to ten years. Provision for deferrals is similar to that in the Guaranteed Student Loan program. Specific details will be outlined prior to the student's signing of the promissory note.

## Middlebury College Loans

The College maintains several revolving loan funds, usually offered only to those students who are ineligible to borrow under the other programs. Payment of principal and simple interest of 5% begins after the termination of studies with no interest being charged while the student is in school.

## Parent Loan Program (PLUS)

Parents of dependent students who find that they need assistance to meet their portion of the expected family contribution may borrow up to $3,000 per year to an aggregate maximum of $15,000 through the PLUS loan program guaranteed by federal and state agencies. These are nonsubsidized loans at 12% interest. Repayment begins not more than 60 days after the date of disbursement. Applications are available through your bank or credit union.

## Middlebury Parent Loan Program (PLP)

Currently, parents of incoming freshmen students *not* receiving financial aid are eligible to participate in this program if their combined income is between $30,000 and $65,000. More information may be obtained from the Comptroller's office and will be mailed to all members of the entering freshmen class.

## Academic Management Services Payment Plan (AMS)

Academic Management Services (AMS) has a simple ten-month payment plan through which Middlebury families can meet their yearly bills. Payments begin on May 1 and continue through January 1. There is a $40 annual fee and no interest is charged.

Information will be sent to you during the Spring concerning the plan.

### Insured Tuition Payment Plan (ITPP)

This program allows parents to pro-rate the bill for College expenses thoughout the year, combined with low-cost life insurance for the designated parent. Information will be sent to all incoming freshmen or you may contact Richard C. Knight, ITPP, 53 Beacon Street, Boston, MA 02108.

### Loan Consolidation

Several states are in the process of developing loan consolidation programs through which students and their families may consolidate several loans. From 1980 to 1983, only the Student Loan Marketing Association (Sallie Mae) could consolidate loans from students who borrowed from different sources. As of this writing, their authority has not been renewed so there is no national or state agency consolidating loans, but legislation is forthcoming that may change that. For more information consult with your state higher education agency and the Office of Financial Aid.

**Distribution of Grants in 1983–84**

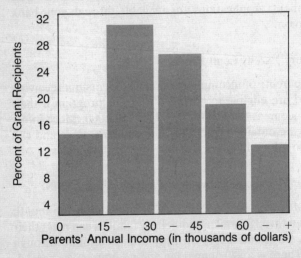

## GIFT AID

This is financial aid awarded to students which does not have to be repaid, although we always hope that students who have received a grant from Middlebury will as alumni acknowledge this generosity with a gift that will benefit another needy student in the future. In 1983–84 Middlebury students received $2.8 million in grant (gift aid) funds. In a larger sense *every* student receives a direct grant from Middlebury. Student fees meet only three-quarters of the cost of a Middlebury education, while gifts from friends of the College, our alumni and our endowment contribute the remaining cost of education for each student every year.

### Pell Grant

Eligibility for this program is determined by the federal government, but funds are disbursed by the school to students in support of their education. Grants will range from $250 to $1,900 for the academic year 1984–85. If you are applying for grant assistance from Middlebury College you must apply for this program by checking the appropriate box (45) on the College Scholarship Service's Financial Aid Form.

The Student Aid Report for the Pell Grant will be mailed to your home address. If you are deemed eligible for this program, and you have decided to attend Middlebury College, *all three copies* of the report must be sent to the Middlebury College Office of Financial Aid for determination of the award amount. If Middlebury has advanced you grant funds to cover this amount, our aid will be adjusted dollar-for-dollar when the final determination is made.

### State Grants

State grants are available to qualified students from Alaska, Connecticut, Maine, Maryland, Massachusetts, New Hampshire, New Jersey, Pennsylvania, Rhode Island, the District of Columbia, and Vermont for use at Middlebury College. We require *all* students from these states to apply for a grant from their state grant agency if they wish to apply for grant assistance from College sources. If Middlebury has advanced you grant funds to cover this amount, our aid will be adjusted dollar-for-dollar when the final determination is made. Application information may be obtained through your State Higher Education Assistance Agency.

## Supplemental Educational Opportunity Grants (SEOG)

Middlebury College participates in this federal grant program which provides funds to students who demonstrate need. By making application to Middlebury College for financial aid, you are also applying for this form of assistance.

## Middlebury College Grants

Grant assistance awarded by the College is provided from institutional operating funds, expendable gifts, alumni annual giving, endowed funds, or restricted funds. The endowed and restricted scholarship funds are described in the Middlebury College General Catalogue; you will be considered for all sources for which you are eligible. No additional application is necessary.

## Outside Scholarships

We encourage you to apply for as many scholarships from sources outside the College as you think you may be eligible for. Local service clubs, organizations devoted to a particular interest (e.g., music) and your high school are especially fruitful sources of scholarship funds. In determining need, federal and state regulations require that we consider all the resources (family contribution, grants, outside scholarship, loan, on-campus work) available to a student and also stipulate that these dollars must not exceed your costs in attending Middlebury. However, although your financial aid will be adjusted if you receive an outside non-federal, non-state scholarship, any initial reduction will first be reflected in the self-help portion of your package, which means that a greater proportion of your financial aid will be coming to you in the form of a grant.

The following examples are derived from those of actual 1983–84 aid recipients at Middlebury College. These examples will give you a good preview of how we will analyze your resources, determine your need, and "package" our aid.

## Example 1

This student is a junior from a family of five—father, mother, and two other children in college. Both parents are employed and the family's yearly income is $30,600. They have a home valued at $54,000 with a $34,000 mortgage. The main wage earner is 47 years old.

| | | |
|---|---|---|
| **Student Budget** | | **$13,800** |
| Parent contribution | 1,300 | |
| Student contribution from savings | 35 | |
| Student contribution from summer earnings | 1,000 | |
| **Family Contribution** | | **2,335** |
| | | |
| Financial Need | 11,465 | |
| Guaranteed Student Loan | 1,931 | |
| **Aid from non-College sources** | | **1,931** |
| | | |
| Remaining Financial Need | 9,534 | |
| Middlebury Grant | 6,940 | |
| National Direct Student Loan | 1,500 | |
| Work Study Job | 1,100 | |
| **Aid from College sources** | | **9,540** |
| | | ———— |
| | | 0 |

## Example 2

This is a freshman student who comes from a family of six with one other child in college. Both parents are employed, earning a total income of $49,555. They own a home valued at $78,000 with no mortgage. The father is 43 years old.

| **Student Budget** | | **$12,950** |
|---|---|---|
| Parent contribution | 4,800 | |
| Student contribution from savings | 48 | |
| Student contribution from summer earnings | 900 | |
| **Family Contribution** | | **5,748** |
| | | |
| Financial Need | 7,202 | |
| Outside Scholarship | 555 | |
| Guaranteed Student Loan | 1,575 | |
| **Aid from non-College sources** | | **2,130** |
| | | |
| Remaining Financial Need | 5,072 | |
| Middlebury Grant | 4,600 | |
| Work Study Job | 480 | |
| **Aid from College sources** | | **5,080** |

## Example 3

This student is a freshman from a family of four. The parents are divorced and the student lives with the mother whose income is $15,850. The father is also employed and is considered to be contributing toward the student's education. There are two children in college. The mother is 43 years old.

| **Student Budget** | | **$12,800** |
|---|---|---|
| Parent contribution | 1,458 | |
| Student contribution from summer earnings | 900 | |
| **Family Contribution** | | **2,358** |
| | | |
| Financial Need | 10,442 | |
| Pell Grant | 925 | |
| Guaranteed Student Loan | 800 | |
| State Grants | 1,000 | |
| **Aid from non-College sources** | | **2,725** |
| | | |
| Remaining Financial Need | 7,717 | |
| Middlebury Grant | 3,000 | |
| Middlebury Scholarship | 2,420 | |

Supplemental Educational Op-
portunity Grant                                    500
Work Study Job                                      800
National Direct Student Loan                      1,000
**Aid from College sources**                                            **7,720**

## Example 4

This student is a sophomore from a family of five. One parent
is employed with one other student in college. Their total income is $61,544. They own a home valued at $94,600 with a
$15,000 mortgage and modest savings and investments. The age
of the older parent is 50.

| | | |
|---|---:|---:|
| **Student Budget** | | **12,900** |
| Parent contribution | 6,040 | |
| Student contribution from savings | 608 | |
| Student contribution from summer earnings | 1,000 | |
| **Family Contribution** | | **7,648** |
| | | |
| Financial Need | 5,252 | |
| Guaranteed Student Loan | 1,900 | |
| **Aid from non-College sources** | | **1,900** |
| | | |
| Remaining Financial Need | 3,352 | |
| Middlebury Grant | 2,660 | |
| Work Study Job | 700 | |
| **Aid from College sources** | | **3,360** |

## NOTIFICATION OF ELIGIBILITY

The Middlebury College Office of Financial Aid will mail a two-
part Award Authorization letter to freshman and transfer applicants along with the letter of acceptance from the Admissions
Office, or shortly thereafter. The second copy of this award
letter must be returned indicating acceptance or declination of
the aid before your award is official and any aid can be credited
to your student account.

As a renewal applicant, you will usually hear as soon after

the end of the spring semester as possible, normally by mid-July. The acceptance/declination letter will have to be returned within the specified time limit before aid can be credited to your student account.

## MAINTAINING ELIGIBILITY

As an institution with highly selective admissions criteria, we normally consider any student who continues to be enrolled in the College to be making satisfactory academic progress. A complete document "Institutional Policy on Standards of Satisfactory Progress to Maintain Financial Aid Eligibility" is available on request in the Office of Financial Aid. Any questions on continuation of eligibility for Middlebury and federal funds will be resolved, in consultation, by the Dean of Students and the Director of Financial Aid.

## INDEPENDENT STUDENTS

Middlebury offers financial aid to meet the gap between educational expenses and family resources but cannot offer assistance to replace that expected contribution. We understand that ultimately the College cannot coerce a contribution from the family, but neither will Middlebury use its resources to compensate for the amount your parents may not provide. Meeting the federal criteria for establishing independence is *not* in itself persuasive evidence of independence, and the College has the ultimate authority in determining your eligibility to apply for aid as an independent student. If you enter Middlebury as a dependent, we will continue to require parental information for all the years you are enrolled at the College even if you re-enter Middlebury after an extended leave of absence.

## MOTOR VEHICLE POLICY

A student receiving financial assistance from the College is permitted to maintain a motor vehicle in Middlebury subject to the existing vehicle regulations affecting all students. However, he or she must plan to use personal funds for all expenses relating to ownership, maintenance, and operation of a motor vehicle. Such costs will not be included in the student budget when determining financial need. The College will take what measures are necessary to ensure that no student aid funds are used to subsidize motor vehicle expenses.

## CONFIDENTIALITY

The family financial information that you and your parents provide to the College is held in the strictest confidence. No information about the amount of the award is released outside the professional aid community without the written approval of the student. Similarly we feel it inappropriate for aid recipients to discuss their awards with anyone other than members of their family or the Office of Financial Aid staff.

# Representative Responses to Moll's *Harper's* Article, "The College Admissions Game"

1. *At time of publication. . . .*

from the Headmistress of the Nightingale-Bamford School, N.Y.C.:

> "Your article in *Harper's* was being handed out wholesale to parents until the Bryn Mawr Director of Admissions told me that it might soon be part of a book; better they should wait and read the whole thing!"

from the Dean of Admissions, Amherst College, Massachusetts:

> "My *Harper's* finally arrived yesterday. What a great article! I'm certain that a few of our counterparts will squirm when they read it, but what you said needed to be said and I'm glad you took the time and trouble to put such straight talk down on paper.
>
> I basically agree with your thesis although Amherst doesn't get very excited about your Category 5."

from the college advisor at Phillips Exeter, New Hampshire:

> "Well, naturally, I read your *Harper's* article. I thought it was fine and accurate. In fact, I have recommended it to all our parents in my column of the Exeter Parents Newsletter. As you may know, your article was quoted extensively last Sunday in the *Boston Globe*."

from an officer of the Public Interest Economics Foundation, Washington, D.C.:

> "Thanks for the lucid, myth-shattering article in *Harper's*. We plan to circulate large numbers of copies, particularly to Washington's local contingent of hysterics."

from the college counselor of the Fieldston School, N.Y.C.:

> "I found your article in *Harper's* to be the most accurate and useful document available to guidance counselors in many a year. I've referred it to all 11th graders and their parents and have also alerted our seniors who are waiting impatiently to receive much painful news from those 'impossible' colleges."

from the Associate Dean of Admissions at Colgate University, Hamilton, N.Y.:

> "I have just finished reading your *Harper's* article and can find fault with you in only one way: why should you be able to capably put into print those sentiments which I at times have difficulty simply conceptualizing? So much for the praise; now back to the 'categorical' decision making."

from the college counselor at the Breck School in Minnesota:

> "Thanks for saying in *Harper's* what should have been said long ago. You have not only enlightened your reader with marvelous insight, but have given students a ray of hope to cling to. My own experience has shown that applicants don't really mind being rejected if they can see some rationale behind the process. Your article gave them a sound explanation."

from the Director of Admissions at Oberlin College, Ohio:

> "Your *Harper's* article does a great job of telling it like it is! As usual, you're right on target."

2. A questionnaire was circulated to over 100 admissions directors of private colleges following publication of the article. The question: "Do you agree with the basic thesis of Moll's *Harper's* article?" The response: a categorical "yes" from such colleges as Bates (Me.), Beloit (Wisc.), Boston College ("Bravo!"), Bucknell (Pa.), Colby-Sawyer (N.H.), Franklin and Marshall (Pa.), Furman (S.C.), Hampshire (Mass.), Lafayette

(Pa.), Manhattan (N.Y.), Manhattanville (N.Y.), Ohio Wesleyan, Ripon (Wisc.), St. Lawrence (N.Y.), Stephens (Mo.),
Susquehanna (Pa.). Other respondents had reservations:

Brandeis (Mass.):

"For the most part, yes. Some schools, I suspect, are more engaged
in this type of admission than others. The other very interesting
question is: who decides how big each interest group's 'share of the
pie' is?—in reality, are not the groups then in direct competition for
seats in the new class?"

Earlham (Ind.):

"Not being in the position of the Ivies, we feel a bit removed from
the issue. Earlham has not been in a position during recent years to
be more than mildly selective. We are saved by students who self-
select us for special reasons and we tell our prospective students just
that."

Knox (Ill.):

"Surely what you say is true for the most selective colleges in the
country. But this has little bearing on the majority of private institutions, and will have less as we move into the eighties."

Lewis and Clark (Oregon):

"I don't doubt your thesis for the most selective colleges. But it
hardly applies to the institutions in our area. Aren't you really talking
about a very small number of colleges?"

Mount Holyoke (Mass.):

"Not completely. Your analysis may lead to the idea that *everyone*
is 'boxed'. There is no uniform standard for making a decision since
much of the process depends on personal judgment and experience
with previous classes. Selection is an art, not a science, and although
special talents, legacies, geography and other factors may play a
part, there is no uniform method of weighting."

University of Richmond (Va.):

"With our volume of applications, I don't feel the candidates fall
into categories as neatly as you have described them."

# Statement of Principles of Good Practice

(ADOPTED BY THE NATIONAL ASSOCIATION OF
COLLEGE ADMISSIONS COUNSELORS)

I. ADMISSIONS PROMOTION AND RECRUITMENT
   A. *College and University Members Agree:*
      1. Admissions counselors are professional members of
         their institution's staff. As professionals, they re-
         ceive remuneration on a fixed salary, rather than
         commission or bonus based on the number of stu-
         dents recruited.
      2. Admissions officers are responsible for the devel-
         opment of publications used for promotional and
         recruitment activities. These publications should:
         a. *State clearly and precisely requirements as to sec-*
            *ondary-school preparation, admission tests, and*
            *transfer-student admission requirements.*
         b. *Include statements concerning admissions cal-*
            *endar that are current and accurate.*
         c. *Include precise information about opportunities*
            *and requirements for financial aid.*

    *d. Describe in detail any special programs such as overseas study, early decision, early admission, credit by examination, or advanced placement.*

    *e. Contain pictures and statements of the campus and community that are current and represent reality.*

3. Colleges and universities are responsible for all persons who may become involved in the admissions promotional and recruitment activities (i.e., alumni, coaches, students, faculty) and for educating them about the principles outlined in this statement.

4. The admissions counselor is forthright, accurate, and comprehensive in presenting his institution to high school personnel and prospective students. The admissions counselor adheres to the following:

    *a. State clearly the requirements, and other criteria.*

    *b. Make clear all dates concerning application, notification, and candidate reply, for both admissions and financial aid.*

    *c. Furnish data descriptive of currently enrolled classes.*

    *d. Avoid invidious comparisons of institutions.*

5. The Admissions Counselor avoids unprofessional promotional tactics, such as:

    *a. Contracting with high-school personnel for remuneration for referred students.*

    *b. Contracting with placement services that require a fee from the institution for each student enrolled.*

    *c. Encouraging a student's transfer if the student himself has not indicated transfer interest.*

B. *Secondary School Personnel Agree to:*

1. Provide a program of counseling which does justice to the college opportunities sought and available.

2. Encourage the student and his parents to take the initiative in learning about colleges and universities.

3. Invite college and university representatives to assist in counseling candidates about college opportunities.

4. Avoid invidious comparisons of institutions.
5. Refuse unethical or unprofessional requests (e.g., for lists of top students, lists of athletes, etc.) from college or university representatives (e.g., alumni, coaches, etc.).
6. Refuse any reward or remuneration from a college, university, or private counseling service for placement of its students.

C. College clearinghouses and matching services which provide liaison between colleges and universities and students shall be considered a positive part of the admissions process if they effectively supplement other high-school guidance activities and adhere to the Principles of Good Practice contained herein.

## II. APPLICATION PROCEDURES
   A. *Colleges and Universities Agree to:*
   1. Accept full responsibility for admissions decisions and for proper notification of those decisions to candidates and, where possible, to secondary schools.
   2. Receive information about a candidate in confidence and to respect completely the confidential nature of such data.
   3. Notify high school personnel when using students on admission selection committee.
   4. Not apply newly revised requirements to the disadvantage of a candidate whose secondary-school course has been established in accordance with earlier requirements.
   5. Notify the candidate as soon as possible if the candidate is clearly inadmissible.
   6. Not deny admission to a candidate on the grounds that the institution does not have aid funds to meet the candidate's apparent financial need, foreign students excepted.
   7. Not require a candidate or his school to indicate the order of the candidate's college or university preference, early decision plans excepted.

8. Permit the candidate to choose without penalty among offers of admission until he has heard from all colleges to which he has applied or until May 1.

9. Not maintain a waiting list of unreasonable length or for an unreasonable period of time.

B. *Secondary School Personnel Agree to:*

1. Provide an accurate, legible, and complete transcript for its candidates.

2. Describe its marking system and its method of determining rank in class.

3. Describe clearly its special curricular opportunities (e.g., honors, advanced placement courses, seminars, etc.).

4. Provide an accurate description of the candidate's personal qualities that are relevant to the admission process.

5. Report any significant change in the candidate's status or qualifications between the time of recommendation and graduation.

6. Urge the candidate to recognize and discharge his responsibilities in the admissions process.

   a. *Complying with requests for additional information in a timely manner.*

   b. *Responding to institutional deadlines on admissions and refraining from stockpiling acceptances.*

   c. *Responding to institutional deadlines on room reservations, financial aid, health records, and prescheduling where all or any of these are applicable.*

7. Not, without permission of the candidate, reveal the candidate's college preference.

III. FINANCIAL ASSISTANCE (WHERE SUCH ASSISTANCE IS BASED UPON NEED):

A. *Colleges and Universities Agree That:*

1. Financial assistance consists of scholarships, grants, loans, and employment which may be offered to students singly or in various forms.

2. They should strive, through their publications and communications, to provide schools, parents, and students with factual information about their aid opportunities, programs, and practices.

3. Financial assistance from colleges and other sources should be viewed only as supplementary to the efforts of the family.

4. In determining the financial contribution of the candidate's family, they use methods which assess ability to pay in a consistent and equitable manner, such as those developed by the College Scholarship Service and the American College Testing Program.

5. They should clearly state the total yearly cost of attendance and should outline for each student seeking assistance an estimate of his need.

6. They should permit the candidate to choose, without penalty, among offers of financial assistance until he has heard from all colleges to which he has applied or until his reply date.

7. They should clearly state policies on renewals.

8. They should not announce publicly the amount of the financial award to an individual candidate because it is a reflection of the family's financial situation.

B. *Secondary School Personnel Agree to:*

1. Refrain, in public announcements, from giving the amounts of financial aid received by students.

2. Advise the student who has been awarded aid by non-college sources that it is his responsibility to notify the colleges to which he has applied of the type and amount of such outside assistance.

3. Provide adequate opportunity within the school for all able students to receive a special recognition for their accomplishments, thus making it unnecessary for colleges to provide such honorary recognition through their financial-assistance programs.

# The Lighter Side

We on one side of the Admissions desk realize that candidates who sit on the other side compare notes and chatter and giggle among themselves about all the unexpected, somewhat zany things that happen along the pathway of "getting into college." Well, we on the "authoritative" side of the desk smile at a few things that happen enroute also. Here are a few tidbits that Directors of Admission have consented to divulge:

Bowdoin (Maine):
  "I interviewed a superb candidate at a College Day in a hotel room. As the forty-minute interview drew to a close, I happened to mention the word 'Bowdoin, and the kid jumped up with alarm . . . He had intended to see the Williams College representative in the next room."

Bucknell (Pennsylvania):
  "Leaning back in my chair during an interview to achieve that perfect projection of the casual and interested air, the rollers on my chair took off, and I did a reverse somersault. The candidate was obviously stunned. His face seemed to say: "Wow, I wonder what this guy does for encores?""

Colgate (New York):
  "About to interview two boys at one of the nation's most prestigious prep schools, I asked the college advisor about the first boy's cre-

dentials. 'He ranks 150 out of 150,' was the response. 'What about the second boy?' I asked. 'He's tied with the other.' "

## Franklin and Marshall (Pennsylvania):

"What *should* I have done when the young man I was interviewing grew so nervous that he wet his pants? But perhaps that incident was only the runner-up. One time I called a young man to tell him that he had won a special scholarship. His mother answered the phone and I said: 'Hello, this is the Director of Admissions of Franklin and Marshall College. Is your son there?' She said, 'No.' I said, 'Well, I'm calling to tell him about a special scholarship he has won.' And she said: 'For heaven's sakes, George, I told you *never* to call me at home!' I repeated my story, and she still thought it was 'George' pulling her leg, and said, 'Please hang up. I can see my husband coming up the walk now.' I hung up and wrote a letter."

## Furman (South Carolina):

"A young man completed the 'Sex' blank on our application by saying: 'Once, in Charlotte, North Carolina.' A young woman, in completing the question which asks about the 'state of your health,' put 'Georgia.' "

## Lafayette (Pennsylvania):

"And why do you think that Lafayette might be a good college for you?

Candidate: "Well, I don't want to go to a real big college or a real small college. I just want a mediocre college like Lafayette."

## Manhattan (New York):

"At a New York City Fair, I tried to hand a young lady an application. She said: 'Oh, no thank you. I've already applicated.' "

## Ripon (Wisconsin):

"One girl told me she was the accompanist for the a capella choir. Best prize: A young man wrote on his application that he first heard about Ripon by reading its name on the wall of the Men's Room in the Boston Public Library."

## St. Lawrence (New York):

"I met a nun at a conference representing another college, who said: 'What I like about most of you men in admissions is that you're young enough to be sexy, but too old to be dangerous.' Also, I remember the guidance counselor's report which arrived saying: 'Prepared in copulation with the principal.' "

Scripps (California):

"The cosmic giggle hasn't happened to me yet. But the possibilities haunt me. . . ."

Stanford (California):

"Several quips from recommendations linger in my mind: The teacher (of typing) who wrote 'Barbara has the fastest hands in the class'; the counsellor who wrote 'John's only weakness is his lack of potential.' And we're still mystified by the principal who wrote 'Burt is in the top third quarter of his class.' "

Tulane (Louisiana):

"A conversation with a high Math, low Verbal applicant for Engineering:

    Counselor: Are you a good student?

    Applicant: I don't do too good in English.

    Counselor: I don't do too <u>well</u> in English.

    Applicant: Me neither."

# Index

Public school applicants, 21, 26, 28, 44, 123, 125
  "Buckley Amendment" and, 154
  typical School and Teacher Reports from, 155

Radcliffe College, 87, 97
  percentage accepted who attend, 8
  percentage of applicants admitted to, 83
Randolph-Macon College, 97
Recruitment efforts of colleges, 173–180
  for black students, 33
  "Ethics Committee" to control improper, 179–180
  lying with statistics, 178–179
Resumes, applicant, 57, 59
Rice University, 87
  scholarships, 12
Rickey, Branch, 88
Ripon College, 89, 121
  future plans of, 174
Rockefeller Foundation Award winners, 88
Rockford College, 177
Roethke Award winners, 88
"Role for Marketing in College Admissions, A," 176
Roommate assignments, 74
Rural colleges, 90
Russwurm, John B., 89

"Safety" application 104
St. Lawrence College, 121, 125, 184
SATs, see Scholastic Aptitude Test (SAT)
Scholarships, 12, 74, 178, 198
  for merit versus need, 100, 101–102
  percentage of students receiving, at sample colleges, 101
Scholastic Aptitude Test (SAT), 115, 125–137
  Bowdoin's dropping requirement of, 76, 134
  coaching before taking, 136

  common questions about, 136–137
  correlation with performance, 9–10, 75–76, 136, 137
  cultural bias of, 137
  definition of, 129
  guessing on, 136
  the handicapped's performance on, 137
  importance of, 9–10, 31, 50, 134
  median scores, for admitting college, 18, 130, 131–133
  number of times taken, 129, 136
  Preliminary (PSAT), 129
  range of scores at four colleges, 131–133
  repeating the tests, 136
  scores of sample candidates, 18, 29, 46, 52, 53, 60, 66, 70–71
  test results, learning, 136
  as uniform means of appraisal, 126, 129–130, 134–135
  verbal aptitude and family income, 170
School Reports, 21–22, 115, 155–160
  comical, 164–165
  on sample applicants, 21–22, 30, 37–39, 41, 47, 58–59, 73
  typical public school, 154–155
  typical private school, 156–163
Scripps College, 97
  advice to applicants, 184
  future plans of, 174
  range of SAT scores at, 133
Selectivity of private colleges, 2, 82–83, 108–109
  future of private colleges and, 167–180
  overstatement of, by college, 178–179, 180
  percentage of applicants accepted, 82, 83
  reasons for reduced, 2–3, 167–173, 180
Selling yourself, 182–185
Seven Sister schools, 97
  list of, 87